Tar Heel Laughter

Tar Heel Laughter

edited by
RICHARD WALSER

The University of North Carolina Press
Chapel Hill

Library of Congress Cataloging in Publication Data

Walser, Richard Gaither, 1908-   comp.
   Tar Heel laughter,

   Bibliography: p.
   1. American wit and humor—North Carolina.
I. Title
PN6162.W29   *817'.008*   *73-15568*
ISBN 0-8078-1219-9

Contents

Foreword

Laughter, it is said, exercises the muscles, invigorates the lungs, and lightens the depressed spirits. As long as we can laugh, neither pollution nor war nor man's lethal creations shall ever destroy us. "For me," wrote O. Henry, "it is to laugh." And O. Henry's fellow North Carolinians, back through the years and up to the present, would seem to agree. Except for an implacable mulligrubbing sourpuss, everyone enjoys a joke. A funny story, told or written with a sense of native art, never goes unappreciated, even in the depths of Gates County's Dismal Swamp. With a laugh, the whole world becomes brighter.

When John Lawson, a happy Londoner exploring the New World, wrote up his journeys of those first dim years of the eighteenth century, the recorded history of North Carolina humor began. Sadly, for more than 120 years thereafter, the records were sparse. Then, during the three decades following Ham Jones's famous "Cousin Sally Dilliard" in 1831, rich comic inventions surged from the minds of fun-loving North Carolinians. At that time, newspapermen, not merely reporters and anecdotists but typesetters as well, were prime chroniclers of North Carolina humor. Salisbury's Ham Jones and Milton's C. N. B. Evans epitomized a southern practice and a southern style in the vein of the old Southwest although they lived on its northeastern periphery. Indeed, Johnson Jones Hooper of Wilmington, North Carolina, was one of the most famous humorists of the old Southwest. In 1835, at the age of twenty, Hooper moved to Alabama and thereafter wrote almost exclusively of his adopted state.

After the Civil War, humor in North Carolina once more moved along steadily, if slowly at times. Gradually such favorite antebellum genres as dialect letters, well-nigh indigestible today except for the historians, professional linguists, and lexicographers, disappeared to be replaced by the stories of gifted raconteurs. With the coming of the twentieth century, journalists, who were no longer typesetters but still anecdotists as well as reporters, reaffirmed an earlier pattern that flowered in the decades following. Eventually the litterateurs appeared, throwbacks to Lawson who had written more than two centuries before.

North Carolinians laughed at the writings of them all. But it must be remembered that fashions in humor, like those in other areas, change with the times. While what North Carolinians laughed at, say, a hundred years ago may not be outrageously funny today, it seems appropriate that, in a survey such as the present collection, examples of our ancestors' humor, whether currently mirth-provoking or not, be set down.

From the pert observations of John Lawson in 1709 to the folk comedy of Paul Green in 1968 and from the satiric bite of William Byrd to the broad risibility of Carl Goerch are obviously appreciable distances. Less lengthy spans extend from the backwoods hoedown of Harden E. Taliaferro to the ethnic leg-pulling of Harry Golden, from the calculated absurdities of Bill Nye to the literary capers of Thomas Wolfe. Yet all make up a Tar Heel's laughter.

Humor, it is generally agreed, is based on the perception of incongruity. The unexpected turn of events, the double entendre, the preposterous exaggeration in a tall tale related by either an unlettered rustic or a novelist of the mid-twentieth century, the surprising concoctions implicit in the solicistic and inelegant vernacular, the ribald and adroit repartee—all are earmarks of North Carolina humor, a humor of rhetorical exhilaration. For the most part it remains a masculine humor of fighters, boasters, hunters, and practical jokers.

There is too, a strange, predictable component in the nature of humor. More than any other type of literary material, humor is a "traveling" commodity. It is not possible that each selection in a book of regional humor can positively be identified as originating in that region. A "wandering anecdote" may be heard in Greensboro on Saturday and repeated almost word for word in San Francisco on Monday. No one knows where the story originated or how it arrived in Greensboro or in San Francisco.

From an earlier day, Zeb Vance presents a similar case in point. Seldom can a collector be positive that Vance was the originator of a certain turn of speech, a certain anecdote, a certain incident. Stories that were of doubtful authenticity gravitated to his oversized personality and soon became associated with him, being told by those who knew him or by those who simply had heard of him. Even among the less questionable Vance anecdotes, the germ of truth was soon refined and magnified by constant telling and re-telling.

Many of the Vance stories, and others found in this collection, resemble various familiar anecdotes heard under other conditions and in other contexts. Their provenance is uncertain and myste-rious. It can be said only that, with the exception of several paragraphs from William Byrd, all entries in this collection have North Carolina sources (not necessarily *origins*) of some sort.

In his "To the Reader" at the beginning of *Look Homeward, Angel,* Wolfe wrote that "a novelist may turn over half the people in a town to make a single figure in his novel" and recalled Dr. Samuel Johnson's remark that "a man would turn over half a library to make a single book." Every collector of humor must duplicate Dr. Johnson's procedure. To make this one book, literally hundreds of books have been turned over, unrewardingly more often than not. A collector's only regret concerns the hundreds of other repositories of unindexed North Carolina humor that were unintentionally passed over.

Since this is a readers' edition and not a scholarly one, moderate alterations from primary sources have been made in such matters as punctuation, spelling, and paragraphing. Titles have been supplied when the authors gave none or when excerpts from longer works have been used. Care has been taken, generally, to leave undisturbed and inviolate the humorists' *words*, even when sentences were ungrammatical or incoherent. Except in rare cases (e.g., *gnat* for *nat*) dialectical spelling remains intact, though a writer like Taliaferro uses *of, ov, uf,* and *uv* without apparent discrimination.

Finally a personal statement: Sometimes books are painful to write or put together, but they must be done, and they *are* done. At other times things go more easily. But in all the history of book-making, I sincerely believe that no anthologist was ever more joyfully employed than I in putting together *Tar Heel Laughter.*

R.W.

Department of English
North Carolina State University
Raleigh, 23 October 1973

Acknowledgments

The editor is grateful to the following authors and publishers for permission to reprint selections from the works listed below:

Bill Adler, ed., *The Wit and Wisdom of Billy Graham* (New York: Random House, 1967). Reprinted by permission of the Billy Graham Evangelistic Association.

Felix E. Alley, *Random Thoughts and the Musings of a Mountaineer* (Salisbury: Rowan Printing Co., 1941). Reprinted by permission of Felix E. Alley, Jr.

Associated Press, *Reader's Digest*, August 1971. Reprinted by permission of the Associated Press. *Fun Fare: A Treasury of Reader's Digest Wit and Humor* (Pleasantville, N.Y.: Reader's Digest Association, 1949). Reprinted by permission of the Associated Press.

Billy Arthur, *The State*, 1 December 1967. Reprinted by permission of *The State*.

Russell Baker, "A New Raconteur Reigns in Senate," *The New York Times*, 13 May 1956. Copyright © by The New York Times Company. Reprinted by permission.

Bugs Barringer, *News and Observer* (Raleigh), 17 June 1967. Reprinted by permission of the author.

Ralph Steele Boggs, "North Carolina White Folktales and Riddles," *Journal of American Folklore* 47 (October-December 1934). Reprinted by permission of the American Folklore Society.

Benjamin Albert Botkin, ed., *A Treasury of Southern Folklore* (New York: Crown Publishers, 1949). Copyright © B. A. Botkin. Reprinted by permission of Crown Publishers, Inc.

John G. Bragaw, *Random Shots* (Raleigh: Edwards and Broughton Co., 1945). Reprinted by permission of Lalla C. Bragaw.

J. Mason Brewer, *Worser Days and Better Times* (Chicago: Quadrangle Books, 1965). Reprinted by permission of Quadrangle Books, Inc. *Negro American Folklore* (Chicago:

Quadrangle Books, 1968). Reprinted by permission of Quadrangle Books, Inc.

J. Street Brewer, *The State*, 1 January 1970. Reprinted by permission of *The State*.

Ben Lucien Burman, *It's a Big Country* (New York: Reynal & Company, 1956). Reprinted by permission of Taplinger Publishing Company, Inc.

Bennett Cerf, *The Laugh's on Me* (New York: Doubleday & Company, 1959). Copyright © 1959 by Bennett Cerf. Reprinted by permission of Doubleday & Company, Inc.

Albert Coates, *In Appreciation . . .* (n.p., 1962). Reprinted by permission of the author. *What the University of North Carolina Meant to Me* (Richmond: p.p., 1969). Reprinted by permission of the author.

Charles Craven, *Charles Craven's Kind of People* (Chapel Hill: Colonial Press, 1956). Reprinted by permission of the author. "Henry Belk Honored at Dinner Here," *News and Observer* (Raleigh), 31 October 1968. Reprinted by permission of the author.

Burke Davis, *The Summer Land* (New York: Random House, 1965). Reprinted by permission of Random House, Inc.

Sam J. Ervin, Jr., "The Hill Country Sayin's of Sam Ervin," *Time*, 16 April 1973. Reprinted by permission from *Time*, The Weekly Newsmagazine; Copyright © Time Inc.

Willie Snow Ethridge, *You Can't Hardly Get There from Here* (New York: Vanguard Press, Inc., 1965). Reprinted by permission of Vanguard Press, Inc.

Carl Goerch, *Carolina Chats* (Raleigh: Edwards and Broughton Co., 1944). Reprinted by permission of the author. *Characters . . . Always Characters* (Raleigh: Edwards and Broughton Co., 1945). Reprinted by permission of the author. *Down Home* (Raleigh: Edwards and Broughton, 1943). Reprinted by permission of the author. *The State*, 15 January 1968, 1 March 1968, 15 September 1968, 1 October 1968, 1 March 1969, 15 May 1969. Reprinted by permission of the author.

Harry Golden, *Enjoy, Enjoy!* (New York: World Publishing Company, 1960). Reprinted by permission of The World Publishing Company. Copyright © 1942, 1944, 1949, 1950, 1954, 1957, 1959, 1960 by Harry Golden. *Ess, Ess, Mein Kindt* (New York: G. P. Putnam's Sons, 1966). Reprinted by permission of G. P.

Putnam's Sons. *For 2¢ Plain* (New York: World Publishing Company, 1959). Reprinted by permission of The World Publishing Company. Copyright © 1943, 1945, 1948, 1952, 1955, 1956, 1957, 1958, 1959 by Harry Golden. *Only in America* (New York: World Publishing Company, 1958). Reprinted by permission of The World Publishing Company. Copyright © 1944, 1948, 1951, 1953, 1954, 1955, 1956, 1957, 1958 by Harry Golden. *So Long as You're Healthy* (New York: G. P. Putnam's Sons, 1970). Reprinted by permission of G. P. Putnam's Sons. *So What Else Is New?* (New York: G. P. Putnam's Sons, 1964). Reprinted by permission of G. P. Putnam's Sons. Copyright © 1942, 1945, 1951, 1957, 1962, 1963, 1964 by Harry Golden. *You're Entitle'* (New York: World Publishing Company, 1962). Reprinted by permission of the World Publishing Company. Copyright © 1962 by Harry Golden.

Paul Green, *Words and Ways*, an issue of *North Carolina Folklore*, December 1968. Reprinted by permission of the author.

Marion Hargrove, *See Here, Private Hargrove* (New York: Henry Holt and Co., 1942). Copyright © by Marion Hargrove. Reprinted by permission of William Morris Agency, Inc.

Crockette W. Hewlett, *Between the Creeks* (Wilmington, p.p., 1971). Reprinted by permission of the author.

Arthur Palmer Hudson, *Journal of American Folklore* 81 (July-September 1968). Reprinted by permission of the American Folklore Society.

F. Roy Johnson, *Witches and Demons in History and Folklore* (Murfreesboro: Johnson Publishing Company, 1969). By permission of the author.

Weimar Jones, *My Affair with a Weekly* (Winston-Salem: John F. Blair, Publisher, 1960). Reprinted by permission of John F. Blair, Publisher.

Joseph M. McCullen, *Publications of the Texas Folklore Society*, 1961. Reprinted by permission of the Texas Folklore Society.

Frank A. Montgomery, Jr., *The State*, 15 January 1968. Reprinted by permission of *The State*.

Joseph Mitchell, *McSorley's Wonderful Saloon* (New York: Duell, Sloan and Pearce, 1943). Reprinted by permission of Harold Ober Associates Incorporated. First published in *The New Yorker*. Copyright © 1940 by Joseph Mitchell. Copyright renewed.

Dave Morrah, *Me and the Liberal Arts* (New York: Doubleday & Company, 1962). Copyright © 1962 by David W. Morrah, Jr. Reprinted by permission of Doubleday & Company, Inc.

J. Alex Mull, *The State*, 1 September 1966. Reprinted by permission of *The State.*

Howard W. Odum, *Cold Blue Moon: Black Ulysses Afar Off* (Indianapolis: Bobbs-Merrill Company, 1931). Reprinted by permission of Mary Frances Odum Schinhan. *Rainbow Round My Shoulder: The Blue Trail of Black Ulysses* (Indianapolis: Bobbs-Merrill Company, 1928). Reprinted by permission of Mary Frances Odum Schinhan.

O. Henry, *Postscripts* (New York: Harper & Brothers, 1923). Reprinted by permission of Harper & Row.

Guy Owen, *The Ballad of the Flim-Flam Man* (New York: Macmillan Publishing Company, 1965). Copyright © Guy Owen. Reprinted by permission of Macmillan Publishing Co., Inc.

Elsie Clews Parsons, *Journal of American Folklore* 30 (April-June 1917). Reprinted by permission of the American Folklore Society.

Thilbert H. Pearce, *How to Sell a Dead Mule* (Freeman, S.D.: Pine Hill Press, 1971). Reprinted by permission of the author.

William T. Polk, *Southern Accent* (New York: William Morrow & Company, 1958). Copyright © 1958 William T. Polk. Reprinted by permission of William Morrow & Company, Inc.

W. Howard Rambeau, *Fun Fair: A Treasury of Reader's Digest Wit and Humor* (Pleasantville, N.Y.: Reader's Digest Association, 1949). Reprinted by permission of Reader's Digest.

Charles A. Reap, *A Story is Told* (Albemarle: p.p., 1968). Reprinted by permission of the author.

A. C. Reid, *Tales from Cabin Creek* (Raleigh: p.p., 1967). Reprinted by permission of the author.

Robert Ruark, *I Didn't Know It Was Loaded* (New York: Doubleday & Company, 1948). Copyright © 1948 by Robert Ruark. Reprinted by permission of Harold Matson Co., Inc.

Chub Seawell, *The State*, 1 November 1969. Reprinted by permission of *The State.*

A. C. Snow, the column "Sno' Fooling," *Raleigh Times*, 14 May 1966, 1 November 1967, 30 October 1968, 7 March 1969, 31

May 1969, 15 August 1969, 25 September 1969, 4 October 1969, 24 March 1970, 29 June 1971, 4 December 1971. Reprinted by permission of the author.

Thad Stem, Jr., *Entries from Oxford* (Durham: Moore Publishing Company, 1971). Reprinted by permission of Moore Publishing Company.

Una Taylor, *Fun Fare: A Treasury of Reader's Digest Wit and Humor* (Pleasantville, N.Y.: Reader's Digest Association, 1949). Reprinted by permission of Reader's Digest.

Roy Thompson, *The State*, 1 February 1970. Reprinted by permission of *The State*.

Glenn Tucker, *Zeb Vance: Champion of Personal Freedom* (Indianapolis: Bobbs-Merrill Company, 1965). Copyright © 1965 by Glenn Tucker. Reprinted by permission of the publisher, The Bobbs-Merrill Company, Inc.

Betty C. Waite, *Fun Fare: A Treasury of Reader's Digest Wit and Humor* (Pleasantville, N.Y.: Reader's Digest Association, 1949). Reprinted by permission of Reader's Digest.

Earl Wilson, syndicated column, "It Happened One Night," *News and Observer* (Raleigh), 25 April 1966. Reproduced by courtesy of Publishers-Hall Syndicate.

Thomas Wolfe, *The Hills Beyond* (New York: Harper & Brothers, 1941). Reprinted by permission of Harper & Row Publishers, Inc. *Look Homeward, Angel* (Charles Scribner's Sons, 1929). Copyright © 1929 Charles Scribner's Sons. Reprinted by permission of Charles Scribner's Sons.

Tar Heel Laughter

John Lawson among the Indians

North Carolina's first humorist was the English explorer John Lawson. In January and February of 1701, he traveled across the colony and some years later in London published an account of the trip as A New Voyage to Carolina *(1709), re-titled* The History of Carolina *in 1714. The book is delightful mainly because of the author's wit and high spirits. Rarely are these traits absent, even when Lawson is describing (in the semi-scientific manner expected in his day) the plants, animals, and natives he observed. Before his death at the hands of the Tuscarora in 1711, Lawson was prominent in the political affairs of the colony.*

The Teaching of English

The *English* Traders are seldom without an *Indian* Female for his Bed-fellow, alledging these Reasons as sufficient to allow of such a Familiarity. First, They being remote from any white People, that it preserves their Friendship with the Heathens, they esteeming a white Man's Child much above one of their getting, the *Indian* Mistress even securing her white Friend Provisions whilst he stays amongst them. And lastly, This Correspondence makes them learn the *Indian* Tongue much the sooner, they being of the *French-*man's Opinion, how that an *English* Wife teaches her Husband more *English* in one Night, than a School-master can in a Week.

Good Eating

At the other House, where our Fellow-Travellers lay, they had provided a Dish, in great Fashion amongst the *Indians,* which was Two young Fawns, taken out of the Doe's Bellies, and boil'd in the same slimy Bags Nature had plac'd them in, and one of the Coun-try-Hares, stew'd with the Guts in her Belly, and her skin with the Hair on. This new-fashion'd Cookery wrought Abstinence in our Fellow-Travellers, which I somewhat wonder'd at, because one of

3

them made nothing of eating *Allegators,* as heartily as if it had been Pork and Turneps.

Crab-Catching Raccoon

The way that this Animal catches Crabs, which he greatly admires, and which are plenty in *Carolina,* is worthy of Remark. When he intends to make a Prey of these Fish, he goes to a Marsh, where standing on the Land, he lets his Tail hang in the Water. This the Crab takes for a Bait, and fastens his Claws therein, which as soon as the *Raccoon* perceives, he, of a sudden, springs forward, a considerable way, on the Land, and brings the Crab along with him. As soon as the Fish finds himself out of his Element, he presently lets go his hold; and then the *Raccoon* encounters him, by getting him cross-wise in his Mouth, and devours him.

Child Discipline

The Bat or Rearmouse, the same as in *England.* The *Indian* Children are much addicted to eat Dirt, and so are some of the Christians. But roast a Bat on a Skewer, then pull the Skin off, and make the Child that eats Dirt, eat the roasted Rearmouse; and he will never eat Dirt again. This is held as an infallible Remedy.

Indian Marriages

When any young *Indian* has a mind for such a Girl to his Wife; he, or some one for him, goes to the young Woman's Parents, if living; if not, to her nearest Relations; where they make Offers of the Match betwixt the Couple. The Relations reply, they will consider of it, which serves for a sufficient Answer, till there be a second Meeting about the Marriage, which is generally brought into Debate before all the Relations (that are old People) on both Sides; and sometimes the King, with all his great Men, give their Opinions therein. If it be agreed on, and the young Woman approve thereof, (for these Savages never give their Children in Marriage, without their own Consent) the Man pays so much for his Wife; and the handsomer she is, the greater Price she bears. Now, it often happens, that the Man has not so much of their Money ready, as he is to pay for his Wife; but if they know him to be a good Hunter, and that he can raise the Sum agreed for, in some few Moons, or any little time, they agree, she shall go along with him, as betroth'd, but he is not to have any Knowledge of her, till the utmost Payment is discharg'd; all which is punctually observ'd. Thus, they lie together under one Covering for several Months, and the Woman remains the same as she was when she first came to him. I doubt, our *Europeans* would be apt to break this Custom, but the *Indian* Men are not so vigorous and impatient in their Love as we are. Yet the Women are quite contrary, and those *Indian* Girls that have convers'd with the *English* and other *Europeans,* never care for the Conversation of their own Countrymen afterwards.

Depriv'd of Reason

They [the Indians] are never fearful in the Night, nor do the Thoughts of Spirits ever trouble them; such as the many Hobgoblins and Bugbears that we suck in with our Milk, and the Foolery of our Nurses and Servants suggest to us; who by their idle Tales of Fairies, and Witches, make such Impressions on our tender Years, that at Maturity, we carry Pigmies Souls, in Giant Bodies and ever after, are thereby so much depriv'd of Reason, and unman'd, as never to be Masters of half the Bravery Nature design'd for us.

Accommodating Son

They are so little startled at the Thoughts of another World, that they not seldom murder themselves; as for Instance, a *Bear-*

River *Indian*, a very likely young Fellow, about twenty Years of Age, whose Mother was angry at his drinking of too much Rum, and chid him for it, thereupon reply'd, he would have her satisfied, and he would do the like no more; upon which he made his Words good; for he went aside, and shot himself dead.

A Vice

Most of the Savages are much addicted to Drunkenness, a Vice they never were acquainted with, till the Christians came amongst them.

A Hanging

. . . they are very resolute in dying, when in the Hands of Savage Enemies; yet I saw one of their young Men, a very likely Person, condemn'd, on a *Sunday*, for Killing a Negro, and burning the House. I took good Notice of his Behaviour, when he was brought out of the House to die, which was the next Morning after Sentence, but he chang'd his Countenance with Trembling, and was in the greatest Fear and Agony. I never saw any Person in his Circumstances, which, perhaps, might be occasion'd by his being deliver'd up by his own Nation (which was the *Tuskeruro's*) and executed by us, that are not their common Enemies, though he met with more Favour than he would have receiv'd at the Hands of Savages; for he was only hang'd on a Tree, near the Place where the Murder was committed; and the three Kings, that but the day before shew'd such a Reluctancy to deliver him up, (but would have given another in his Room) when he was hang'd, pull'd him by the Hand, and said, *Thou wilt never play any more Rogues Tricks in this World; whither art thou gone to shew thy Tricks now?*

Ulcer Cure

Another Instance (not of my own Knowledge, but I had it confirm'd by several Dwellers in *Maryland*, where it was done) was, of an honest Planter that had been possess'd with a strange Lingring Distemper, not usual amongst them, under which he emaciated, and grew every Month worse than another, it having held him several Years, in which time he had made Tryal of several Doctors, as they call them, which, I suppose, were Ship-Surgeons. In the beginning of this Distemper, the Patient was very well to pass, and was possess'd of several Slaves, which the Doctors purged all away, and the poor Man was so far from mending, that he grew worse and worse every day. But it happen'd, that, one day, as his Wife and he were commiserating his miserable Condition, and that he could not expect to recover, but look'd for Death very speedily, and condoling the Misery he should leave his Wife and Family in, since all his Negro's were gone. At that time, I say, it happen'd, that an *Indian* was in the same Room, who had frequented the House for many Years, and so was become as one of the Family, and would sometimes be at this Planter's House, and at other times amongst the *Indians*.

This Savage, hearing what they talk'd of, and having a great Love for the Sick Man, made this Reply to what he had heard. *Brother, you have been a long time Sick; and, I know, you have given away your Slaves to your* English *Doctors: What made you do so, and now become poor? They do not know how to cure you; for it is an* Indian *Distemper, which your People know not the Nature of. If it had been an* English *Disease, probably they could have cured you; and had you come to me at first, I would have cured you for a small matter, without taking away your Servants that made Corn for you and your Family to eat; and yet, if you will give me a Blanket to keep me warm, and some Powder and Shot to kill Deer withal, I will do my best to make you well still.* The Man was low in Courage and Pocket too, and made the *Indian* this Reply. *Jack, my Distemper is past Cure, and if our* English *Doctors cannot cure it, I am sure, the* Indians *cannot.* But his Wife accosted her Husband in very mild terms, and told him, he did not know, but God might be pleased to give a Blessing to that *Indian's* Undertaking more than he had done to the *English;* and farther added; *if you die, I cannot be much more miserable, by giving this small matter to the* Indian; *so I pray you, my Dear, take my Advice, and try him;* to which, by her Persuasions, he consented. After the Bargain was concluded, the *Indian* went into the Woods, and brought in both Herbs and Roots, of which he made a Decoction, and gave it the Man to drink, and bad him go to bed, saying, it should not be long, before he came again, which the Patient perform'd as he had ordered; and the Potion he had administred made him sweat after the most violent manner that could be, wherby he smell'd very offensively both to himself, and they that were about him, but in the Evening, towards Night, *Jack* came, with a great Rattle-Snake in his Hand alive, which frightned the People almost out of their Senses; and he told his Patient, that he must take that to Bed to him; at which the Man was in a great Consternation, and told the *Indian*, he was resolv'd, to let no Snake come into his Bed, for he might as well die of the Distemper he had, as be kill'd with the Bite of that Serpent. To which the *Indian* reply'd, he could not bite him now, nor do him any Harm; for he had taken out his Poison-teeth, and shew'd him, that they were gone. At last, with much Persuasion, he admitted the Snake's Company, which the *Indian* put about his Middle, and order'd nobody to take him away upon any account, which was strictly observ'd, although the Snake girded him as hard for a great while, as if he had been drawn in by a Belt, which one pull'd at, with all his strength. At last, the Snake's Twitches grew weaker and weaker, till, by degrees, he felt him not; and opening the Bed, he was found dead, and the Man thought himself better. The *Indian* came in the Morning, and seeing the Snake dead, told the Man, that his Distemper was dead along with the Snake, which prov'd so as he said, for the Man speedily recover'd his Health, and became perfectly well.

No-Nose Doctors

The Struma is not uncommon amongst these Savages, and another Distemper, which is, in some respects, like the Pox, but is attended with no *Gonorrhoea*. This not seldom bereaves them of their Nose. I have seen three or four of them render'd most miserable Spectacles by this Distemper. Yet, when they have been so negligent, as to let it run on so far without curbing of it; at last, they make shift to patch themselves up, and live for many years after; and such Men commonly turn Doctors. I have known two or three of these no-nose Doctors in great Esteem amongst these Savages.

The Sale of Rum

But when they happen it safe, (which is seldom, without drinking some part of it, and filling it up with Water) and come to an *Indian* Town, those that buy Rum of them have so many Mouthfuls for a Buck-Skin, they never using any other measure; and for this purpose, the Buyer always makes Choice of his Man, which is the one that has the greatest Mouth, whom he brings to the Market with a Bowl to put it in. The Seller looks narrowly to the Man's Mouth that measures it, and if he happens to swallow any down, either through Wilfulness or otherwise, the Merchant or some of his Party, does not scruple to knock the Fellow down, exclaiming against him for false Measure. Thereupon, the Buyer finds another Mouthpiece to measure the Rum by; so that this Trading is very agreeable to the Spectators, to see such a deal of Quarrelling and Controversy, as often happens, about it, and is very diverting.

William Byrd's Lubberland

William Byrd II (1674-1744) of Westover on the James River had such a potent gift for satire that he has come to be recognized as one of America's first humorists. In 1728 he served as one of the Virginia commissioners to settle the boundary dispute between his colony and North Carolina. Some eight or ten years after the survey, he completed a History of the Dividing Line *with the now-famous uncomplimentary remarks on the habits of the North Carolinians he met. It took at least two hundred years before dwellers in Lubberland (his name for North Carolina) could read Byrd with the pleasure—and begrudging forgiveness—he so deserves.*

March 10. The Sabbath happen'd very opportunely to give some ease to our jaded People, who rested religiously from every work, but that of cooking the Kettle. We observed very few corn-fields in our Walks, and those very small, which sem'd the Stranger, to us, because we could see no other Tokens of Husbandry or Improvement. But, upon further Inquiry, we were given to understand People only made Corn for themselves and not for their Stocks, which know very well how to get their own Living.

Both Cattle and Hogs ramble in the Neighbouring Marshes and Swamps, where they maintain themselves the whole Winter long, and are not fetch'd home till the Spring. Thus these Indolent Wretches, during one half of the Year, lose the Advantage of the Milk of their cattle, as well as their Dung, and many of the poor Creatures perish in the Mire, into the Bargain, by this ill Management.

Some, who pique themselves more upon Industry than their Neighbours, will, now and then, in compliment to their Cattle, cut down a Tree whose Limbs are loaden with the Moss aforemention'd. The trouble wou'd be too great to Climb the Tree in order to gather this Provender, but the Shortest way (which in this Country is always counted the best) is to fell it, just like the Lazy Indians, who do the same by such Trees as bear fruit, and so make one Harvest for all. By this bad Husbandry Milk is so scarce, in the Winter Season, that were a Big-belly'd Woman to long for it, She would lose her Longing. And, in truth, I believe this is often the Case, and at the same time a very good reason why so many People in this Province are markt with a Custard Complexion.

The only Business here is raising of Hogs, which is manag'd with the least Trouble, and affords the Diet they are most fond of. The Truth of it is the Inhabitants of N Carolina devour so much Swine's flesh, that it fills them full of gross Humours. For want too of a constant Supply of Salt, they are commonly obliged to eat it Fresh, and that begets the highest taint of Scurvy. Thus, whenever a Severe Cold happens to Constitutions thus Vitiated, tis apt to improve into the Yaws, called there very justly the country-Distemper. This has all the Symptoms of the Pox, with this Aggravation, that no Preparation of Mercury will touch it. First it seizes the throat, next the Palate, and lastly shews its spite to the poor Nose, of which tis apt in a small time treacherously to undermine the Foundation.

This Calamity is so common and familiar here, that it ceases to be a Scandal, and in the disputes that happen about Beauty, the Noses have in some Companies much ado to carry it. Nay, tis said that once, after three good Pork years, a Motion had like to have been made in the House of Burgesses, that a Man with a Nose shou'd be incapable of holding any Place of Profit in the Province; which Extraordinary Motion could never have been intended without Some Hopes of a Majority.

Thus, considering the foul and pernicious Effects of Eating Swine's Flesh in a hot Country, it was wisely forbidden and made an Abomination to the Jews, who liv'd much in the same Latitude with Carolina.

March 11. . . . Nor were these worthy Borderers content to Shelter Runaway Slaves, but Debtors and Criminals have often met with the like Indulgence. But if the Government of North Carolina has encourag'd this unneighbourly Policy in order to increase their People, it is no more than what Ancient Rome did before them, which was made a City of Refuge for all Debtors and Fugitives, and from that wretched Beginning grew up in time to be Mistress of a great Part of the World. And, considering how Fortune delights in bringing great things out of Small, who knows but Carolina may, one time or other, come to be the Seat of some other great Empire?

March 15. . . . At the End of 18 Miles we reacht Timothy Ivy's Plantation, where we picht our Tent for the first Time, and were furnisht with every thing the Place afforded.

We perceiv'd the happy Effects of Industry in this Family, in which every one lookt tidy and clean, and carri'd in their countenances the chearful Marks of Plenty. We saw no Drones there, which are but too Common, alas, in that Part of the World. Tho', in truth, the Distemper of Laziness seizes the Men oftener much than the Women. These last Spin, weave and knit, all with their own Hands, while their Husbands, depending on the Bounty of the Climate, are Sloathfull in every thing but getting of Children, and in that only Instance make themselves useful Members of an Infant-Colony.

March 16. . . . Tis a wonder no Popish Missionaries are sent from Maryland to labour in this Neglected Vineyard, who we know have zeal enough to traverse Sea and Land on the Meritorious Errand of making converts.

Nor is it less Strange that some Wolf in Sheep's cloathing arrives not from New England to lead astray a Flock that has no shepherd. People uninstructed in any Religion are ready to embrace the first that offers. Tis natural for helpless man to adore his Maker in Some Form or other, and were there any exception to this Rule, I should expect it to be among the Hottentots of the Cape of Good Hope and of North Carolina.

March 17. . . . [O]ur Brethren of North Carolina . . . live in a climate where no clergyman can Breathe, any more than Spiders in Ireland.

For want of men in Holy Orders, both the Members of the Council and Justices of the Peace are empower'd by the Laws of that Country to marry all those who will not take One another's Word; but for the ceremony of Christening their children, they trust that to chance. If a Parson come in their way, they will crave a Cast of his office, as they call it, else they are content their Offspring should remain as Arrant Pagans as themselves. They account it among their greatest advantages that they are not Priest-ridden, not remembering that the Clergy is rarely guilty of Bestriding such as have the misfortune to be poor.

One thing may be said for the Inhabitants of that Province, that they are not troubled with any Religious Fumes, and have the least Superstition of any People living. They do not know Sunday from any other day, any more than Robison Crusoe did, which would give them a great Advantage were they given to be industrious. But they keep so many Sabbaths every week, that their disregard of the Seventh Day has no manner of cruelty in it, either to Servants or Cattle.

March 25. . . . Surely there is no place in the World where the Inhabitants live with less Labour than in N Carolina. It approaches nearer to the Description of Lubberland than any other, by the great felicity of the Climate, the easiness of raising Provisions, and the Slothfulness of the People.

Indian Corn is of so great increase, that a little Pains will Subsist a very large Family with Bread, and then they may have meat without any pains at all, by the Help of the Low Grounds, and the great Variety of Mast that grows on the High-land. The Men, for their Parts, just like the Indians, impose all the Work upon the poor Women. They make their Wives rise out of their Beds early in the Morning, at the same time that they lye and Snore, till the Sun has run one third of his course, and disperst all the unwholesome Damps. Then, after Stretching and Yawning for half an Hour, they light their Pipes, and, under the Protection of a cloud of Smoak, venture out into the open Air; tho', if it happens to be never so little cold, they quickly return Shivering into the Chimney corner. When the weather is mild, they stand leaning with both their arms upon the corn-field fence, and gravely consider whether they had best go and take a Small Heat at the Hough: but generally find reasons to put it off till another time.

Thus they loiter away their Lives, like Solomon's Sluggard, with their Arms across, and at the Winding up of the Year Scarcely have Bread to Eat.

To speak the Truth, tis a thorough Aversion to Labor that makes People file off to N Carolina, where Plenty and a Warm Sun confirm them in their Disposition to Laziness for their whole Lives.

March 27 . . . . Within 3 or 4 Miles of Edenton, the Soil appears to be a little more fertile, tho' it is much cut with Slashes, which seem all to have a tendency towards the Dismal.

This Town is Situate on the North side of Albemarle Sound, which is there about 5 miles over. A Dirty Slash runs all along the Back of it, which in the Summer is a foul annoyance, and furnishes abundance of that Carolina plague, musquetas. They may be 40 or 50 Houses, most of them Small, and built without Expense. A Citizen here is counted Extravagant, if he has Ambition enough to aspire to a Brick-chimney. Justice herself is but indifferently Lodged, the Court-House having much the Air of a Common Tobacco-House. I believe this is the only Metropolis in the Christian or Mahometan World, where there is neither Church, Chappel, Mosque, Synagogue, or any other Place of Publick Worship of any Sect or Religion whatsoever.

What little Devotion there may happen to be is much more private than their vices. The People seem easy without a Minister, as long as they are exempted from paying Him. Sometimes the Society for propagating the Gospel has had the Charity to send over Missionaries to this Country; but unfortunately the Priest has been too Lewd for the People, or, which oftener happens, they too lewd for the Priest. For these Reasons, these Reverend Gentlemen have always left their Flocks as arrant Heathen as they found them. Thus much however may be said for the Inhabitants of Edenton, that not a Soul has the least taint of Hypocrisy, or Superstition, acting very Frankly and above-board in all their Excesses.

Provisions here are extremely cheap, and extremely good, so that People may live plentifully at triffleing expense. Nothing is dear but Law, Physick, and Strong Drink, which are all bad in their Kind, and the last they get with so much Difficulty, that they are never guilty of the Sin of Suffering it to Sour upon their Hands. Their Vanity generally lies not so much in having a handsome Dining-Room, as a Handsome House of Office: in this kind of Structure they are really extravagant.

They are rarely guilty of Flattering or making any Court to their governors, but treat them with all the Excesses of Freedom and Familiarity. They are of Opinion their rulers wou'd be apt to grow insolent, if they grew Rich, and for that reason take care to keep them poorer, and more dependent, if possible, than the Saints in New England used to do their Governors.

March 31. . . . We Christen'd two of our Landlord's children, which might have remained Infidels all their lives, had not we carry'd Christianity home to his own Door.

The Truth of it is, our Neighbors of North Carolina are not so zealous as to go much out of their way to procure this benefit for their children: Otherwise, being so near Virginia, they might, without exceeding much Trouble, make a Journey to the next Clergyman, upon so good an Errand.

And indeed should the Neighbouring Ministers, once in two or three years, vouchsafe to take a turn among these Gentiles, to baptize them and their children, twould look a little Apostolical, and they might hope to be requited for it hereafter, if that be not thought too long to tarry for their Reward.

Old-Time Tomfoolery

Our forefathers were prone to laugh at much the same things that we find laughable today. The primary differences were in matters of style and emphasis. The unsophisticated homespun quips in the columns of the Raleigh Rasp *poked outrageous and sometimes almost libelous fun at poetmongers, simpletons, and smart alecks. On another level, our ancestors' interest in verbal play—in words as words, in dialect—was keener than ours. Dialect in "The Debating Society and Other Matters" is used for comic effect as well as a means of satirizing the pomposity of the local pseudo highbrows. Our greatgrandfathers rolled upon the floor at the anticipated absurdities in doggerel. To the art of exaggeration, they set no limits. Unlike their more tolerant and charitable descendants of a later age, they delighted in the hilarious exposure of presumption and affectation. For example, John N. Bunting turned red with humorous ire at the mere thought of pretense, particularly in fashion. Dossey Battle called weddings "benedictal victimizations" and proceeded to poetize his amazing marriage notices. The comic intent of Felix E. Alley's anecdotes concerning Boney Riddley is apparent. All in all, our forefathers were a lusty and raucous folk, and very much alive.*

Quarter

During the Revolutionary War when draughts were made from the militia to recruit the continental army, a certain Captain gave liberty to the men who were draughted from his company to make their objections, if they had any, against going into the service. Accordingly, one of them, who had an impediment in his speech, came up to the Captain and made his bow.

"What is your objection?" said the Captain.

"I ca-a-an't go," answers the man, "because I st-st-ut-ter."

"Stutter!" says the Captain. "You don't go there to talk, but to fight."

"Ay, but they'll p-p-put me upon g-g-guard, and a man may go ha-ha-half a mile before I can say, 'Wh-wh-who goes there?' "

"O, that is no objection, for they will place some other sentry with you, and he can challenge, if you can fire."

"Well, b-b-but I may be ta-ta-taken and run through the g-g-guts before I can cry, 'Qu-qu-quarter!' "

This last plea prevailed, and the Captain, out of humanity, laughing heartily, dismissed him.

[*Raleigh Register*, 29 July 1800.]

The Tavern Bill
Or a new method to drive away Rats

As a pennyless beau from a tavern withdrew,
He call'd on his host for his bill—
It was merely a whim, just to learn what was due,
For payment exceeded his skill.
The landlord in haste (no doctor could quicker)
Exhibits his items for victuals and liquor.
With dread and surprise the beau views the account,
His money so little—so great the amount—
But prudently silent, betrays not his pain,
For he who can't pay should at least not complain.
  Meanwhile the huge host the misfortune regrets,
That his house is eternally pester'd with rats,
And eagerly asks what fit poison can chase,
From his mansion forever, that damnable race.
"My good friend," quoth the beau, with a countenance
  grum,
"I think I have hit on a plan.
Present this account to the rats when they come—
They'll scamper as fast as they can."

[*Edenton State Gazette*, 12 February 1789.]

Anecdote

In a country party, during the summer, a young lady of high rank, who knew that she had very handsome legs, declared, in a laughing careless manner, that she would certainly bring short petticoats into fashion the next winter, that the town might see what a pretty ancle she had—What think you, said she to a certain wit, of the fashion of short petticoats?—It is the particular fashion, Madam, replied he, that I admire above all others, *and I care not to what HEIGHT it is carried.*

[*North-Carolina Minerva* (Raleigh), 3 December 1799.]

Raspings from the Raleigh Rasp

UGLY MAN.—There is a man in this city so ugly that we know of nothing to which he can be compared. Our Zeke [the editor's make-believe assistant], however, who is always at our elbow looking over, says the only thing he can compare him to is a stack of black cats with their tails cut off.

[25 September 1841.]

LAZY MAN.—There is a man in this city who is so extremely lazy that he carries a kitten under each arm to breathe for him.

[26 February 1842.]

POETRY MACHINE.—That Zeke of ours is a dangerous customer. He is quite a moral youth, and is quite seldom absent from the church when opportunity offers. A few evenings since, his devotional feelings were assailed by an attack on his olfactories by a very disagreeable scent of unclean feet, and returning home in a fit of anger, he got hold of our Machine, and ground out the following, in revenge upon the assailant for his filthiness:

> There is a youth in our town
> > Whose foot's so mighty large,
> His shoe, seen floating down the stream,
> > Was taken for a barge.

> A stranger, seeing, hastened on,
> > T'examine keel and hull,
> But smelling strong the stench which rose,
> > Cried, "Contagion, it is *dreadful.*"

    Now warning take, who go to church
      And by him get a seat,
  For I can tell, you're sure to smell
      A pair of stinking feet.

[5 March 1842.]

GO IT, LITTLE 'UN.—A chap about eight years old lately stepped into one of our oyster houses, chewing his quid like an old tar, and squirting his tobacco juice in every direction. Strutting up to a table where a gentleman was indulging in a dish of boiled eggs, he said, "Stranger, I'll take a little of that salt."

"What do you want with it?" inquired the gentleman.

"To eat with one of your eggs."

"Well, my little chap, who's your father?"

"My father! Why, he is the greatest man in the country. He can whip all the bullies, and mamma can lick him just as slick as that," said the chap, who suiting the action to the word, gulphed down the gentleman's glass of beer. His mamma knew he was out. No danger of his starving in a *free* country.

This is the boy who stopped at our office door and called out to Zeke: "Mister, can't you give me a drink of water? I am so hungry, I don't just know where I shall sleep tonight!"

[26 March 1842.]

TAKE HIM AWAY.—A youngster in this city addressed the following lines to his "ladye-love," who, after perusing them, sent them to us for publication. We cheerfully publish them.

    u luvly gurl i Dus luv u
    Wy cant u luv pore i
    to git won kis wot wod i du
    i think ide ner bout di

    u Bets i axed u tu luv me
    but u told me u kuddent
    ide luv u like bawk dus a tree
    but then u sed i shuddent

    i lase my hand rite on my hart
    an sez Bets i luvs u

an twel u takes a worser part
to u i will pruv tru.
[28 May 1842.]

THE BET.—A dandy was one day sitting in a tavern porch, dressed in tights, when a wagoner came along, said, "Stranger, I'll bet you a bottle of wine that with my whip I can cut your tights and not touch your skin."

"Done," said the dandy, and at the word the wagoner drew his whip with all his might and cut the fellow to the bones, at the same time calling for the wine and declaring that he had lost the bet.
[27 August 1842.]

ROOM FOR ALL.—A little fellow asked his mammy who was going to sleep in that-ar bed with Jim and John and Jack and Jo and Kate and Bet and Moll and Jane and Su and Dick and the baby and that strange man what's here to-night!

The old lady brought the little 'un a slap across the face, and pushing her spectacles on top of her head, answered, "Why, me and your daddy! to be sure! and plenty room for Israel and his wife, if they chance to come."
[3 September 1842.]

AWFUL SITUATION!—One of our chums informs us that a few nights since, his rest was disturbed in the following manner: He heard in his sleep two distinct voices exclaiming, "More rope on this side! Don't pull the left one so fast!"

He awoke from his sleep and, to his utter astonishment, he found himself on the floor, and his feet out of the window, with two huge fleas pulling at each leg, trying to carry him off. He said it was with great difficulty he could extricate himself from their grasp, but when he did, he took down his gun and shot one, the head of which weighed four pounds and ten ounces!
[3 September 1842.]

SLEEPING BY THE WHOLESALE.—A curious kind of fellow, whose name we can't exactly recollect, from some cause unknown had been robbed of sleep for eleven nights in succession. He at length determined to make up for lost time, and accordingly put

up at a tavern and rented a room with eleven beds in it.

After the night had cleverly shut the light in, a company of gentlemen who were travelling called at the tavern for lodgings, but the good lady of the house told them that she could not accommodate them, that, true, she had eleven beds in one room, but *one* man occupied the whole. This being the case, the travelling party said they must be entertained, and accordingly proceeded to the chamber door of eleven beds and rapped. No answer was returned. They essayed to open the door; it was locked. They shouted aloud, but received no reply. At last, driven to desperation, they determined upon bursting open the door.

They had no sooner done so than they discovered every bedstead empty and all the eleven beds piled up in the center of the room, with the traveller sound asleep on their top. They aroused him with some difficulty and demanded what in the world he wanted of all those beds.

"Why, look here," said he. "Strangers, I ain't had no sleep these here eleven nights, so I just hired eleven beds to get rested all at once and make up what I have lost. I calculate to do up a considerable mess of sleeping—I've hired all these beds and paid for them and, hang me, if I don't mean to have eleven nights' sleep out of 'em before morning!"

[10 September 1842.]

[The weekly *Rasp* (1841-42) was intended by its nineteen-year-old editor, Wesley Whitaker, Jr., "to rasp down the immoral callosities of the folks" in his home town. Most of the barbs were presumably written by the young editor or his brother, J. B. Whitaker, who joined the venture for five months in 1842.]

To a Bottle

'Tis very strange that you and I
Together cannot pull;
For you are full when I am dry,
And dry when I am full.

[*Milton Chronicle*, 21 May 1858.]

North Carolina Ballroom

"Miss, can I have the pleasure of dancing with you next cotillion?"

"Well, I don't know—"

"Engaged, perhaps?"

"Well, ef you must know, I ain't quite done *chawing my raw-zum!*"

[*The Live Giraffe* (Raleigh), 14 May 1859.]

The Debating Society and Other Matters

Wilumston, Ma 27.

Mr. Editu, Greebul to promise i set mi self doun to rite you about the things that is transpirin in this scluded willage of Wilumstun. in my last i promist for to tel you bout what hapind at the baten scity at the next meten. wel i wus thar an yu wuld ben mused to seen them how tha acted, wel thar wont no boad as how most of the spekurs wernt thar, but tha got to makin motions for to du this & du that & bored the man what tha all caled mr President most Tu deth. at last sum wun got up i bleve it wur leander And made a mottion tu find the tresrur for not bieing curtin bucks for the sciety. wel the tresrur, or the laffin man as sum of the fellurs calls him, gumped cited most tu deth & made a half dusin speches caus he dident wont tu pay that dollar & the little lim uf the lau he got up & thunderd away at a mity rate about the constution not sain any thing about finding the tresrur, while all the rest uf the fellurs wur laffin in thar sleves at them, i thote old fussy lip wud kil hisself laffin. he sed he wonted tu make a spech but wus fraid tha wuld laf at him like tha did at the rest. at last tha broke up all mity wel pleased speculy leander as buttons wernt thar to pich into him.

wel sence then thar has been rite smart gwine on round town And the most spessul was a wedden tuk place at the piscupul church, i tel yu What the bride finale waturs lucked good nuf tu ete standin up in a row all Dresed in White and lookin as plesen as a basket uf chips. wel mr editur i bleve i wil close by Sain suthin bout the 4 juli metin as tuck place at the cort hous las frida nite that lected a oritur & redurs for the prochin 4 guly &c tu or thre on im tride tu make speches & torked bout the fire uf fredum burnin thar brest, but If it did burn it must Have ben mity dim, sorter like thes heer slo maches as tha uses tu blo up rocks with a long thime before it Bustid which wernt the case with nun of them fellurs but sevrul of them curlapsed. in My next i wil rite suthin bout bachlers Hall so tha better mind out.

Yourn til deth
A OBSERVIN MAN

[*Williamston Mercury,* 8 June 1859]

Raleigh Gals

Raleigh, January 12, 1857.—I have concluded to drop you another letter from this city to inform you that Mose has shaken the dust from his feet as a testimony against this old rat town. It's decidedly the darnedest town this side of sunset, except in constables, they are thick here as mosquitoes are in Sampson—and their *bills* more piercing. The people generally try to look so devilish rich, proud, learned, wise, grand and noble, that they completely annihilate "upper tens" into "where did you come from?"

As for the women portion, I never did see the like!—they are just as common as blackberries in their season.—And, Mr. Editor, it is amazing to see how every one of these gals expect to marry, and that too, to some *lion* who is worth his millions and has his hundreds of kinky-heads out in the Far West! In fact, they had the audacity to tell me, *right up to my teeth*, that they wouldn't belittle themselves enough to have as common a fellow as our Mose—and that too, Mr. Editor, without knowing whether or not they could get our Mose! As Cousin [John W.] Syme of the [Raleigh] Register would say, "Joking is joking, and poking is poking," but I be-dad-slapped if any of these gals can poke a crooked stick down a straight man's throat like mine! And such right down hifalutin nonsense as they carry on is insulting to say the least. But, gals, as I don't want to get mad, and as I am going to leave and never return to your flea-hopping city of oaks, I will tell you what I will do. I agree, if I don't marry a prettier, smarter, richer and more religious gal than any of you are, I will consent to give you my head for a soap gourd the balance of my existence.

Now, Mr. Editor, it is amazingly astonishing, to think [that] what bothered, fretted, tormented and troubled Solomon of old, who, it is said, was the wisest and most learned man that ever lived, these Raleigh gals can overcome in a minute. It's no more trouble to them than eating, and they can eat forever, if you will be fool enough to buy them sweet things.

Somewhere in the Songs of Solomon, he says: "We have a little sister, and she hath no *breasts:* what shall we do for our sister in the day she shall be spoken for?"

Now, Mr. Editor, let one of these Raleigh gals be spoken for, and she has no *breasts!* I will wager you all of my victuals for two months, and my new hat and trowsers, that she will make full breasts, and all in five minutes out of *cotton!* What a pity that Solomon couldn't even think of—cotton! And bless your life, that is not all. These Raleigh gals can paint, pad, stuff and fix up the devilishest, ugliest, old-looking maid in christendom, and pack her off on a good, christian-looking man who is unsuspecting, for a lovely sweet-sixteen angel just from the skies!

They even had the boldness to try to play this counterfeit off upon tall Mose, but I soon smelt a rat, and told them that I intended to see my own time in these nuptial affairs, and that I had no notion of going it blind and find myself in a few days (as soon as the paint could wear off) married to an old wrinkled-face maid. That I wasn't so overish anxious to get married as all that. And they got so mad that they gritted their teeth at me, and said I wasn't worthy even of an old maid! They are the worst gals that ever lived on Uncle Sam's domain. The very d——l is in 'em. And as me and that distinguished individual don't pull in the same team, I have concluded to leave the place and go to the country, where gals are gals, not made of cotton, straw, bed-quilts, paint, baby-clothes, grape-vines, barrel hoops, and other household plunder.

[John N. Bunting, *Mose's Letters: Life As It Is, or, The Writings of "Our Mose," Written by "Tall Mose," Correspondent of "The Live Giraffe"* (Raleigh: Whitaker & Bunting, 1858). Little is known about Bunting, except that in the late 1850s he was associated with R. Harper Whitaker in the editing and publication of *The Live Giraffe,* a humorous newspaper along the lines of the earlier *Rasp.* For the *Giraffe,* he was a traveling reporter and commentator as well as subscription agent. Forty-three of his contributions were collected in *Mose's Letters.* In 1857, he was defeated when he ran for clerk of court in Wake County.]

Cheap John's

STATEMENT.

To all whom it may concern:

Bill Gaskin's wife says that Mrs. Thomason told her that she heard Mr. Clawson's wife say that Jno. Lumsden's wife told her that Granny Abby House heard that there was no doubt that the widow Cook said that Capt. Watts' wife thought Col. Williams' wife believed that old Mrs. Grundy reckoned positively that Tim Smith's wife told Miss Kate Jones, that her Aunt declared to the world that it was generally believed that Mother Watson had said in plain terms that she heard Weikel's wife say that her sister Florintina had said that it was well known around Raleigh that Sam Dodd's wife made no bones in saying that in her opinion that it was a matter of fact and of great public interest that Mr. Bradley had said that Mr. Ballard told him that Mr. Brown said that Bunting did declare and circulate that if you want to get first-class

Clothing, Notions, Crockery,

AND EVERYTHING ELSE AT PRICES LOWER
THAN THE LOWEST, GO TO

CHEAP JOHN'S

No. 59 Fayetteville Street,

OPPOSITE MARKET HOUSE,

RALEIGH, N. C.

DAILY NEWS PRINT, RALEIGH, N. C.

[Broadside, 1870s, original owned by Curtis Booker.]

Dossey Battle's Marriage Notices
In the Tarborough Southerner

Married.—At the residence of Mr. Henry Leonard on the 13th inst., by J. J. Cockrell, Esq., Mr. J. A. Barnes to Miss Ida Lane. May their barnes be full of happiness, and the lane be the straight one that leads to glory.
[21 January 1876.]

—In Edgecombe County, on 12 inst., at the residence of the bride's aunt, Mrs. Kenny Mabry, near Killquick, Mr. T. E. Powell, of Nash County, was harnessed matrimonially with Miss Lizzie Cloman, by Rev. Mr. Burns.
Mr. Powell, for life, has got a true woman—
None sweeter or better than fair Lizzie Cloman.
[20 December 1877.]

—John Izzard to Miss Esther A. Bissett.
She aimed a dart at John Izzard
And hit him square in the gizzard.
His target was the heart of Miss Bissett;
The result shows he didn't miss it.
[31 January 1878.]

—Rev. T. J. Eastman, in Wilson County, on 20th January, drew up in solemn array before him W. Burt Ferrell, of Bull-bitch-swapping suit fame, and Miss Mehala Bottoms. This couple hailed from Nash.
Clang the cymbal—send forth the herald
To sound the nuptials of W. Burt Ferrell.
In double harness let him trot so gaily
With exhaustless Bottoms, he and Mehala.
[7 February 1878.]

—Willie J. Macon and Miss Susie J. Wilson.
E. E. Allen and Miss E. D. Davis.
Our congratulations to Messrs. Macon and Allen
On their good luck while going a-gallin';

Our lowest bow to Misses Wilson and Davis—
Your lovers have got each a *rara avis.*
[27 March 1879.]

—Wm. H. Ward and Miss Johnetta Proctor.
 "Oh, me! Help us, O Lord!"
 Spoke in anguish Wm. H. Ward;
 "With a big chunk o' love I'm surely knocked, or
 Som'thin', by the lovely Miss Proctor."
 The prayer was heard and th' thing was brought on
 By timely assistance of Rev. O. C. Horton.
[12 June 1879.]

—M. Dowdy and Miss Alethia Owens.
 When first he approached, he said, "Howdy,"
 Did the gallant Mr. M. Dowdy;
 "My love is yours, I want yowins,
 My dear Miss Alethia Owens."
 She consenting, the sly little mouse,
 They were hitched up for life by Col. Woodhouse.
[17 July 1879.]

—R. H. Baker and Miss Zilphia Massey.
 A woman does well to marry a baker

Or a butcher or candlestick maker.
We trust the Baker, in getting a Massey,
Kind and most dutiful wife he has a.
[24 July 1879.]

—D. S. Pope and Miss Pattie Bishop.
Ambition's reign, when given full scope,
Would make a Bishop sigh to be a Pope.
If th' parity of reason you dish up,
Of course the Pope would want a Bishop.
[8 October 1879.]

—Samuel Eshon, in his 87th year, and Miss Sarah Miller,
only 22.
'Tis nice to see these gay old colts
Frisking like they do.
You should not ask the old man's age,
She is only twenty, too.
[23 October 1879.]

—W. H. Finch and Miss Ann Lewis.
As a wife, Miss Ann Lewis,
Like the snow, pure is.
May poverty's finger never pinch
The home and heart of W. H. Finch.
[13 January 1880.]

—David A. Ray to Miss Ruth McDowell.
He had his "Day in Court"-
Ing, and succeeded—of a truth—
He's a good man and deserved well
To capture such a Ruth.
[29 January 1880.]

—J. L. Ballard, Jr., and Miss Maggie Moore.
A duckie sweet, a duckie mallard,
Is the duckie of J. L. Ballard.
When duckies small fill the floor,
He'll think o' the day he wanted Moore.
[29 April 1880.]

—Robert Vick and Miss Annie Etheridge.
> Mr. Robert Vick,
> Don't play a trick
> But keep your Annie sated
> With plenteous joy
> Without alloy
> While you be Annie mated.

[6 January 1881.]

—E. M. Hyman, Esq., and Miss Hattie Hyman.
> If a Hyman adds a Hyman
> To the happy flock,
> And there are two happy Hymans,
> It shouldn't feelings shock.

[10 February 1881.]

—George F. Parrott and Miss Julie F. Bissell.
> Under the mistle-
> Toe, Julie Bissell
> Has entered into matrimonial joys.
> From cellar to garret
> May the happy *pere* Parrott
> Listen to the warblings of small girls and boys.

[8 September 1881.]

[Dossey Battle (1842-1900), editor of the *Tarborough Southerner* from 1875 to 1890, once wrote, "Matrimony is raging in some portions of the state. So are measles and hog cholera." He also observed, "Other fevers come and go, but matrimonial fever catches a man early in life, and he never thoroughly recovers from it. Those who have not got it, want it and want it bad." Battle, formerly a lieutenant in the Confederate army, practiced law while editing the *Southerner* and became a Superior Court judge a year before his death.]

Earthquake

That reminds us of stories they tell about Southport residents during the Charleston earthquake just before the turn of the century. Some of the folks got out of their houses for fear they would topple down upon them. Then, convinced that this must be the end of the world, they headed for the cemetery so they could see the people come up out of their graves.

["Waterfront," in *State Port Pilot*, reprinted in *The State*, 15 March 1971.]

Boney Ridley, Mountain Boozehound

Boney "protracted" [a] spree until it was thought that he was going to die. All day long on Sunday the neighbors had been gathered at his bedside singing, "Hark, from the tomb a doleful sound" and other songs of like encouraging import. Finally Boney sent for Aunt Polly, his wife, and said to her: "Polly, you have always had great faith in prayer. I'm afraid I'm dying and if there is anything in prayer, I want you to pray for me now." Aunt Polly, good old religious soul that she was, dropped to her knees, and began to pray in this manner: "O, Lord, please have mercy on my poor old drunken husband." When she got that far, Boney interrupted her and said, "O, damn it, Polly, don't tell Him I'm drunk. Tell Him I'm sick."

Long before the time of our prohibition laws, the Methodist minister at Franklin announced that on a certain Saturday he was going to deliver a temperance lecture at Highlands in the upper part of Macon County. At this time Uncle Boney was upwards of eighty-two years of age, but he was as straight and erect as a Cherokee brave.

On the morning of the day that the lecture was to be delivered, Boney had walked across the mountains from his cabin home on the Cowee to Highlands, a distance of some twelve or fifteen miles. Some mischievous young men, after apprising Boney of their intention, introduced him to the minister, assuring him that Boney had walked all this distance across the high mountains for the sole purpose of hearing the temperance lecture. He was about three sheets in the wind at the time, but of course the minister did not know it. When the minister had delivered the first half of his lecture he said: "Now I am going to give you people a living illustration of what temperance will do for a man. Back there sits brother Boney Ridley, who is now eighty-two years of age; but he has walked fifteen miles over a mountain path this morning in order that he may hear me deliver this temperance lecture. Brother Ridley, stand up back there and tell these people what temperance has done for you."

"Brother" Ridley arose to his full stature of six feet and three inches, and said, "Well, preacher, I am bound to confess that for the greater portion of my life I drank to excess. But some twenty years ago I commenced *tapering* off; and it has got so now that if I drink more than a pint at any one time, it has a terrible tendency to fly to my head!"

One night Boney came in about two o'clock A.M., full of "corn." In getting to his bed in the darkness he fell over a chair and made such a racket that Aunt Polly was awakened, and she proceeded to give Boney "a piece of her mind." After awhile Boney awoke with a terrible thirst. In trying to reach the water bucket over in the corner, he fell over another chair which again aroused Aunt Polly. During the night the wind had blown a ball of thread of goose egg proportions off the wall-plate into the water bucket. Boney grabbed the gourd and hurriedly drank about a quart of water, and in the process swallowed this ball of thread. As the ball had fallen, a strand of the thread unwound. After swallowing the thread, Boney felt something between his lips. He commenced pulling it, and as he pulled it he could feel the ball of thread revolving around in his stomach. He began to scream and called for Aunt Polly. She jumped out of bed, fell over one of the chairs Boney had upset, and stormed at him: "You old drunken sot, this is the third time you have disturbed me. What is the matter now?" Boney replied: "Polly, don't abuse me now, of all times, for I do believe that I am *onraveling* from the inside!"

Boney had an enormously large mouth. On one occasion down at Franklin, when Boney was pretty well soaked with corn juice, one of his friends offered to bet five dollars that Boney could put a goose egg in his mouth and then close his lips without breaking the egg. An egg was procured and Boney put it in his mouth and closed his jaws, with the result that he swallowed the egg. He became very much frightened and ran into Dr. Lyle's office exclaiming: "Doctor, I have swallowed a goose egg and I want you to do something for me at once." The doctor told him not to be alarmed, that he was in no danger at all; to which Boney replied: "But, Doctor, you don't understand; I have swallowed a goose egg *whole, shell and all.* I fear that if I move or walk around, it may break inside of me; and if I stay still the darned thing is liable to hatch!"

After Boney went to Franklin to live with his sister, one of his friends one night found him about midnight leaning against a brick building. He was holding a piece of white paper against the wall with his left hand, and with a pencil in his right hand he appeared to be writing a letter. His friend inquired: "Boney, what are you doing?" "I am writing a letter," said Boney. "Who are you writing to?" his friend inquired. "I am writing a letter to myself," Boney replied. "What are you writing to yourself?" his friend desired to know. Boney replied: "How in the h—— do you think I would know? I won't get it till the mail comes tomorrow."

[Felix E. Alley, *Random Thoughts and the Musings of a Mountaineer* (Salisbury: Rowan Printing Co., 1941). Judge Alley (1873-1957), born in Jackson County, wrote the words and music for the popular ballad "Kidder Cole."]

Ham Jones

One of the most acclaimed humorous sketches of antebellum days was "Cousin Sally Dilliard," beloved by Abraham Lincoln and widely imitated. So well-known was it that other pieces by Hamilton Chamberlain Jones (1798-1868) were commonly identified as being "By the Author of 'Cousin Sally Dilliard.'" Though born in Virginia, Ham Jones spent his youth in North Carolina and graduated from its University. As a sideline to his law practice in Salisbury, he edited the Carolina Watchman *there from 1832 to 1839, and for it he occasionally wrote sketches in the vein of "Cousin Sally Dilliard." Later, William T. Porter invited him to contribute to the* Spirit of the Times, *a national sporting weekly that was at that time the principal purveyor of popular American humor. While it would be expected that some of Ham Jones's sketches reflect his experiences in the primitive and chaotic law courts of the day, he was also capable of spinning out variations on two of the most popular subjects of antebellum humor: the country bumpkin in the city and the periodic militia muster days of unsoldierly rustics at the crossroads.*

Cousin Sally Dilliard
Scene: A Court of Justice in North Carolina.

A beardless disciple of Themis rises, and thus addresses the court: May it please your Worships, and you, Gentlemen of the Jury, since it has been my fortune (good or bad I will not say) to exercise myself in legal disquisitions, it has never before befallen me to be obliged to denounce a breach of the peace so enormous and transcending as the one now claiming your attention. A more barbarous, direful, marked and malicious assault—a more willful, violent, dangerous, and murderous battery—and finally, a more diabolical breach of the peace has seldom happened in a civilized country; and I dare say it has seldom been your duty to pass upon one so shocking to benevolent feelings as this, which took place over

at Captain Rice's, in this county—but you will hear from the witnesses.

The witnesses being sworn, two or three were examined and
deposed—one, that he heard the noise, but didn't see the fight—
another, that he saw the row, but don't know who struck first—and
a third, that he was very drunk, and couldn't say much about the
scrimmage.

Lawyer Chops: I am sorry, gentlemen, to have occupied so
much of your time with the stupidity of the witnesses examined. It
arose, gentlemen, altogether from misapprehension on my part.
Had I known as I now do, that I had a witness in attendance, who
was well acquainted with all the circumstances of the case, and who
was able to make himself clearly and intelligibly understood by the
Court and jury, I should not so long have trespassed on your time
and patience. Come forward, Mr. Harris, and be sworn.

So forward comes the witness, a fat, chuffy-looking man, a
"leetle" corned, and took his corporal oath with an air.

Chops: Mr. Harris, we wish you to tell all about the riot that
happened the other day at Captain Rice's, and as a good deal of
time has been already wasted in circumlocution, we wish you to be
as compendious and at the same time as explicit as possible.

Harris: Edzactly. (Giving the lawyer a knowing wink, at the
same time clearing his throat.) Captain Rice, he gin a treat, and
Cousin Sally Dilliard, she came over to our house and axed me if my
wife, she moughtn't go. I told Cousin Sally Dilliard that my wife
was poorly, being as how she had a touch of the rheumaties in the
hip, and the big swamp was in the road, and the big swamp was up,
for there had been a heap of rain lately; but howsomever as it was
she, Cousin Sally Dilliard, my wife, she mought go. Well, Cousin
Sally Dilliard then axed me if Mose, he moughtn't go. I told Cousin
Sally Dilliard that Mose, he was the foreman of the crop, and the
crop was smartly in the grass; but howsomever as it was she, Cousin
Sally Dilliard, Mose, he mought go.

Chops: In the name of common sense, Mr. Harris, what do you
mean by this rigmarole?

Witness: Captain Rice, he gin a treat, and Cousin Sally
Dilliard, she came over to our house and axed me if my wife, she
moughtn't go. I told Cousin Sally Dilliard—

Chops: Stop, sir, if you please. We don't want to hear anything about Cousin Sally Dilliard and your wife. Tell us about the fight at Rice's.

Witness: Well, I will, sir, if you will let me.

Chops: Well, sir, go on.

Witness: Well, Captain Rice, he gin a treat, and Cousin Sally Dilliard, she came over to our house and axed me if my wife, she moughtn't go—

Chops: There it is again! Witness, witness, I say, witness, please to stop.

Witness: Well, sir, what as you want?

Chops: We want to know about the fight, and you must not proceed in this impertinent story. Do you know anything about the manner before the Court?

Witness: To be sure I do.

Chops: Will you go on and tell it, and nothing else?

Witness: Well, Captain Rice, he gin a treat—

Chops: This is intolerable! May it please the Court, I move that this witness be committed for a contempt. He seems to me to be trifling with the Court.

Court: Witness, you are now before a Court of Justice, and unless you behave yourself in a more becoming manner, you will be sent to jail; so begin and tell what you know about the fight at Captain Rice's.

Witness: (Alarmed.) Well, gentlemen, Captain Rice, he gin a treat, and Cousin Sally Dilliard—

Chops: I hope that this witness may be ordered into custody.

Court: (After deliberating.) Mr. Attorney, the Court is of opinion that we may save time by telling the witness to go on in his own way. Proceed, Mr. Harris, with your story, but stick to the point.

Witness: Yes, gentlemen. Well, Captain Rice, he gin a treat, and Cousin Sally Dilliard, she came over to our house and axed me if my wife, she moughtn't go. I told Cousin Sally Dilliard that my wife was poorly, being as how she had the rheumaties in the hip, and the big swamp was in the road, and the big swamp was up; but howsomever, as it was she, Cousin Sally Dilliard, my wife, she mought go. Well, Cousin Sally Dilliard then axed me if Mose, he moughtn't go. I told Cousin Sally Dilliard as how Mose, he was the foreman of the crop, and the crop was smartly in the grass; but howsomever, as it was she, Cousin Sally Dilliard, Mose, he mought

go. So on they goes together, Mose, my wife, and Cousin Sally
Dilliard, and they comes to the big swamp, and the big swamp was
up, as I was telling you. But being as how there was a log across the
big swamp, Cousin Sally Dilliard and Mose, like genteel folks, they
walks the log, but my wife, like a d——d fool, hoists up her petticoats and waded, and, gentlemen, that's the height of what I know
about it.

[*Atkinson's Saturday Evening Post* (Philadelphia), 6 August 1831.]

A Buncombe Story

But this that I am gaun to tell,
Which lately on a night befell,
Is just as true's the Devil's in h——l
    Or Dublin City.

        Burns

A real raw of a chap went with his intended to Asheville to get
license to be married, but the Clerk was not there. He lived a few
miles in the country, so they did not know what to do. They were
informed, however, that Mr. C., a merchant in the place, delivered
out licenses for the Clerk in his absence. Away they posted to the
store and asked "if they had marriage licenses to sell there." The
merchant answered that he usually kept licenses there for the Clerk,
but that the whole stock was exhausted.

This was awkward again. The two lovers had a consultation. It
was too late to go to the Clerk in the country, and there seemed no
alternative but a postponement of the wedding—when of a sudden
the gloomy prospect was cleared up. Dan Wilson, a merry constable, saw that the bridegroom was a flat. He saw, too, the awk-
wardness of their predicament, and beckoning the fellow to one
side, he asked him who was to marry him.

"Squire W.," was the answer.

"I can give you license," said the constable.

"Can you?" said the countryman, and his heart leapt for joy.

The writing was drawn, and it ran nearly thus:

Old W——
    You d——d old fool,

You are hereby commanded to bind this rascal
in the bonds of matrimony with this b——ch, firm
and tight, and be d——d to you.
                                        Signed
                                        Nobody

Squire W——, a good, easy, conscientious man, lived in the
border of the town of Asheville. Thither the devoted two repaired
and made known their business. The squire simply asked if they
had a license. On the fellow's answering that he had, he proceeded
without further parley to tie the knot. Shortly thereafter, the effec-
tual rite of *stowing away* (as the sailors have it) was duly performed.

And now, we must for a while leave the parties to their happiness while we change the scene for a moment; and this carries us
back to Asheville.

Dan Wilson was so full of his joke that he whispered it first in
one ear and then in another until every wag of a merchant's clerk in
the village had got wind of it. So after the stores were closed for the
night and supper was over, several of them marched down to the
squire's to see how the thing had taken with him.

"Well, squire," says one of them, "we heard there was to be a
wedding here tonight, and we have come down to see it."

"You are too late," says the squire. "The wedding is over and
the parties are gone to bed."

"But," inquired the spokesman of the party, "did they have a
license, squire?"

"Why yes," said he, "I suppose they had. I asked the man and
he said he had."

"Well, but did you see it? It is well enough to look into these
things. You know there is a heavy penalty for marrying people without authority, and we learn that the fellow did not have license."

"I did not see it," said Squire W., "but I *will* see it."

Accordingly he pushed into the apartment of the wedded ones,
and presently brought forth a paper, which he commenced reading
partly to himself and partly aloud, soliloquizing as he read, pretty
much thus:

"Old W——. What's this, what's this? *Fool*— I'm dished, I
am tricked—ruined! *Bind this rascal*—. Dan Wilson, just like him.
Hum, hum, hum—*firm and tight*. Yes, It's Dan! *Signed, Nobody!*
GET UP! GET UP!" roared the squire as loud as he could bawl.

"GET UP!You ain't married! You ain't half married! The license ain't good! GET UP!"

And before the bedded couple could comprehend head or tail of the fuss, he rushed into the chamber, and seizing the first foot he could get hold of, which happened to be that of the man, he dragged him out of bed and left him sprawling on the floor.

The result was that the disturbed bridegroom had to ride off several miles to the Clerk and get a lawful warrant, whereby he was legally tied "tight and firm" about daybreak.

[*Carolina Watchman* (Salisbury), 16 April 1836.]

McAlpin's Trip to Charleston

In the county of Robeson, in the State of North Carolina, there lived in times past a man by the name of Brooks who kept a grocery for a number of years, and so had acquired most of the land around him. This was mostly pine barrens of small value, but nevertheless Brooks was looked up to as a great landholder and big man in the neighborhood. There was one tract, however, belonging to one Col. Lamar, who lived in Charleston, that *"jammed in upon him so strong,"* and being withal better in quality that the average of his own domain, that Brooks had long wished to add it to his other broad acres. Accordingly he looked around him and employed, as he expressed it, "the smartest man in the neighborhood," to wit, one Angus McAlpin, to go to Charleston and negotiate with Col. Lamar for the purchase of this also. Being provided pretty well with bread, meat, and a bottle of *pale-face,* which were stowed away in a pair of leather saddle bags, and, like all other great Plenipotentiaries, being provided with suitable instructions, Mac mounted a piney-woods-tacky named Rasum and hied him off to Charleston.

The road was rather longer than Brooks had supposed, or his agent was less expeditious, or some bad luck had happened to him, or something was the matter that Angus did not get back until long after the day had transpired which was fixed on for his return. Brooks in the meantime had got himself into a very fury of impatience. He kept his eyes fixed on the Charleston road, he was crusty towards his customers, harsh towards his wife and children, and scarcely eat or slept for several days and nights, for he had set his whole soul upon buying the Lamar land.

One day, however, Angus was descried slowly and sadly wending his way up the long stretch of sandy road that made up to the grocery. Brooks went out to meet him, and, without further ceremony, he accosted him.

"Well, Mac, have you got the land?"

The agent, in whose face was anything but sunshine, replied somewhat gruffly that "he might let a body get down from his horse, before he put at him with questions of business."

But Brooks was in a fever of anxiety and repeated the question—

"Did you get it?"

"Shaw, now, Brooks, don't press upon a body in this uncivil way. It is a long story and I must have time."

Brooks still urged and Mac still parried the question till they got into the house.

"Now, surely," thought Brooks, "he will tell me." But Mac was not quite ready.

"Brooks," says he, "have you anything to drink?"

"To be sure I have," said the other, and immediately had some of his best forthcoming. Having moistened his clay, Mac took a seat and his employer another. Mac gave a preliminary *hem!* He then turned suddenly around to Brooks, looked him straight in the eyes, and slapped him on the thigh.

"Brooks," says he, "was you ever in Charleston?"

"Why, you know I never was," replied the other.

"Well, then, Brooks," says the agent, "you ought to go there. The greatest place upon the face of the earth! They've got houses there on both sides of the road for five miles at a stretch, and d——n the horse-track the whole way through! Brooks, I think I met five thousand people in a minute, and not a chap would look at me. They have got houses there on wheels. Brooks! I saw one with six horses hitched to it, and a big driver with a long whip going it like a whirlwind. I followed it down the road for a mile and a half, and when it stopt I looked and what do you think there was? Nothing in it but one little woman sitting up in one corner. Well, Brooks, I turned back up the road, and as I was riding along I sees a fancy-looking chap with long curly hair hanging down his back, and his boots as shiney as the face of an up-country nigger! I called him into the middle of the road and asked him a civil question—and a civil question, you know, Brooks, calls for a civil answer all over the world. I says, says I, 'Stranger, can you tell me where Col. Lamar lives?' and what do you think was his answer—'*Go to h——l, you fool!!*'

"Well, Brooks, I knocks along up and down and about, until at last I finds out where Col. Lamar lived. I gets down and bangs away at the door. Presently the door was opened by as pretty, fine-spoken, well-dressed a woman as ever you seed in your born days, Brooks. *Silks!* Silks *thar* every day, Brooks! Says I, 'Mrs. Lamar, I presume, Madam,' says I. 'I am Mrs. Lamar, Sir.' 'Well, Madam,' says I, 'I have come all the way from North Carolina to see Colonel Lamar—to see about buying a track of land from him that's up in our parts.' Then she says, 'Col. Lamar has rode out in the country, but will be back shortly. Come in, Sir, and wait a while. I've no doubt the Colonel will soon return.' And she had a smile upon that pretty face of hers that reminded a body of a spring morning.

"Well, Brooks, I hitched my horse to a brass thing on the door, and walked in. Well, when I got in, I sees the floor all covered over with the nicest looking thing! Nicer than any patched-worked bed quilt you ever seed in your life, Brooks. I was trying to edge along round it, but presently I sees a big nigger come stepping right over it. Thinks I, if that nigger can go it, I can go it, too! So right over it I goes and takes my seat right before a picture which at first I thought was a little man looking in at a window.

"Well, Brooks, there I sot waiting and waiting for Col. Lamar, and *at* last—he didn't come, but they began to bring in dinner. Thinks I to myself, here's a scrape. But I made up my mind to tell her, if she axed me to eat—to tell her with a genteel bow that I *had no occasion to eat*. But, Brooks, she didn't ax me to eat—she axed me if I'd be so good as to carve that turkey for her, and she did it with one of them lovely smiles that makes the cold streaks run down the small of a feller's back. 'Certainly, Madam,' says I, and I walks up to the table.

"There was on one side of the turkey a great big knife as big as a bowie knife, and a fork with a trigger to it on the other side. Well, I falls to work, and in the first *e*-fort I slashed the gravy about two yards over the whitest table cloth you ever seed in your life, Brooks! Well! I felt the hot steam begin to gather about my cheeks and eyes. But I'm not a man to back out for trifles, so I makes another *e*-fort and the darned thing took a flight and lit right in Mrs. Lamar's lap! Well, you see, Brooks, then I was taken with a blindness, and the next thing I remember I was upon the *hath* a-kicking. Well, by this time I began to think of navigating. So I goes out and mounts Rasum, and cuts for North Carolina! Now, Brooks, you don't blame me! Do you?"

[*Spirit of the Times* (New York), 11 July 1846.]

Going to Muster in North Carolina

John S. Guthrie, Esq., of Chatham [County], long a member of the Legislature, was distinguished for his good sense, fine wit, and occasionally some of the most extraordinary bursts of eloquence. . . . The fact is, if there was any painter on earth who could have apprehended the expression of John's face when he was in the proper vein—that broad, kind, habitual smile, the quizzical leer of that impatient grey eye, and above all, the longitudinal expansion of that mouth, with its peculiar curves and angles—I would have the picture for my frontispiece. . . .

He says that when he arrived at the age of eighteen, he was put upon the muster roll, and duly warned by the orderly of the company to appear on next Saturday morning at the usual parade ground, equipped according to law. John says that he knew well enough that he was eighteen years old, but the thought of bearing arms in the service of his country had never once crossed his brain; but when the idea was brought home to him by the summons of the subordinate of Captain Diddler, he says he did not know what he should do—so near being a man! So he went and whipped a big boy that had always kept him under, and took a dose of medicine for fear he should grow too fast!

Well, Saturday at length came, and off he starts, after an early breakfast, towards the glorious spot where he was to "shoulder arms" for the first time in his life as a sure-enough soldier, and if he had not been stopped, he would have been at the muster-ground an hour at least before anyone else. But as he was passing by old Mr. Emerson's, he was hailed by that worthy to know where he was going. He quickly made known his destination—when the old man told him to come in and wait a while, for that he was going that way himself. John says he paused to consider what he should do; it looked like checking him in the dawn of his career to glory, but the old fellow insisted, and in he went.

He sat for a while, and watched the slow and deliberate preparations of his proposed companion, and he thought he should have dropped down with impatience, but still the old man pursued the "even tenor of his way." He went to the kitchen, and got a tin cup of hot water; he then took out a rusty razor, and strapped—strapped—strapped it, until—until he could have seen it drawn across the old chap's weasand. He then quietly lathered his face, and then tugged and grinned, and re-lathered and tugged away again. He thought at length, by way of relief, of taking a conversation with the old lady, who was sitting by, knitting; but here comes the crisis of our story. Old Mrs. Emerson was obviously in no very serene condition of temper, and his reception in this quarter was anything but entertaining.

"Mrs. Emerson," says he, "how do you come on raising chickens this year?"

"I don't know," replied she, in a quick, barking kind of voice.

Falls short, thinks John, but after sitting a while, he resolves to try her again—

"Mrs. Emerson, how do the girls come on getting sweethearts?"

"I don't know! I reckon you know as much about that as I do," says she.

He turned and discovered that there was a pent-up storm in her face. Her knitting needles were urged together with such emphasis that they sounded like castanets, and as she tossed the thread over the busy points, she had the air of throwing off her indignation from her forefingers. John then turned to notice the old man.

Having performed the operations of scraping and scouring, he moved to a large chest, and taking out a shirt, pantaloons, waistcoat, and stockings, he proceeded towards the door of an adjacent room with his clothes in his hand. But just about the time he had accomplished half that distance, Mrs. Emerson boiled over.

"Old man!" said she, straightening herself up and pointing with a long skinny finger right at him. The old fellow stopped and made a sort of half face to the right. "Old man!! Now you are going to that nasty muster, and there you'll get drunk and spend all your money. And you'll wallow in the dirt, and I shall have your clothes to wash. You *shan't go!!*—YOU RAILY SHAN'T GO!!!"

"Well, old woman," says he, "there was no use in making such a terrible to-do about it, for I had partly gin it out anyhow!"

John said he didn't wait for any excuse from the old man, but went forward and got to muster in full time.

[*Spirit of the Times* (New York), 18 July 1846.]

John Winslow's Billy Warrick

Following a three-installment run in the Spirit of the Times, *editor William T. Porter included the anonymous "Billy Warrick's Courtship and Wedding" in his collection* The Big Bear of Arkansas and Other Tales *(1845). More than a hundred years later Norris W. Yates* (Papers of the Bibliographical Society of America, *1954 Second Quarter) identified the author as the Fayetteville lawyer John Winslow. Winslow was a graduate of The University of North Carolina at Chapel Hill and a brother of Governor Warren Winslow. According to one account, John Winslow was so "especially fond of hunting" that his law practice suffered. The Billy Warrick sketches are among the best examples of the popular humor that took the form of atrociously spelled letters written by lively folk in the backcountry.*

Billy Warrick's Courtship and Wedding
A Story of "The Old North State"—By A County Court Lawyer

Chapter I. Warrick in Distress
Piney Bottom in Old North State
Jinuary this 4, 1844

Mr. Porter—Sir:—Bein' in grate distrest, I didn't know what to do, till one of the lawyers councilled me to tell you all about it, and git your apinion. You see, I are a bin sparkin' over to one of our nabors a cortin of Miss Barbry Bass, nigh upon these six munse.

So t'other nite I puts on my stork that cum up so high that I look'd like our Kurnel paradin of the milertary on Ginral Muster, tryin' to look over old Snap's years—he holds sich a high hed when he knows that he's got on his holdsturs and pistuls and his trowsen and sich like, for he's a mity proud hoss. I had on a linun shurt koller starched stif that cum up monstrus high rite under my years, so that evry time I turn'd my hed it putty nigh saw'd off my years, and they are so sore that I had to put on sum Gray's intment, which draw'd so hard, that if I hadn't wash'd it in sopesuds I *do* bleve it would a draw'd out my branes. I put on my new briches that is new fashon'd and opens down before, and it tuck me nigh on a quarter of a houre to butten em, and they had straps so tite I could hardly bend my kneas. I had on my new wastecoat and a dicky bussam with ruffles on each side, and my white hat. I had to be perticlar nice in spittin' my terbaccer juce, for my stork were so high I had to jerk back my head like you have seed one of them Snapjack bugs. Considrin' my wiskurs hadn't grow'd out long enuff, as I were conceety to think that I look'd middlin' *peart,* and my old nigger 'oman Venus said I look'd nice enuff for a Bryde.

It tuck one bale of good cotting and six bushils of peese to pay for my close. Dod drot it, it went sorter hard; but when I tho't how putty she *did* look last singin' school day—with her eyes as blue as indiger, and her teath white as milk, and sich long curlin' hare hangin' clear down to her belt ribbun, and sich butiful rosy cheaks, and lips as red as a cock Red-burd in snow time, and how she squeased my hand when I gin her a oringe that I gin six cents for—I didn't grudge the price.

Mr. Porter—when I got to old Miss Basses bars, jist after nite, sich streaks and cold fits cum over me worse than a feller with the Buck agur, the furst time he goes to shute at a dear. My kneas got to trimblin', and I could hardly holler "get out" to Miss Basses son Siah's Dog, old Troup, who didn't know me in my new geer, and cum out like all creashun a barkin' amazin'. Ses I to myself, ses I, what a fool you is—and then I thort what Squire Britt's nigger man Tony, who went to town last week, told me about a taler there, who sed that jist as soon he got thru a makin' a sute of close for a member of assembly to go to Rawley in, he 'spected to come out a cortin' of Miss Barbry. This sorter rased my dander—for he's shockin' likely, with black wiskurs, 'cept he's nock-nead—with his hare all comded to one side like the Chapel Hill boys and lawyers.

Then I went in, and after howdying and shakin' hands, and sorter squeasin' of Barbry's, I sot down. There was old Miss Bass,

Barbry, and Siah Bass, her brother (a monstrus hand at possums), old Kurnel Hard, a goin to cort and stopp'd short to rite old Miss Basses will, with Squire Britt and one of the nabors to witness it all rite and strate.

This kinder shock'd me—till Kurnel Hard, a mighty perlite man, sed, ses he, "Mr. Warrick, you are a lookin' oncommon smart."

"Yes," ses I, "Kurnel" (a sorter cuttin' my eye at Barbry), "middlin' well in body—but in mind. . . ."

"Ah, I see," ses he (cuttin' off my discoorse), "I understand that you are—" (Mr. Porter, I forget the Dixonary words he sed—but it were that I were in *love*.)

If you *could* have seed my face and felt it burne, you *would* a tho't that you had the billyous fever—and as for Barbry, now want she red as a turkey cock's gills—and she gump'd up and said, "Ma'am," and run outer the room, tho' nobody on yearth that I heerd on called her—and then I heerd Polly Cox—drot her pictur!—who is hired to weeve—a sniggrin at me.

Arter a while, Squire Britt and the nabor went off—and Siah he went a Coonin' of it with his dogs, but driv old Troup back, for he's deth on Rabbits—and old Miss Bass went out, and Kurnel Hard, arter taken a drink outen his cheer box, he got behin' the door and shuck'd himself and got into one of the beds in the fur eend of the room. Arter a while, old Miss Bass cum back, and sot in the chimbly corner and tuck off her shoes—and then tuck up her pipe and went to smokin'—the way she rowl'd the smoke out was astonishin'—and evry now and then she struck her head and sorter gron'd like. What it were at, I don't know, 'cept she were bother'd 'bout her consarns—or thinkin' 'bout her will which she had jist sined.

Bimeby Barbry cum back, and sot on a cheer clost by me. She was a workin' of a border that looked mity fine.

Ses I, "Miss Barbry, what is that you're seamstring so plagy putty?"

Ses she, "It teent nothin'."

Up hollered old Miss Bass. "Why," ses she, "Mr. Warrick, it's a *nite cap*, and what on the Lord's yearth young peple now a days works and laces and befrils nite caps fur *I* can't tell—it beets me—bedizin' out their heads when they're gwain to bed, just as if anybody but their own peple seed 'em; and there's young men with wiskurs on there upper lip, and briches upenin' before—it want so in my day—but young peple's got no sense—bless the Lord—oh me."

"Lord, mammy," ses Babry, "do hush."

Ses old Miss Bass, "I shaant—for its the nat'ral truth."

I sorter look'd at my briches— and Mr. Porter, I were struck into a heap—for if two of my buttons want loose, so that one could see the eend of my factry homespun shurt! I drap't my handkercher in my lap, and run my hand down and hapen'd to button it putty slick—but it gin me sich a skeer—I shall never ware another pare.

Miss Barbry then begun a talkin' with me 'bout the fashuns, when I were in town, but old Miss Bass broke in, ses she, "Yes, they tells me that the gals in town has injun rubber things blowed up and ties aroun' there wastes, and makes 'em look bigger behin' than afore—for all the world like an 'omen was sorter in a curous way behind."

Thinks I, what's comin' next—when old Miss Bass, knockin' the ashes outer her pipe, gethered up her shuse and went off.

Then Barbry blushed and begun talkin' 'bout the singin' meetin', and kinder teched me up 'bout bein' fond of sparkin' Dicey Loomis—jist to see how I'd take it.

"Well," ses I, "she's 'bout the likeliest gal in this settlement, and I reckon mity nigh the smartest—they tells me she kin spin more cuts in a day, and card her own rolls, and danse harder and longer, and sing more songs outer the Missunary Harmony, than any gal in the country."

You see, Mr. Porter, I thot I'd size her pile.

Ses she, sorter poutin' up and jist tossin her head, "If them's your sentiments, why don't you cort her? For my part, I knows sevral young ladies that's jist as smart and can sing as many songs—and dance as well—and as for her bein' the prettiest—Lawz a Mersy! sher—you shouldn't judge me for sposin' *I* was a man!"

I thot I'd come again, but was sorter feard of runnin' the thing in the groun'. Then I drawd up my cheer a leetle closer, and were jist about to talk to the spot, when I felt choky, and the trimbles tuck me uncommon astonishin'.

Ses Barbry, lookin' rite up in my face, and sorter quivrin in her talk, ses she, "Mr. Warrick, goodness gracious, *what does* ale you?"

Ses I, hardly abel to talk, "It's that drotted three-day agur I cotch'd last fall a clearin' in the new grouns—I raly bleve it will kill me, but it makes no odds,—daddy and mammy is both ded, and I'm the only one of six as is left, and nobody would kear."

Ses she, lookin' rite mornful, and holdin' down her hed, "Billy, what *does* make you talk so?—you auter know that there's one that would kear and greve too."

Ses I, peartin up, "I should like to know if it ar an 'oman—for if it's any gal that's spectable and creddittable, I could love her like all creashun. Barbry," ses I, takin of her hand, "ain't I many a time, as I sot by the fire at home, all by my lone self, ain't I considered how if I *did* have a good wife how I could work for her, and do all I could for her, and make her pleasant like and happy, and do evry thing for her?"

Well, Barbry she look'd up to me, and seemed so mornful and pale, and tears in her sweet eyes, and pretendin' she didn't know I held her hand, that I could not help sayin', "Barbry, if that sumbody that keard was only *you*, I'd die for you, and be burryd a dozen times."

She trimbld, and look'd so pretty, and sed nothin'. I couldn't help kissin' her, and seein' she didn't say "quit," I kissed her nigh on seven or eight times; and as old Miss Bass had gone to bed, and Kurnel Hard was a snorin' away, I wan't perticillar, and I spose I kissed her too loud, for jist as I kissed her the last time, out hollered old Miss Bass.

"My Lord!—Barbry, old Troup is in the milk-pan!—I heerd him smackin his lips a lickin of the milk. Git out, you old varmint!—git out!"

Seein' how the gander hopped, I jumped up, and hollered, "Git out, Troup, you old raskel!" and opened the door to make bleve I let him out. As for Barbry, she laffed till she was nigh a bustin' a holdin' in, and run out; and I heerd Kurnel Hard's bed a shakin' like he had my three-day agur. Well, I took tother bed, after havin' to pull my britches over my shuse, for I couldn't unbutten my straps.

Next morning I got up airly, and Siah axed me to stay to breakfast, but I had to feed an old cow at the free pastur, and left. Jist as I got to the bars, I meets old Miss Bass, and ses she, "Mr. Warrick, next time you see a dog a lickin up milk, don't let him do it loud enuff to wake up evry body in the house, perticerlar when there's a stranger 'bout."

And Barbry sent me word that she's so shamed that she never kin look me in the face agin, and never to come no more.

Mr. Porter, what shall I do? I feel oncommon sorry and distrest. Do write me. I see a letter from N. P. Willis tother day in the Nashunal Intelligensur where he sed he had a hedake on the top of his pen; I've got it at both eends, for my hands is crampped a writin, and my hart akes. Do write me what to do.

No more at pressence, but remane

Wm. Warrick.

Chapter II. Warrick in Luck

"I'd orfen heerd it said ob late,
Dat Norf Carolina was de state,
Whar hansome boys am bound to shine,
Like Dandy Jim of de Caroline." Etc.

Piney Bottom, in Old North State
March 21, this 1844

Mr. Porter,—I rode three mile evry Satterdy to git a letter outer the Post Offis, spectin' as how you had writ me a anser; but I spose what with Pineter dogs, and hosses, and Kricket, and Boxin', and Texas, Trebla, and three Fannys, and Acorns, and Punch in perticlar, you hain't had no time. I'm glad your *Speerit* is revivin'; so is mine, and, as the boy sed to his mammy, I hopes to be better acquainted with you.

Well, I got so sick in my speerits and droopy like that I thot I should ev died stone ded, not seein' of Barbry for three weeks. So one evenin' I went down, spectin' as how old Miss Bass had gone to Sociashun—for she's mity religus, and grones shockin' at prayers—to hear two prechers from the Sanwitch Ilans, where they tells me the peple all goes naked—which is comikil, as factry home-spun is cheap, and could afford to kiver themselves at nine cents a yard. When I went in, there sot old Miss Bass and old Miss Collis asmokin' and chattin' amazin'. I *do* think old Miss Collis beats all natur at smokin'.

Old Miss Collis had on her Sundy frock, and had it draw'd up over her kneas to keep from skorchin', and her pettykoats rased tol-erble high as she sot over the fire to be more comfortabler like, but when she seed me she drop'd 'em down, and arter howdying and civerlizin' each other I sot down, but being sorter flusticated like, thinkin' of that skrape, last time I was here, about old Troup lickin' of the milk, and my briches that is open before comin' unbotten'd and showin' the end of my sheert, I didn't notis perticlar where I sot. So I sot down in a cheer where Barbry had throw'd down her work when she seed me comin' at the bars, and run—and her nedle stuck shockin' in my—into *me*, and made me jump up oncommon and hollered!

I thought old Miss Collis woulder split wide open a laffin', and old Miss Bass like to a busted, and axed my parding for laffin', and I had to give in, but it was laffin' on t'other side, and had to rub the place.

Arter a while we got done—but it looked like I had bad luck, for in sittin' down agin I lik'd to have sot on Barbry's tom cat, which if I had, I shoulder bin like Kurnel Zip Coon's wife, who jump'd into a holler log to mash two young panters to deth, and they scratched her so bad she couldn't set down for two munse! I seed this 'ere in a almynack. Old Miss Bass, seein' I was bothered, axed me to have a dram, but I thank'd her, no.

Ses she, "Mr. Warrick, you ain't one of the Temprite Siety?"

Ses I, "No, but I hain't got no casion, at presence!"

Ses she, "You is welcome."

Well, we chatted on some time 'bout prechin, and mumps, and the measly ointment, and Tyler gripes, and Miss Collis she broke out and sed, "I never *did* hear the beat of them Tyler gripes! I have hearn talk of all sorter gripes, and dry gripes, and always thought that the gripes was in the stomic, before now, but bless your soul, Miss Bass, this here gripes is in the hed! I told my old man that no good would come of 'lectin' Tyler, but poor old creeter, he's sorter hard-headed, and got childish, and would do it. O me! Well, we're all got to come to it and leve this world! Bless the Lord! I hope I'm ready!''

And then she struck her hed, and spit out her terbaccer juce as slick as a Injun.

"That's a fact," ses old Miss Bass, "youre right, Miss Collis; old men gits uncommon stubborn; a hard, mity hard time, I had with my old man. But he's ded and gone! I hope he's happy!" And they both groaned and shet their eyes, and pucked up their mouths. Ses she, "He got mity rumitys and troubled me powerful, and the old creetur tuck astonishin' of dokter's stuff, and aleckcampane and rose of sublimit—but he went at last! The Lord's will be done! —Skat! you stinkin' hussy, and come out of that kibbard!" ses she to the cat. "I *do* think cats is abominable, and that tom cat of Barbry's is the 'scheviousest cat I ever *did* see!"

Ses Miss Collis, "Cats *is* a pest, but a body can't do well without 'em; the mice would take the house bodily," ses she. "Miss Bass, they tells me that Dicey Loomis is a-gwying to be married. Her peple was in town last week, and bort a power of things and artyfishals, and lofe sugar, and ribbuns, and cheese, and sich like!"

"Why," ses Miss Bass, "you don't tell me so! Did I ever hear the beat o' that! Miss Collis, are it a fact!"

"Yes," ses Miss Collis, "it's the nat'ral truth, for brother Bounds tell'd it to me at last class meetin'."

Ses Miss Bass, hollerin' to Barbry in t'other room, "Barbry, do you hear that Dicey Loomis is gwying to git married? Well! well! it beats me! bless the Lord! I wonder who she's gwying to git married to, Miss Collis?"

Ses Miss Collis, "Now, child, yure too hard for me; but they do say it's to that taler from Town. Well, he's a putty man, and had on such a nice dress, 'cept he's most too much nock nead, *sich* eyes and *sich* whiskers, and now *don't* he play the fiddle!"

Ses Miss Bass, "Well, Dicey is a middlin' peart gal, but for my part I don't see what the taler seed in *her*."

"Nor I nuther," ses Miss Collis," but she's gwine to do well. I couldn't a sed no if he'd a axed for our Polly."

Then in comes Barbry, and we howdy'd and both turned sorter red in the face, and I trimbl'd tolerable and felt agurry. Well, arter we talk'd a spell, all of us, Miss Bass got up and ses she, "Miss Collis, I want to show you a nice passel of chickens; our old speckled hen come off with eleven yisterdy, as nice as ever you *did* see."

Then old Miss Collis riz up, and puttin' her hands on her hips, and stratened like, and ses, right quick, "Laws a massy! my poor back! Drat the rumatics! It's powerful bad; it's gwyne to rain, I know!—oh me! me!"—and they both went out.

Then Barbry look'd at me so comikil and sed, "Billy, I raly *shall* die thinkin' of you and old Troup!" And she throw'd her self back and laffed and laffed.

And she look'd so putty and so happy, ses I to myself, "Billy Warrick, you must marry that gal and no mistake, or brake a trace!" And I swore to it.

Well, we then talk'd agreeable like, and sorter saft, and both of us war so glad to see one another—till old Miss Bass and Miss Collis come back; and bimeby Miss Collises youngest son come for her, and I helped her at the bars to get up behin' her son, and ses she, "Good bye, Billy! Good luck to you! I know'd your daddy and mammy afore you was born on yerth, and I was the furst one after your granny that had you in the arms. Me and Miss Bass *talk'd it over! You'll git a smart, peart, likely gal!* So good bye, Billy!"

Ses I, "Good bye, Miss Collis," and ses I, "Gooly, take good kear of your mammy, my son!" You see, I thot I'd be perlite.

Well, when I went back, there sot old Miss Bass, and ses she, "Billy! Miss Collis and me is a bin talkin' over you and Barbry, and seein' you are a good karickter and smart, and well to do in the world, and a poor orphin boy, I shan't say *no!* Take her, Billy, and be good to her, and God bless you, my son, for I'm all the mammy you've got!" So she kiss'd me, and ses she, "Now kiss Barbry. We've talk'd it over, and leave us now for a spell, for it's hard to give up my child!" So I kiss'd Barbry and left.

The way I rode home was oncommon peart, and my old mare pranced and was like the man in skriptur who "waxed fat and kickd," and I hurried home to tell old Venus, and to put up three shotes and some turkies to fatten for the innfare. Mr. Porter, it's to be the third Wensday in next month, and Barbry sends you a ticket—and if it's a boy, I shall name it arter you, hopin' you will put it in your paper—that is, the weddin'.

So wishin' you a heap of subskribers, I remane in good helth and speerits at presence.
Your Friend,

Wm. Warrick.

Chapter III. Warrick's Wedding

Described in a letter by an "old flame" of his.

To Miss Polly Stroud, nigh Noxvil in the State of Tennysee, clost by where the French Broad and Holsin jines.

Piney Bottom, this July 9, of 1844.
Miss Polly Stroud—dere maddam: I now take my pen in hand of the presence oppertunity to let you know how we are all well, but I am purry in sperits, hopin this few lines may find you the same by gods mercy as I have been so mortyfide I could cry my eyes out bodily. Bill Warrick, yes Bill Warrick, is married to Barbry Bass!

I seed it done—a mean trifllin, deceevinist creetur—but never mind. Didnt I know him when we went to old field skool—a little raggid orflin Boy, with nobody to patch his close torn behin a makin of a dicky-dicky-dout of himself—cause his old nigger 'oman Venus was too lazy to mend em? Didnt I know him when he couldnt make a pot hook or a hanger in his copy book to save his life? As for making of a S, he always put it tother way, jist so Ƨ backwards. And then to say I were too old for him and that he always conceited I was a sort of a sister to him! O Polly Stroud, he is *so* likely, perticlar when he is dressed up of a Sunday or a frolick—and what is worser his wife is prutty too, tho I dont acknowlige it here.

Only too think how I doated on him, how I used to save bosim blossoms for him, which some people call sweet sentid shrubs, and how I used to put my hand in an pull them out for him, and how I used to blush when he sed they was sweeter for comin from where they did? Who went blackberryin and huckleberryin with me? Who always rode to preechun with me and helped me on the hos? Who made Pokebery stains in dimons and squares and circles and harts and so on at quiltins for me? (And talkin of Poke, I do hope to fathers above that Poke will beat Clay jist to spite Bill, for he is a rank distracted Whig and secreterry to the Clay Club.) Who always threaded my nedle and has kissed me in perticler, in playing of kneelin to the wittyist, bowin to the puttyist, and kissin of them you love best, and playing Sister Feebe, and Oats, Peas, Beans, and Barly grows, at least one hundred times? Who wated as candil holder with me at Tim Bolins weddin, and sed he knowd one in the room he'd heap rather marry, and looked at me so uncommon, and his eyes so blue that I felt my face burn for a quarter of a hour? Who, I *do* say, was it but Bill Warrick—yes, and a heap more. If I havent a grate mind to sue him, and would do it, if it wasnt I am feared he'd show a Voluntine I writ to him Feberary a year ago. He orter be exposed, for if ever he is a widderer, he'll fool somebody else the same way he did me. Its a burnin shame, I could hardly hold my head up at the weddin. If I hadnt of bin so mad and too proude to let him see it, I could of cried severe.

Well, it was a nice weddin—sich ice cakes and minicles and rasins and oringis and hams, flour doins and chicken fixins, and four oncommon fattest big goblers rosted I ever seed. The Bryde was dressed in a white muslin figgured over a pink satin pettycote, with white gloves and satin shoes, and her hair a curlin down with a little rose in it, and a chain aroun her neck. I dont know whether it was raal gool or plated. She looked butiful, and Bill did look nice, and all the candydates and two preechers and Col. Hard was there, and Bills niggers, and likeliest nine of them you ever looked at, and when I did look at em and think, I raly thought I should or broke my heart. Well, sich kissin—several of the gals sed that there faces burnt like fire, for one of the preechers and Col. Hard wosnt shaved clost.

Bimeby I was a sitting leanin back, and Bill he come behin me and sorter jerked me back, and skeared me powerful for fear I was fallin backwards, and I skreamed and kicked up my feet before to ketch like, and if I hadnt a had on pantalets I reckon somebody would of knowd whether I gartered above my knees or not.

We had a right good laff on old Parson Brown as he got through a marryin of em. Says he, "I pronounce you, William Warrick and Barbry Bass, man and 'oman." He did look so when we laffed, and he rite quick sed, "man and wife. Salute your

Bryde," and Bill looked horrid red, and Barbry trimbled and blushed astonishin severe.

Well, its all over, but I dont keer—theres as good fish in the sea as ever come outen it. Im not poor for the likes of Bill Warrick, havin now three sparks, and one of them from Town, whose got a good grocery and leads the Quire at church outer the Suthern Harmony. The Missonry Harmony is gone outer fashion.

Unkle Ben's oldest gal Suky is gwine to marry a Virginny tobacker roler named Saint George Drummon, and he says he is a kin to Jack Randolf and Pokerhuntus. Who they is, the Lord knows. Our Jack got his finger cut with a steal trap catchin of a koon for a Clay Club, and the boys is down on a tar raft, and ole Miss Collis and mammy is powerful rumatic, and the measly complaint is amazin. I jist heard you have got two twins agin. That limestone water must be astonishin curyous in its affects. What is the fashuns in Tennysee? The biggist sort of Bishups is the go here. My love to your old man, your friend,

Nancy Guiton.

Old Miss Collis and mammy is jist come home. Betsy Bolin is jist had a fine son and they say she is doin as well as could be expected and the huckleberry crop is short on account of the drouth.

Evans's Fool Killer

North Carolina's most distinctive contribution to American folk humor is the Fool Killer, a destruction-dealing moralist created by Charles Napoleon Bonaparte Evans (1812-83), editor of the Milton Chronicle *in Caswell County from 1841 until his death. Letters from the Fool Killer appeared from time to time in Evans's weekly newspaper as though sent in by a subscriber. It was the Fool Killer's role in life to chastise the fools of this world by "slaying" and "slathering" them with a big club often called a "jo-darter." Among those that knew about and loved the violent but righteously indignant fellow was O. Henry, whose short story "The Fool-Killer" was inspired by Jesse Holmes's altruistic mayhem. Only five Fool Killer letters have been found in the few scattered extant issues of the* Chronicle.

High Rock, N. C., Feb. 1857

Thanks be to a merciful Providence, I still live. But depend on it, Editor, the old man's constitution can't stand many thermometers 12 degrees below zero. I confess that this has been the coldest winter I ever experienced, and the snow retarded my operations considerably, although it saved me lots of labor, for many persons drank spirits copiously during the snow storm to keep warm, when it caused them to freeze as stiff as a poker. Silly individuals! They hadn't sense enough to know that a man in liquor will freeze much sooner than one out of it. . . .

On the 29th Dec. I slayed a party at Durham's [Station] which had been "sold" by the report that Professor H. of Salisbury would then and there ascend in a ballon, carrying up with him a six-horse wagon and team. The good people from the regions of Red

Mountain and S. Lowell flocked there to behold the scene, among the number some pretty girls, a little dumpy farmer, a couple of S. L. [South Lowell] students (one a duck-legged chap and the other a long-legged customer whose pedestals stood out like bench legs), and another customer who was neither a farmer, a mechanic, a student, a man nor a boy. I made these "express" subjects, because they went there by express—depend on it I gave them fits. In bobbin' around I met up with a youth (I took him to be a S. L. student) who looked like he had swallowed an old British ramrod, abusing Fillmore and the Americans. I gave him a blow and lo! his head was transformed into a mush-tub. I am sure if I had turned him around twice, the chap would never have found his way home! If, however, his learning had equalled his vanity and presumption, he'd have been fit for a trustee of some old field school.

The gal who thinks more of herself than anyone thinks of her has been slayed. And divers youngsters and old frisky widowers have bit the dust in these diggins. Editor, a soft-headed youth is not so much to be blamed for making himself a lady's poodle dog as a widower. I find bachelors generally very prudent men. Now and then, however, I have one to maul. I find but few girls with a thimble full of sense. Their thoughts seldom learn to stray beyond beau-catching and flirting. . . .

Shouldering my death-dealing club, I wended my way to Alamance en route for Danville, Va. At Vincent's Store I slathered a party of red-nose chaps who were holding a special court over a poor Negro, charged with making dirk knives. They were all badly frightened when I stepped up and pitched into judge and jury for making a mountain out of a mole hill. . . .

Going to High Falls I met up with a certain J.P., considerably bloated but whether from R.G. [rot gut] Whiskey or self-importance I could not determine. Understanding that he was in the habit of swearing good Christians on the devil's thumb-paper (the [Raleigh] *Standard*) instead of the Bible, I dealt him a double-distilled jo-darter that spread him at my feet as flat as a pancake. Several *Standards* oozed out at his heels! . . .

From here I followed the scent of R.G. Whiskey which brought me once more to Morton's Store (I don't say he keeps the truck—his visitors may carry the smell with them, for all I know.) On looking around the crowd, who should I see but the old bell-weather of the unsophisticated, with a *Standard* in hand and his mouth puckered up as if he'd been eating green persimmons, dodging and trying to hide from me. He had been reading to and lecturing the faithful, not dreaming but what I was in Raleigh. —Says I, "Are you there, old True Penny? How stands the goose question now?" He looked confused, and would have bolted if he'd got the chance, but collaring the old sinner (he belongs to the church, but talks politics when he ought to be praying, and sometimes is almost tempted to bet on elections), I lifted him out of his boots. Then turning around on his faithful disciples, I mauled the goose grease out of them about right. . . .

[12 February 1857.]

Sitting on the Right Side of the R. & D. R. R.
March, 1859

My last letter left me at Leasburg regulating Post Office affairs, but finding that I could not fix things up right without going to Washington (where I am almost afraid to go, lest my morals should get contaminated) and mauling the Postmaster General, I concluded to let the people of Leasburg chew their own tobacco, eat their own gunger-bread and fight their own Post Office battles. And just as I had shouldered my club to go to Raleigh and adjourn one of the most worthless Legislatures that ever disgraced the State, a venerable and mighty clever man came to me and, taking me behind a house in a chimney corner where no one could see or hear us, says he,

"Mr. Holmes, some one fooled me out of a mighty fine turkey last night, and I'd be 'mazen' glad to find out who did it!"

"Describe your bird," said I. He did so, and just as I began to bob around, I heard a mighty noise like the tramping of many horses' feet. Looking around, I descried the Don Quixote Invincibles or Santa Anna's Ragamuffin Guard on parade. The chaps were all disguised, and one of the larks was decked off in the identical feathers of the stolen turkey. Collaring the chap, says I, "Youngster, you'll pass mighty well for an owl without feathers to help you out," and then I proceeded to maul the feathers off him, when the whole Guard rushed on me, led by a Shanghai-looking chap who soon bit the dust, and the balance of the party soon took to their heels.

Going on to Raleigh, I encountered a chap en route who seems to have heard enough about me to know me at sight and, taking me one side, he said that he supposed I knew everything, and as he was courting a girl who had a wealthy aunt and who, report said, intended giving her all of her property when she (the aunt) died, he would like to know of me if he could rely on the report as being true.

"Why do you wish to know?" I inquired.

"Because," he replied, "if it is true, I'll marry that girl before Saturday night, as her old aunt can't live long. And if it is not true, I don't want her, as her daddy has but little plunder."

"See here, old fel," said I, "are you flying around that girl and pretending to be in love with her?"

"I am," was the reply.

"And are you making *plunder* the consideration of your marriage?"

Perceiving me warm up and glance my eye at my faithful club, he lifted his hat and began to scratch his head as if embarrased for a reply, when I walked up to him and, putting my hand in his collar, I told him that I was about the last man that he had any business with, that he would probably fare better to thrust his head in the angry lion's mouth or tilt his pate against forked lightning—that he was my property and mine alone. "You are," said I, "pretending to be monstrously in love with a young lady, but it seems that you love her aunt's property more." And thereupon I pitched into him with all the savageness of skinning skunks, and mauled him about right.

Arriving in Raleigh, I went to the *Standard* office to confer with Holden about breaking up the Legislature, and as I entered his sanctum he mistook me for the Rascal Whaler [the Fool Killer's colleague], jumped out at a back window, and ran like a quarter horse. But I made his devil chase him down and bring him in. On his return, finding it was me and remembering that I put him on parole in the early part of the session, he danced around the room, kissed my club, and cut all sorts of monkey shines for joy. He said he was so glad I was not the Rascal Whaler he didn't know what to do. . . .

"Holden," says I, "I think this is the all-firedest, meanest Legislature you've got here that I ever met up with, and I've come down here to break it up."

"Mr. Holmes," said he in a tremulous whisper, while his eyes stared in every direction as if afraid that some eavesdropping democrat might overhear him, "it's a disgrace to the democracy, and the sooner you break it up the better, but I beg you to keep dark and let no one know that *I* say so."

. . . Holden and myself walked to the Senate chamber, and catching the eagle eye of my friend from Person [County], Col. Cunningham, I beckoned him aside and told him I'd be dod rot if I could stand this Legislature any longer, that I had gone down there to adjourn it or smash up things like an earthquake, that even my old friend from Caswell [County], in whom I had so much confidence, has had his equanimity so disturbed that the ghosts of federalism haunt him in his dreams, and the alien and sedition laws danced like dire spectres perpetually before his eyes. Col. C., seeming to consider for a moment, asked me to keep my hands off the Senate twenty-four hours, and pledged to adjourn it, sine die, in that time—to which I agreed, and gave him to understand that I had no fault to find with his course, although he moved himself a little in the way of my club when he voted for those caucus-trustees for the University.

I then went to the House and calling my old friend Kerr out, I told him to go back and wind that body clean up instantly, or by the eternal I would smash it. Kerr laughed and said he didn't think I'd get much brains if I did smash it. Says I, "Old fel, I think you have shown good sense in making no effort to show off in a body where so many small potatoes are tyring to make themselves very conspicuous. But go and adjourn the House, and don't you and John Morehead let me catch you here again."

So the House was immediately adjourned, but hearing a fuss in the Senate, I peeped in and found a handful of Senators wrangling over a letter from Charley Fisher, President of the N. C. Rail Road. Perceiving that here was work and a plenty of it for the Rascal Whaler who was down about Petersburg on his way to Kempsville, Va., I threw myself on the cow-catcher of the Gaston Road and, soon intercepting him, sent him on to Raleigh to take the Senate in hand.

I concluded to return to Carolina by the Richmond and Danville Rail Road, and en route slathered more subjects than Sampson slew Philistines with the jawbone of a John Donkey.

Near Vernon Hill I heard a mighty fuss in the night, and repairing there I met a parcel of women running as if for their lives and screaming at every jump. A wheelwright chap, it appeared, had made a paper balloon, and a crowd had assembled to see him send it up, but in his efforts the balloon got burnt up, and the balloonist came near burning up with it. Mauling the whole party, I next exercised my club on the head of the man that had a certificate written for a widow to sign before she promised to marry him. . . .

But I must close, and yet I have told you but little about my maulings. Tell all who are anxiously looking out for me to take their subjects in hand, to hold their horses for a week or two and, in pointing subjects out to me, to be always sure that they do not need mauling worse than the subjects they select.

[10 March 1859.]

Down about Norfolk, Va., June, 1861

. . . Editor, I am way down here in Norfolk having a parcel of bowie knives manufactured bearing my name ("Fool Killer"), and woe to the Black Republican wretch who comes in contact with one of them. Where's the Rascal Whaler? I need his services to maul the fuss and feathers out of that archtraitor Winfield Scott. . . .

Before coming down here to try my hand at slathering Black Republican fools, I mauled the goose grease out of a man and his wife near Kentuck meeting house for consulting a witch to tell them the whereabouts of their lost cow. The man was sick in bed and, his cow straying off, he sent his wife to an old dame reputed to be a witch to get her to tell them what had become of their cow. The old hag told them that two men who she described, living in the neighborhood, had made beef of her, one half of which they had sold for whiskey. So they sent to a magistrate to get out a search warrant, but he refused to give it, whereupon they abused him awfully. A few days subsequent the cow was found in a big gully with a broken neck! The weird sister was demolished.

Meeting up with an old coon and asking him his profession, he replied, "I'm a secessionist!" My club dropped him in his tracks.

Passing by Bethel Church in Person County and discovering that preaching was going on, I peeped in and descried a cloven-footed, box-ankled, bandy-shanked lark with his head thrown back, mouth open and full of flies, snoring so loud as to disturb the whole congregation. One tap of my club landed him on the other side of Jordan.

In the vicinity of Buncombe Hall I overheard a customer begging a member of the Legislature to have him appointed a magistrate so as to escape fighting in the war. One jo-darter from the old man's club knocked the cowardice out of him. He received an extra blow because he had been a strong immediate secessionist.

But I have not time to give you a detailed statement of my maulings, so excuse my shortcomings. . . .

[28 June 1861.]

Pace's Rock, Person Co., N.C.
Feb. I don't know what, 1876

Ho! ye fools, knaves, rascals, and rapscallions, I'm once more on your war-path, and my agents everywhere are hereby commanded to report to me immediately. . . .

Shouldering my death-dealing club, I stalked forth in quest of customers and, hearing of a protracted meeting, thither I went to learn if the same religion was  preached that our forefathers inculcated. Arriving there, I heard a mighty good sermon and found a revival going on. The crowd covered a quarter acre of ground, and while the choristers sang a revival hymn, I descried a tall, red-nose and bench-legged chap rise up and, wildly waving his hands above his head, he spanked them together and cowarted around considerably without uttering a word. Sister Sally, Cousin Jinny, and a dozen other female relatives gathered around the lark rejoicing over his conversion, and Cousin Jinny said she thought he would be a converted man soon when he joined the good Templar order. The red nose of the man and the blood-shot eye excited my suspicions and, leading him aside, I interrogated him as to where he got his liquor. (The old man felt like a drop or two "for the stomach's sake" would do *him* no harm!) But the sinner protested that he hadn't "teched a drap," whereupon a gentle tap of my club made him disgorge a full quart of "branch whiskey." I then played into his bread-basket in old-fashioned style and made him show me a gallon jug he had hid under a log in the woods.

Passing on, I came to a house where there was much noise proceeding from a dozen or more legatees consisting of men and women, and they all wanted to fight over the division of a small estate. I walked in and, slathering the entire party, restored friendship and made them all agree not to fall out about a few dollars.

Near Bethel Hill (no matter where situated) I lifted a merchant out of his boots for knocking the head out of a barrel of molasses in mistake for liquor and deluging the floor with molasses. When asked his reason for wanting the head of the liquor barrel knocked out, he said it was frozen and wouldn't run out! The same merchant went to a party where he found no one but an old man and his daughter and a boy with one foot nearly cut off. He danced all night with the girl and slept so sound the next day that his customers couldn't arouse him to get into the store.

I everlastingly wore out a planter who "took in" his tobacco on the Milton market, carried it elsewhere, and got a third less for it. But Editor, business calls and I must shoulder my club and push along. . . .

[16 February 1876.]

Mountain Cave, Jan. 30th 1879

. . . Between Woodsdale and Clarksville I intercepted a young man on the highway with a load of chickens and, perceiving the tears standing in his eyes, I waved my club and, halting him, demanded an explanation. He said he was troubled, that he took his sweetheart to a party a few nights before, and that while there an old bachelor came to him at a late hour and told him he would see the young lady home when she wanted to go, that he (the young man) saw his jularkey on the subject and she said it was all right, that he then left. "But," said he with a loud boo-hoo, "don't you think that cruel old bachelor took my gal at three o'clock that night to a magistrate's house and married her!" And then he bellowed right out, but I dealt my chicken a jo-darter that knocked the pin-feathers out of him and dried him up, telling the lark there were as good fish in the seas as ever a bachelor or any other quadruped in the shape of man pulled out.

Going on, I descried a young man from near Concord swimming Hyco at the peril of a watery grave. Elevating my club, I brought him to a stand and demanded to know who was dying or dead, as I supposed it was a case of life or death with him. He meekly replied that he was going courting! "And who are you flying around?" said I. He told me and it turned out to be the same girl who married the bachelor, but he had not heard of the marriage, although I was then on the bachelor's warpath for riding all over the neighborhood the day after his marriage telling the people he was married and how happy he did feel. One tap of my club lifted the youngster out of his boots.

Near Mt. Carmel in Halifax [County, Virgina], three young men going to a Christmas party got the corn juice mauled out of them very unexpectedly. I was following them up (for I knew they had more whiskey than brains), and near Mt. Carmel they met my Christian friend Chas. Butts going home, when I heard them in a great glee tell him they were "going to heaven," and they wanted him to go with them, that they would pull him through to the New Jerusalem, &c. I could stand it no longer, but springing upon the soft and empty-headed larks, I everlastingly made them out-bellow bull-calves for thus trifling with a pious and worthy hard-working man.

Sitting at the X-roads near Cunningham's Store, New Year's night, I throttled a party I mistrusted for the robbers of A. T. Stewart's remains, and for awhile I thought my fortune was made in securing the large reward. But they proved to be three young men going to a party near McGehee's Mill. One had a box that looked like a coffin, and another had a fiddle wrapped up like a child in a blanket. The third lark looked quite humpbacked, but I found he carried a fiddle also run up under the back of his coat to keep it dry. They were all married men and said they were going to a "pound party" to make music. I let them go on, and after awhile I dropt down on the "pound party" and lo! the musicians were the only guests present. They were discoursing music to the youngster who invited them to the party, but he had forgotten to invite anyone else!

I walked in and, collaring the young lark, "pounded" him about right and made the musicians double-quick it home to their families.

Passing on to Turbiville's Store, an old colored woman besought me to go for these same musicians, saying they stopped at her house to warm, and stole her children's Christmas candy toys. I soon overhauled them and demanded the plunder. Two of them cut their eyes at each other and owned up, but they had eaten the dog. And pushing on I caught the other lark, who had the old woman's cat (made of candy), carrying it home to give to his nephew, he said. After shaming them about taking [an] old Negro's toys while she was busy making them a fire, I mauled the daylights out of them.

Shooting over into Person [County], I attended a party between Long's X-roads and Paine's old tavern, where all the men seemed to be tight except one, and he was a good Templar. When I got there, the landlord was chasing the good Templar over the yard with a jug in one hand and a rope in the other, his aim being to catch the Templar and, tying him, pour the liquor down him. But I smashed the jug and mauling a half gallon of the coffin brand out of mine host, I routed the party.

Not far from North Hyco, I took the starch out of the sails of a young man who was sleigh-riding some ladies in more mud than snow. He upset the ladies and, the mud pulling off a lady's overshoe, he displayed great gallantry in putting it on her foot. It was not discovered until she got home that the shoe had been put on the wrong foot and over another overshoe. I hated to do it, but it was my duty to shake my club at the lady, and I did so with an admonition.

I caught the same ladies out rabbit-hunting in the cold snow and warming their hands by holding them in a rabbit's bed out of which they had just flushed a Molly cottontail. I could but laugh at them.

I slathered the goose grease out of a Capt. Lea's Cavalry company—of the callithumpian gender—during the Christmas holidays while it was on parade in Yanceyville. The boys were charging and coworting about town on horseback, each fellow armed with a fence rail and carrying one or two of John Barleycorn's spurs in his head, when I put in appearance with my death-dealing club, and they outran a Yankee retreating cavalry company, but it was no use, they were my meat.

I looked around town for a bean-shooting party and caught a young man with a bean shooter in his pocket and blood in his eye. He said he carried the deathly instrument to shoot a youngster who had been trying to steal his gal and marry her. I expostulated with him, and he promised to hurt nothing but birds with his bean shooter, and not to shoot them on Sundays. The balance of the shooters dodged me.

Hearing of a man near New Hope Church in Caswell, who was feeding his horse on sugar to fatten it up, I spat in my hand and went for him. When I got there, his brother who had borrowed the beast and which it seems had run away with his wagon and smashed it, arrived with the sugar-fed animal and, delivering him to his brother, remarked, "Here, take your d——d horse. You had no business giving him that sugar!" I collared the sugar man and made him dance to the tune of "Sugar in the Gourd."

Near Milton I made a clever old farmer jump the chinquapin bushes for telling a young man how to take warts off his hands, the advice being to cut one more notch on the north side of a persimmon tree than he had warts. . . .

[13 February 1879.]

Harden E. Taliaferro

The most enduring book of antebellum North Carolina humor is unquestionably Fisher's River (North Carolina) Scenes and Characters, By "Skitt, "Who Was Raised Thar" (*1859*). *Writing about the frisky high jinks of Surry County backwoodsmen, the author (1818-75) drew his portraits from real life and upon occasion even used actual names. Though he spent his adult years as a Baptist preacher in Alabama, he was born and brought up in Surry County, and his book was prompted by a visit back home in 1857. Additional sketches were later contributed to the* Southern Literary Messenger *in Richmond. The outlandish exaggerations of his tall tales, in the tradition of those related by the famed Baron Munchhausen, came directly, it seems, from the folklore of his native mountains.*

The Chase

"I had a hog claim over beyant Moor's Fork" [said Uncle Davy Lane], "and I concluded I'd take old Bucksmasher (his rifle), and go inter the big huckleberry patch, on Round Hill, in sarch for 'um. Off I trolloped, and toddled about for some time, but couldn't find head nur tail uv'um. But while I was moseyin' about, I cum right chug upon one uv the biggest, longest, outdaciousest coachwip snakes I uver laid my peepers on. He rared straight up, like a May-pole, licked out his tarnacious tongue, and good as said, 'Here's at you, sir. What bizness have you on my grit?' Now I'd hearn folks say ef you'd look a vinimus animil right plump in the eyes he wouldn't hurt you. Now I tried it good, just like I were trying to look through a mill-stone. But, bless you, honey! he had no more respect fur a man's face and eyes than he had fur a huckleberry, sure's gun's iron. So I seed clearly that I'd have to try my trotters.

"I dashed down old Bucksmasher, and jumped 'bout ten steps the fust leap, and on I went wusser nur an old buck fur 'bout a quarter, and turned my noggin round to look fur the critter. Jehu Nimshi! thar he were right dab at my heels, head up, tongue out, and red as a nail-rod, and his eyes like two balls uv fire, red as chain lightnin'. I 'creased my verlocity, jumped logs twenty foot high, clarin' thick bushes, and bush-heaps, deep gullies, and branches. Again I looked back, thinkin' I had sartinly left it a long gap behind. And what do you think? By jingo! he'd hardly begun to run—jist gittin' his hand in. So I jist put flatly down again faster than uver. 'Twasn't long afore I run out'n my shot-bag, I went so fast, then out'n my shirt, then out'n my britches—luther britches at that—then away went my drawers. Thus I run clean out'n all my linnen a half mile afore I got home; and, thinks I, surely the tarnul sarpunt are distanced now.

"But what do you think now? Nebuchadnezzar! thar he were, fresh as a mounting buck jist scared up. I soon seen that wouldn't do, so I jumped about thirty-five foot, screamed like a wildcat, and 'creased my verlocity at a monstrous rate. Jist then I begun to feel my skin split, and, thinks I, it's no use to run out'n my skin, like I have out'n my linnen, as huming skin are scarce, so I tuck in a leetle.

"But by this time I'd run clean beyant my house, right smack through my yard, scaring Molly and the childering, dogs, cats, chickens—uvry thing—half to death. But, you see, I got shet uv my inimy, the sarpunt, fur it had respect fur my house, ef it hadn't fur my face and eyes in the woods. I puffed, and blowed, and sweated 'bout half an hour afore I had wind to tell Molly and the childering what were the matter.

"Poor old Bucksmasher staid several days in the woods afore I could have the pluck to go arter him."

[From "Uncle Davy Lane," in Fisher's River (North Carolina) Scenes and Characters, By "Skitt," "Who Was Raised Thar" (New York: Harper & Brothers, 1859).]

The Fast-Running Buck

"Now I'd smashed up so many master old bucks 'bout Fisher's Gap, Blaze Spur, Flour Gap, clean round to Ward's Gap, I 'cluded they mout be gittin' scass, and I'd let 'um rest a spell, and try my luck in other woods; so I toddled off to the Sugar Loaf.

"Now I know'd it were the time uv year fur old bucks to be hard'nin' thar horns, so I tuck the sunny side uv the Sugar Loaf. I kep' my eyes skinned all the way up, but nuver seen any thing tell I got nairly to the top, when up jumped one uv the poxtakedest biggest old bucks you uver seen. He dashed round the mounting faster nur a shootin' star ur lightnin'. But, howsomever, I blazed away at him, but he were goin' so fast round the Loaf, and the bullet goin' strait forrud, I missed him. Ev'ry day fur a week I went to that spot, allers jumped him up in ten steps uv the same place, would fire away, but allers missed him, as jist norated.

"I felt that my credit as a marksman, and uv old Bucksmasher, was gittin' mighty under repair. I didn't like to be outgineraled in any sich a way by any sich a critter. I could smash bucks anywhar and any time, but that sassy rascal, I couldn't tech a har on him. He were a perfect dar-devil. One whole night I didn't sleep a wink—didn't bolt my eyes—fixin' up my plan. Next mornin' I went right smack inter my blacksmith shop, tuck my hammer, and bent old Bucksmasher jist to suit the mounting, so that when the pesky old buck started round the mounting the bullet mout take the twist with him, and thus have a far shake in the race.

"I loadened up, and moseyed off to try the 'speriment. I 'ruv at the spot, and up he jumped, hoisted his tail like a kite, kicked up his heels in a banterin' manner, fur he'd outdone me so often he'd got raal sassy. I lammed away at him, and away he went round the mounting, and the bullet arter him—so good a man, and so good a boy. I stood chock still. Presently round they come like a streak uv sunshine, both buck and bullit, bullit singin' out, 'Whar is it? whar is it?' 'Go it, my fellers,' says I, and away they went round the Loaf like a Blue Ridge storm. Afore you could crack yer finger they was around agin, bucklety-whet. Jist as they got agin me, bullit throwed him.

"I throwed down old Bucksmasher, out with my butcher-knife, jerked off my shot-bag and hung it on the horn uv one uv the purtiest things you uver seen. I thort I'd look at it better when I stuck my buck. I knifed him monstrous quick, and turned round to look at the curious thing I'd hung my shot-bag on, and it were gone most out'n sight. I soon seen it were the moon passin' along, and I'd hung my shot-bag on the corner uv it. I hated mightily to lose it, fur it had all my ammernition in it, and too 'bout a pound uv Thompson's powder.

But I shouldered my old buck, moseyed home, skinned and weighed him, and he weighed 150 pounds clean weight. I slep' sound that night, fur I'd gained the victory. I went next day to look fur the moon, and to git my shot-bag, pervided it hadn't spilt it off in moseyin' so fast. Sure 'nuff, it come moseyin' along next day, jist at the same time o' day, with my shot-bag on its horn. I snatched it off, and told it to mosey on 'bout its business.

"Now thar's some things I'll describe the best I can, and I'm a tolluble hand at it, though I say it; but I nuver will tell a human critter how that moon looked. But I'll say this much: all that talk of 'stronimy and 'lossify 'bout the moon are nonsense; *that's what I know*. They can't fool this old 'coon, fur what I know I know—what I've seen I've seen."

[From "Uncle Davy Lane," in *Fisher's River (North Carolina) Scenes and Characters, By "Skitt," "Who Was Raised Thar"* (New York: Harper & Brothers, 1859).]

Johnson Snow at a "Hottle"

Profit and curiosity prompted two rare men to visit Raleigh, North Carolina—Sam Lundy and Johnson Snow. Sam went for profit, Johnson for curiosity. Sam went rarely even to a neighbor's house without his one-horse wagon, loaded with "gingy cakes," beer, chestnuts, chinqupins, "haze nuts," "hickry nuts," "wannits," "wannit goody," and the like: and you did a brave job if you resisted his importunities to purchase. And of

course, going to Raleigh, he would "toddle off" with such a load, and make it pay. But Johnson had no such motives.

"Ha, ha! See here, Sam Lundy, lem me go wi' you to Rolly, that big town, whar the big Legislater men make ur laws. Hello, ole fel, I want ter see the town, and the big State House, and drink some knockemstiff with the Legislater men, perticler wi' Bill Dobson, ur Siniter. Ha, ha! gist lem me go wi' you, and I'll make fire, cook, toat water, ur do anything else you ax me, ef you'll gist lem me eat and stay wi' you thar and back."

Sam wanted company—the proposition was accepted, and they "mosied off" for Raleigh, over two hundred miles—Sam with his one-horse "waggin," loaded as above. I shall not stop to record the transpiration of many funny incidents on the way, but begin with them at the last camping place before they reached the city. Early in the morning they rose, Johnson walking ahead of the wagon, looking out "fur the big town," at every turn of the road. They soon reached the suburbs of the city, rather sorry looking houses, and Johnson's contempt rose to fever heat, and he burst forth soliloquizingly:

"Ha, ha! hello! Is this Rolly? That big town that I've hearn so much about? Ef I had a midlin o' bacon, I'd grease it and let the dogs hide it, certin. I wouldn't give a drink o' knockemstiff fur any sich a place. A good mess o' hog's gullicks and turnup greens is worth a dozen sich places. And here's whar they cum tu make their laws? Ha, ha! the place is gist like thar laws, they ain't much account, no how. Ef people would gist keep the laws uf the Bible, there'd be no use fur man laws, certin. But, stop! I tried keepin' Bible laws a spell while I was in Passen Beller's Church, and made a ding shacklin out of it, certin. So, reckon huming laws is needful, but why cum to sich a place to make um?"

Just as Johnson ended his last sentence, he had arrived at the top of a hill, and the city presented itself magnificently before him. He was a few paces before Sam's wagon, and threw up his hands with perfect amazement, and there he stood till Sam reached his stand-point.

"Ha, ha! Beautiful as Girzah, comely as Jeruzlum, and turebul as an army with banners, as saith that good man, Passen Beller, in his soul-sarchin sarmins."

Struck with the steeples upon the Churches and other public

buildings, more than with anything else, he continued:

"Hello, Sam! What sharp pinted, slim things is them at the eend uv some uv thar houses? Ar they big haystacks? Hello! that won't do, for the wind would blow um off, like the chaff of the summer thrashin floor. Ha! I've gist thought what ther fur. They ar pigin houses on top uv thar dwellin houses. Mighty heap o' pigins here, I reckin. Look good, Sam, and see ef you can see any Grocery, fur I'm monstus dry."

They soon descended the hill, and it was not long before they entered the main business street of the city, with its numerous sign boards, gazing on every side as they advanced—Johnson stumping his toes occasionally from side looking. Johnson could not read, nor even spell, and he was right after a Grocery. Sam could read a little, by spelling every word as he went; a bad speller at that. Besides spelling poorly, he would syllable his words very badly. The first sign board of any note was at a Livery Stable, and Johnson said:

"Hello, Sam! It's high time to begin to spell out some uv these big signs; we are sartinly gettin into the regions uv some knockemstiff. Try your hand at that one."

Sam stopped his wagon, fixed his cross eyes as well as he could upon the sign board, but committed quite a blunder in orthography. He put a *b* in the place of *v*, and a *t*, between the *r* and *y*, and spelled it "Liberty Stable," and pronounced it accordingly, whereupon Johnson indignantly responded:

"Liberty fiddlesticks! No sound of Grocery in that, certin. Who uver hearn uv a Liberty Stable afore. Ha, ha! I wonder what it means, anyhow? Good menny hosses in thar, I reckin; I s'pose they keeps liberty hosses thar. Less toddle, Sam, fur this is no place fur a thirsty Jewker."

On they went, in the middle of the broad street, gazing rustically at the sign boards on each side, till they came to a Drug Store, the sign over the door being painted in large gilt letters. They halted, and Johnson blurted out:

"Hello! monstus fine letters! Goal letters, at that, certin. Ha, ha! You must be lousy wi' goal, to put it on yer sign boards. Jeruzlum! Sam, gist look at the bottles! What curious shaped things they ar. They don't look like knockemstiff bottles, at all, howsomever. Nur thar ain't nobody thar that looks like they war re-

freshen tharselves. Nobody of the grit 'peers to be about the door.
Take a rest, Sam, and spell it out."

Sam took aim, but missed the mark sadly again. He left out the
r, and spelled it "Dug Store." This was too much for the dry and
impatient Johnson, and he indignantly left.

"Hello! A huckleberry fur yer Dug Stores! Ha, ha! Knock-
eemstiff ain't *dug* out'n the yerth, certin. It's made in Still-
houses—'bout the interestenest places now on these mundacious
shores of mortality. Mosey up yer waggin, Sam, I'm gittin dryer and
dryer. I shall soon turn to a powder horn, at these licks."

Sam popped his whip, and on they "mosied," gazing as ever on
each side of the street, scanning every sign board of any note. At
last Johnson halted, and exclaimed:

"Ureeko!" as saith Silas Jones, the larnt Schoolmaster. Look a
thar, Sam, wi' yer cross peepers, at them fellers in that house, and
look at them bottles! They're ra-al knockemstiff bottles—got the
right shape. And them thar fellers has the right actions, and the
right gab. Set yer eyes straight, and spell that sign."

Unfortunately for Johnson, Sam's eyes were sadly at fault
again. He had all the letters in this time, but syllabled wrong, and
pronounced wrong. It was a "sure-enough" Grocery, but Sam made
it something else—thus: Groc-e-ry, *Grokery*.

"Hello!" said Johnson. "That shoot didn't bring the hide and
taller neither. Thar it is agin! Grokery, grokery! Bull-an-Injuns!
who keers for yer Liberty Stables, Dug Stores, and Grokeries. Ha,
ha! I'm dry, that's what's what; I'm arter a Grocery, a knockemstiff
Grocery, not a Grokery, though that sounds a. leetle more like it
than tothers. Less pike on, Sam, mebbee we'll find it d'rectly."

On they went till they came broadside with a large brick Hotel,
on the wall of which was painted in large capitals—HOTEL—and
over one door in front imposingly appeared the common append-
ages, BAR-ROOM. These, of course, attracted the attention of our
heroes. They halted, and Johnson with distended eyes, broke
silence:

"Thunder an lightnin! That takes the rag off ov the bush. Ha!
ha! two signs on one house. 'That caps the stack, and saves the
grain,' as saith Passen Beller, when he proves his pints o' Scripter
doctrin. Hello, Sam, some tall spellin done here, certin."

Sam put on extra dignity in looks, and held gravely forth: "Hot-el, *Hottle*."

"Hottle! Hottle!!" exclaimed the vexed Johnson. "Pox take yer Hottles. Uvry thing in thar dignation hot, I reckin. Arter all it's a right good sound, fur thar ain't much diffunce in the sound ov *Hottles* and *Bottles*, though thar mout be right smart diffunce in thar innards. Hello! Sam! spell that tother sign afore we leave, fur I see some fellers goin in and coming out'n thar smacking thar lips, and wipin thar mouths, a monstrous good sign. It looks knockemstiff fashion, certin."

Sam spelled and pronounced right this time: "B-a-r R-oo-m, *Bar Room*." This was enough; Johnson grew nervous, and roared out:

"What on yeth have they got bars here fur? A room full on un, and some to spar, I reckin! Ha, ha! I thought when we left the Blue Ridge, we was out'n all danger of bars, but here's a room chug full ov um, and runnin over. Hello, Sam, take keer ov yer own gizzard, save your own tabernickle! I'm agwine to leave here in sarch ov Bill Dobson, at the State House, he knows whar to take a feller, and what the knockemstiff are, too; uvry man fur hisself, Sam."

And away sped Johnson, as fast as a fat man ever waddled. The day being hot, and it but a few minutes before twelve o'clock, he was in a lather of sweat when he rapidly ascended the steps of the State House. Almost out of breath, he anxiously inquired of the first man he met:

"Hello, friend, whar kin I find Bill Dobson?"

"In the Senate Chamber. Go to yonder door."

Johnson "buckled off" to the door of the Senate Chamber, and soon encountered the doorkeeper.

"Stand back!" said the doorkeeper, fiercely.

"Git out'n the door, you poke-o-moonshine, else I'll knock daylight through you quicker nor a cat can lick its paw," responded Johnson, with clenched fists.

"I'll call the Sergeant-at-Arms," replied the doorkeeper.

"Who keers!" bawled Johnson. "Ha! ha! I kin lick him and the whole Legislater to back him. Whar's Bill Dobson? and hush yer nonsense, ef you've any feelin fur yer tabernicle."

Fortunately the Legislature just then adjourned for dinner,

ending the confab. Johnson rushed abruptly into the Senate Chamber, seized the hand of Dobson, and shook it heartily.

"Hello, Bill, I nuver was so glad to see you sense my peepers seed daylight! I'm most used up, fur the want ov some knockemstiff, and suthin ter eat."

Dobson was equally glad to see Johnson, for he was a man of wit, and quite a wag as well as a man of decided ability, and saw a good opportunity to have quite a batch of fun. He readily invited Johnson to a hotel for dinner. Just before they reached the place, Johnson looked up and saw they were going into Sam Lundy's "Hottle." He halted and said:

"Hello! ha! ha! what you gwine inter that Hottle fur? Stop! that's too hot a place fur me jist now, while the train ile is runnin' out'n me so."

"Why do you call it a Hottle?" inquired Dobson.

"It's so, certain, for Sam Lundy spelt it so!" replied Johnson, emphatically.

"Sam's no scholar," replied Dobson; "he spelled it wrong. It is a Hotel—a Tavern, as you have always heard them called. I board here, and I assure you they have fine eating."

"Well, sense you're a Legislater man, I'll give it up," responded Johnson. "Ha! ha! Bill, afore we go in let us have some knockemstiff; I'm thirsty as a sucker in a salt bail."

"Agreed," said Dobson, well knowing the more "knockemstiff" Johnson imbibed the more fun would come out, and they started for the bar-room of the "Hottle." Just as they reached the door, Dobson leading, Johnson looked up and saw the fearful sign, and abruptly stopped.

"Hello, Bill! Bull-an-injuns, just stop! Dry as I am, I don't feel like fightin bars fur all the knockemstiff in the world, and the hog's gullicks and turnup greens ter boot."

"Fighting bears? What do you mean?" inquired Dobson, greatly amazed.

"Ha! ha! jist read that sign over yer noggin, and trimble," replied Johnson, nervously. "Sam Lundy spelt it *Bar Room*, and its full o' bars, certain."

"He spelled it right," said Dobson, "but there isn't a bear this side of the Blue Ridge, I assure you upon the honor of a Senator.

They keep the best of liquors in there, as you will find if you will just enter and sample for yourself. Stewart's Creek and Fisher's River whiskey is nothing to it."

Johnson had unbounded confidence in Dobson and in they went, Johnson however, scanning every nook and corner for "bars." Dobson, of course, had to "treat," which he did willingly and freely, to stir up Johnson's wit for dinner at the "Hottle." After "refreshment" at the "Bar's Den," as Johnson ever afterwards called it, they went into the "Hottle," took their seats with the crowd, and awaited dinner. Johnson's wit and fluency of speech delighted the crowd, while Dobson was well paid for his outlay in the "Bar's Den." Presently one of the largest, and one of the most discordant gongs that John Chinaman ever made, rang out uproarously, stopping Johnson in the middle of one of his wittiest sentences. His eyes flared, his mouth flew open like a fly-trap, he sprang from his seat, made for the door, exclaiming as he went, at the top of his voice, not a weak one at that, "The Hottle's a fallin! the Hottle's a fallin! Run, Bill! run!"

Running about fifty steps, he turned and looked, and saw the "Hottle" still standing. He returned, saw he was "sold," and by his adroitness made the crowd believe that he merely intended to create a little amusement.

The dinner bell then rang out its inviting tones, and there was a general rush to the diningroom. Dobson gallanted Johnson leisurely to the table, telling him that he intended to introduce him to the members of the Legislature at the dinner table, and instructed him what to say in response. Arriving at the door, Dobson, in the courtly manner, said:

"Members of the Legislature of North Carolina, and gentlemen, one and all, I have the pleasure of introducing to you one of my honorable constituents, Mr. Johnson Snow, of Stewart's Creek, Surry County."

Johnson made a rustic bow, and replied:

"Gentle*men*, one an all, and ye sons ov Solon in perticler, yer most obedient sarvunt," and took his seat by the side of his friend Dobson.

The eyes of all were fastened upon Johnson, trying to read him, particularly those who had seen his rapid flight from the gong. While they were eyeing Johnson, he was narrowly scanning the barren table, with not a thing upon it but the plates before him, bottom upwards, and a napkin upon the bottom of each. He had never seen the like before. He could stand it no longer.

"Hello, Bill! we have sot down too soon. The wimmin hain't sot the vittles on the table yit. Less git up."

"Sit still," responded Dobson, "it's the fashion here."

"Fashion!" exclaimed Johnson. "Ha! ha! plague on sich a fashien. I can't live on dish rags, clean as this one is on my plate. It takes hog's gullicks and turnup greens fur the gizzard ov this boy."

The crowd laughed and inwardly pronounced Johnson a "regular take in," not one suspecting he was in earnest. The waiters now began to fly around the table, and one approached Johnson, and said:

"Masser, what yer hev on yer plate?"

"Ha! ha! I don't see nothin on the table here but plates and dish rags," replied Johnson, "an' you ax me what I'll hev on my plate! Set yer vittles down afore me, and let me take my choice, like we do on Stewart's Creek, in good old Surry."

"That's not the way we does, Masser," responded the waiter, with a polite bow, "we allers fetches what Masser wants, makes no odds [what] him wants. Name him, Masser, an this nigger fetch him quick."

Johnson seemed perplexed, but rallied.

"Ha! ha! sense you so well off fur things, fetch me a well-loadened plate o' hog's gullicks and turnup greens."

Waiter was nonplussed, and perplexingly replied:

"Well, Masser, I mus coknowledge you's got dis nigger dis time. I knows turnup greens, donno what ye means by hog's gullipes, as ye call im."

"Git out'n here, you ignerrammus!" shouted Johnson, "bin liven here under the very drappins of the Legislater, and don't know what hog's gullicks is! Take my plate and loaden it well with the same kind o' truck you put on Bill Dobson's. Toddle! mosey! pike! quick!"

Away went darkie, darting like a pike fish, quite crestfallen at being outdone in the name of an article of food. The crowd snickered all 'round the table at the Stewart's Creek wit, to all of which Johnson paid no attention, but kept up a running conversation with his friend Dobson. Darkie soon returned with a heavily freighted plate, with quite a variety, and with a flourish, reported:

"Well, Masser, here he am, jis like Masser Dobson's; much alike as two black-eye peas."

Johnson "mosied" into the plate, and said but little during his heavy assault upon the "truck," darkie every now and then replenishing, for fear of another tirade. After a while Johnson suspended hostilities. Darkie seized the plate and started off, whereupon Johnson halted him.

"Hello! stop, and mark time! you knock-kneed thief. Ha! ha! bring back that plate. I ain't half done yit; hain't got half the wuth ov my money. Set it down here! and bring on some more ov yer truck and turn over."

"Lor bless you, Masser! I thought you done eatin 'stantials, and dis chile gwine ter bring yer de-*sert*. Skuse me, Masser."

"Ha! ha! that's the last thing I'll excuse you fur, fur wanting to bring me my de-serts. I've bin trying to shirk my deserts all my life. Ef I had um, I would not be here in this Hottle today, eating," giving Darkie a severe and serious look.

"Masser, I's sorry we don't onderstand one anudder. I no onderstand yer hog's gullips, and ye no onderstand my de-sert. Masser, I means puddin, pies, cakes, and soforf, all on um sweetened with sass. Dat do, Masser?"

"Why didn't you say that at fust, instid o' lettin out yer big quality werds here? Mosey on, and fetch a Benjamin's mess on um."

Darkie soon returned, and Johnson, wordless the rest of the dining, made sad havoc of darkie's "soforfs."

Dinner over, the hour for the Legislature to meet arrived, and Dobson gave Johnson a polite invitation to accompany him to the State House. Whereupon he earnestly replied:

"Ha! ha! Bill, I was a fool fur wantin to come to this quality place anyhow; I'm done with it certin. I'll no more of yer Liberty Stables, Dug Stores, Grockeries, Hottles and Bar Rooms. I shall hunt up Sam Lundy, and leave. I can't keep up wi this place, certain. You go on making laws, and I'll pike fur Stewart's Creek."

Dobson left for the Senate Chamber, and Johnson to hunt Sam, whom he found just as he had sold his last nut, and pint of "wannut goody," and they left for Surry; Sam satisfied with his profits, and Johnson's curiosity fully gratified.

[*Southern Literary Messenger*, February 1863. Reprinted in *Carolina Humor: Sketches by Harden E. Taliaferro*, edited by David K. Jackson (Richmond, Va.: Dietz Press, 1938).]

Legal Wit

Lawyers, more than members of any other profession, have spawned a sumptuous harvest of anecdotes. Doctors and teachers lag far behind, even preachers. Perhaps the reason is that the court- room itself is a place where ingenuity and humor have positive value. An abundance of legal wit, especially the North Carolina ge- nus, is somewhat traceable to earlier days when, like Ham Jones, judges and lawyers rode the circuit and resided at inadequate hotels in tiny county seats. There they passed the otherwise dull hours by spinning yarns around dining-room tables and, later in the evening, outside on the broad piazza. Whatever its provocation, legal wit in North Carolina has produced some exceptional stories.

Epigram

Two lawyers, when a knotty cause was o'er,
Shook hands, altho' they wrangled hard before,
Zounds, says the client that was cast, pray how,
Are you such friends that were such foes just now?
Thou fool says one, we Lawyers tho' so keen,
Like sheers, ne'er cut ourselves, but what's between.

[*North Carolina Journal* (Halifax), 7 November 1792.]

The Hardest Kick Yet

There is an attorney practicing in our Courts who attained great notoriety, among numerous other things, for bullying witnes- ses on the opposing sides of cases where he is concerned. As it would not be polite to give the full name right out, we will merely call him "Wyke" for short.

There was a horse case—a very common case upon our magistrate's docket—trying before Esq. Surebaker one day, in which Wyke happened to be "fernent" the horse. A slow and easy witness had been called to the stand by the Plaintiff, who in a plain straightforward manner made the other side of the case look rather blue. The Plaintiff's attorney being through, Wyke commenced a regular *cross*-examination which was cut short in the following manner:

"Well, what do *you* know about a horse? You a *horse doctor?*" said the *barbarian* in his peculiar contemptuous and overbearing manner.

"No, I don't pretend to be a horse doctor, but I know a good deal about the nature of the beast."

"That means to say you know a horse from a jackass when you see them," said Wyke in the same style, looking knowingly at the Court, and glancing truimphantly around the crowd of spectators with a telegraphic expression which said, "Now I've got him on the hip."

The intended victim, gazing intently at his legal tormentor, drawled out—

"Oh, ye-as—jes so—*I'd never take you for a horse!*"

[*Greensboro Patriot*, 25 November 1848.]

The Effect of a Strong Plea

A man in North Carolina who was saved from conviction for horse-stealing by the powerful plea of his lawyer, after his acquital by the jury, was asked by the lawyer:

"Honor bright, now, Bill, you did steal that horse, didn't you?"

"Now, look a-here, judge," was the reply, "I allers did think I stole that hoss, but since I hearn your speech to that 'ere jury, I'll be doggoned if I a'n't got my doubts about it."

[Melville D. London, *Wit and Humor of the Age* (Chicago: Star Publishing Company, 1890).]

Settling an Estate

Shortly after Cleveland's first inauguration [Zeb B.] Vance met a fellow Senator who had been to see the President in reference to some matter of patronage in his State and who complained of the treatment he had received at the White House, saying the President was indifferent, if not disrespectful. "Oh," said Vance, "you need not complain of that; it is his way. He treats me so; he treats everybody so. I went to see him a few days ago and he treated me so indifferently that I was reminded of a case I had in court up in Buncombe County soon after I began to practice law.

"An old man had died leaving a small estate, mostly of land in the mountains, and his two sons, Bill and Jim, the only heirs, employed me to settle up the estate, pay off the debts, and divide the balance of the money between them. The land had been sold under an order of court, but the creditors were making some disturbance, and for one cause and another the final hearing and decree had been postponed for several terms. The boys grew very impatient, but I assured them I was confident the case would be finally disposed of at the ensuing term.

"Court came, the boys were in the courthouse in high expectation. The case was called, and after considerable wrangling and disputation was again continued.

"At recess the clients were in the attorney's office talking the matter over when the elder turned to the other and said, 'Well, Jim, you seen how that was done and you know our lawyer was not to blame; he done all he could and I am satisfied.' 'Well, I am not,' answered Jim, 'I seen it all and know our lawyer is not to blame, but, Bill, I will tell you what's a fact, there has been so much bother about this case, so many disputes, references and continuances, I am so disgusted with the whole business that durned if I ain't almost sorry the old man died.'"

[Clement Dowd, *Life of Zebulon B. Vance* (Charlotte: Observer Printing and Publishing House, 1897).]

Elimination

I tried a very old colored man for larceny. He had no lawyer. After the solicitor had passed the jury, I advised the defendant:

"Uncle Charlie, are you willing for those twelve men over there to hear your case?" Uncle Charlie looked over the twelve, there being six men on each of the two rows of seats. After a careful inspection Uncle Charlie said: "Well, suh, I don't know, suh." I then said: "Well, under the law you have the right to stand aside as many as six of them without assigning any reason for it." Uncle Charlie again looked over the twelve men sitting on the two rows of seats, turned to me and said: "Well, suh, if it's all the same to you, suh, I believes I will 'liminate de fus' row."

[Felix E. Alley, *Random Thoughts and the Musings of a Mountaineer* (Salisbury: Rowan Printing Co., 1941).]

The Doctor Whose Patients All Died

This story has to do with a lawyer who spake for his client and spared not his friend. . . .

Taylorsville was the home of the great trial lawyer, Romulus Z. Linney. . . . His intimate friend, Dr. Long, has been summoned from the adjoining county of Iredell to testify against the interests of a client of Mr. Linney, who had filed a caveat to the will of an old lady, the caveat being based on the ground that she was mentally incapable. The jury were rugged countrymen from the isolated hills. Dr. Long, of sombre and stately mien, whose flowing snow-white beard and bodily structure were peculiarly appropriate to his name, had approached the witness chair with deliberate, elephantine dignity, comfortably located his person, qualified as an expert, and testified with an air of finality that he had been professionally and personally well acquainted with the testatrix and that, in his opinion, she was of sound mind and mentally qualified to devise her property. Counsel for propounders having announced, "The witness is with you, Mr. Linney," that gentleman focused his penetrating eyes upon the complacent doctor and questioned him as follows, the last word of each interrogatory being accentuated by a rising inflection:

"Excuse the necessity of a slight repetition, but what is your name? What is your age? Where do you reside, and what is your avocation?"

There was a glint of surprise and indignation on the countenance of the witness; he was well known by the lawyer and in the neighboring community, though (as Mr. Linney surmised) not so well known by all the jurymen. But he slowly growled:

"My name is Jabez Long; I am 65 years old; I reside in Statesville, and I am a practicing physician."

"Ah! A really practicing physician; and how long have you practiced?"

"Thirty-eight years."

"T-h-i-r-t-y-e-i-g-h-t- years! And have you practiced medicine in this county?"

The witness glared at the lawyer and answered doggedly:

"Not extensively. My practice has been almost confined to Iredell County."

"Ah! I am well acquainted with many of the good people of Iredell. Let me see—did you ever practice in the family of Mr. John Alexander?"

"I did."

"You *did*. What do you infer by *did*? But that reminds me; I do not recall having seen Mr. Alexander recently. Has he moved from Iredell County?"

"Alexander is dead. You attended his funeral."

"Dead! You don't tell me. And did you attend him in his last illness?"

"I did."

"And he died?"

"I have just answered that question. You know he is dead; but he—"

"Tut! Tut! Never mind about that. Oblige the court by confining your reply to the scope of my inquiry. And Mr. Alexander's good wife, I knew her as a winsome maiden. Has she removed from Iredell County?"

"She is dead."

"Dead! Indeed! And did you attend her during her last illness?"

"I did. But you know yourself that was twelve years ago and she—"

"Oh, that is quite sufficient. We are not tabulating dates. You administered to the physical ailments of Mistress Alexander and she died? She died, did she not?"

"Oh, yes, she died; she was—oh, all of us have—"

"And Mr. Reuben Hinkle, that splendid specimen of vigorous manhood—I do not recall having recently observed his benign countenance—is he, too, a victim of your professional skill? Were you ever his physician?"

"I was Reuben Hinkle's physician, and he is dead; but I protest against—"

"So Mr. Hinkle sleeps with his fathers and you tried to cure him?"

Vigorous objections by opposing counsel are not here noted, but similar inquiries by Mr. Linney concerning numerous deceased persons slipped by—the trial judge evidently enjoying Mr. Linney's methods—and all of the witness' answers disclosed the information that he was the attending physician of many who had departed this life. But it was worse, and the witness became pallid from rage when Linney soared to a high key, stuck his finger toward the witness, and loudly inquired, "Just what measure of success have you acquired, anyway, in treating afflicted humanity? Dead! Dead! They are all dead. You practiced your profession on every person I have mentioned, and they died! They d-i-e-d!"

And then, in addressing the jury—"Why, gentlemen, this grizzled, pompous, bewhiskered old patriarch has the consummate and astounding egotism and effrontery to pass judgment on the mental qualification of that poor unfortunate woman to apportion her vast estate, when he admits under solemn oath that he attempted to cure every person I named and that they died."

Those who knew Mr. Linney were not surprised that his compelling loquacity appeased the outraged feelings of his friend, the doctor, and that the doctor himself afterward related the occurrence as a good joke on himself.

[Joseph Lacy Seawell, *Law Tales for Laymen* (Raleigh: Alfred Williams and Company, 1925). Seawell (1869-1936) was clerk of the North Carolina Supreme Court, 1911-23.]

In August

A judge in North Carolina was sentencing a big, loose-jointed Negro who had been convicted of murdering another Negro.

"George Earley," his honor said, "you have been found by a

jury of twelve men tried and true to be guilty of murder in the first degree for having killed, in cold blood, Moses Stackhouse, and it is the sentence of this court that on the tenth day of August the sheriff of Polk County take you to a place near the county jail and there hang you by the neck until you are dead, dead, dead! And may God have mercy on your soul. Have you anything to say for yourself?"

The Negro shifted from one foot to the other and twisted and untwisted the old felt hat he held in his hands. All eyes in the courtroom were upon him. Finally, rolling his eyes up at the judge, he said:

"Look y'here, Jedge, you-all don't mean this comin' August, does you?"

[Robert Rudd Whiting, comp., *Four Hundred Good Stories* (New York: Baker & Taylor, 1910).]

Colonel Jones and His Witness

As a rule, women do not make good witnesses, by the way. They get nervous. This is especially true about women who know nothing about courtrooms except from reading newspapers, and imagine that lawyers earn their living by the merciless examination of witnesses. This fact was illustrated a year or so ago when the Summerrow-Baruch libel case was being tried. One of the witnesses was a Charlotte lady who happened to be in the Baruch store when Mrs. Summerrow received the alleged insults. The examination of the witness had been delayed for two days, and when she at length came to the stand she was visibly agitated. One understood her feeling. She imagined that some one intended to twist her up and force her to seem to tell an untruth. And, in spite of her fright, it could be seen that she had determined that she, a lone woman who was about to be badgered and browbeaten, should not be made to tell a lie. The examination was something like this:

"Madam," said Colonel Hamilton C. Jones, a most courtly man, "please go ahead and tell what happened in the store. Tell it in your own way, and—"

"Now, Colonel Jones," interrupted the witness, "don't try to lay any trap for me. I came here to tell the truth and the truth I will tell, for—"

"But, madam," interrupted Colonel Jones, "I assure you—"

"Colonel Jones, don't attempt to get me excited or mix me up. I don't know much about this case, and—"

"Madam," said the colonel a trifle sternly, "I have no wish to mix you up. All I want you to do is to give a plain recital of the facts. Now please go ahead and give your testimony. What took place in the store at the time you were there?"

"There you are, Colonel Jones, there you are trying to get me bothered," said the witness, who was tremendously excited. "If you will only let me alone—"

"But, madam, I am doing nothing to you. You are a witness in this case, and I must ask you to proceed with your evidence."

"Oh, I see you have laid a trap for me, Colonel Jones. I know I am only a woman and don't know anything about courts, but I would have thought, Colonel Jones—"

"But, madam—"

"I beg of you, Colonel Jones, not to persist in trying to make me tell a lie. As I said before—"

"Madam, I—"

"I came here as a witness who had no feeling one way or the other, and—"

"But, madam, I only want you to tell the truth, and I am doing nothing to disturb you."

"Oh, yes, you are, Colonel Jones. You know you are. I can plainly see that you have made up your mind to catch me in some way, and I must request you not to do that, Colonel Jones, for—"

"Stand aside, madam," said Colonel Jones, as he mopped the perspiration from his brow.

[Isaac Erwin Avery, *Idle Comments* (Charlotte: Avery Publishing Co., 1905). Colonel Jones (1837-1904) was son of the Salisbury humorist Ham Jones. Avery (1871-1904), native of Burke County, was city editor of the *Charlotte Observer*, 1900-1904.]

Two Anecdotes

Judge [Samuel] Lowrie, while a practitioner at the bar, unexpectedly lost a case for a client who was a justice of the peace, and in his own opinion a very learned one. The Judge was at a loss to know how to explain the cause satisfactorily to him when they met, but he did it as follows:

"Squire, I could not explain it exactly to any ordinary man, but to an intelligent man like you, who are so well posted in law and law phrases, I need only to say that the Judge said that the case was *coram non judice.*"

"Ah!" said the client, looking very wise and drawing a long breath, "if things had got in that fix, Mr. Lowrie, I think we did well to get out of it as easy as we did."

The following response was made to an inquiry of a character witness in a suit in Wilkes County.

Ques.—Do you know the general character of F——?

Ans.—I do.

Ques.—What is it?

Ans.—Well, for passing and repassing, entertaining and being entertained, in a social point of view, it is good; but in matters of business where he is financially interested, and especially in winding up dead men's estates, his character is bad.

[Z. V. Walser, *Flashes of Wit and Humor of the North Carolina Bench and Bar: An Address at the Annual Meeting of the North Carolina Bar Association, at Morehead City, July 2d. 1908* (n.p., n.d.). Walser (1863-1940), a Lexington lawyer, was attorney general of North Carolina, 1897-1900.]

A Trio of Stories

I am reminded of the judge who sentenced the man to die. . . . He asked him if he had anything to say. So, he stood up and said, "Yes, your Honor, no doubt many people look up to your Honor, many respect your Honor, and some may love your Honor, but you done and ruint yourself with me."

[1 November 1969.]

A client of mine named Will Sanders who has long since gone on to glory told me one time that he had made more liquor than any other man in North Carolina, 'specially countin' that that he made in South Carolina.

I says, "Well, Will, you must have bumped into Judge Johnson J. Hayes at some time or other."

He says, "Oh, yes, I knows him well, knows him well. He sent me to Atlanta one time, but he did it in such a kind manner and explained everything so fully I have sort of felt under obligations to him ever since."

[15 November 1970.]

One time an old colored man was standing in front of Judge Hayes in Greensboro, his hair was right white, and the judge says, "Uncle, have you got a lawyer?"

And he answered and said, "No, Jedge, I ain't got nary lawyer."

And Judge Hayes says, "Do you want the court to appoint some lawyer to represent you?"

And he says, "Nawsir, Jedge, I don't believe I wants the court to pint some lawyer to recommend me. I was up here one time before and some jedge he pinted some lawyer to recommend me, and you know what that jedge done? That jedge put me in jail and turnt that lawyer loose. If it's all the same to you, Jedge, I'm jest gonna throw myself on the ignorance of the court."

[15 November 1970.]

[Chub Seawell, *The State*. H. F. "Chub" Seawell, Jr., is a Carthage lawyer well known for his speeches and writings.]

Tending to Business

While a distinguished North Carolina judge was holding court in one of the Great Smoky counties, the session was disturbed by an old banjo picker and singer who was bawling out the comic Irish ballad, "Paddy and the Barber," in the courtyard below.

"Mr. Sheriff," ordered the judge, "go down and tell that old fool to shut up."

When the sheriff returned and business resumed, so did the song.

"Mr. Sheriff, didn't you tell that old fool what I said?"

Replied the sheriff, "Yes, your Honor, but he said, 'You go back an' tell the jedge to 'tend to his business and I'll 'tend to mine.' "

[Arthur Palmer Hudson, *Journal of American Folklore* 81 (July-September 1968). This story, as recalled by Professor Hudson, was told to him by folklorist Dr. I. G. Greer (1881-1967).]

Second Chance

My brother, who now lives in South Carolina, tells about one time he was in Judge Meekins' court as a spectator. The jury had just convicted a man of making whiskey and Judge Meekins called him to stand for sentence. The Judge looked at him and said, "Young man, the jury has convicted you and I could send you to prison but I am not going to do it yet. You are too nice a looking young man to be mixed in such a lowly and trifling traffic as whiskey-making. I want to give you a chance and see you make something out of yourself. Sentencing will be withheld. You go home and don't have any more to do with those lowly characters with whom you have been associated. Go to church services regularly, get a job and go to work. Find a nice girl and marry her, establish you a home and raise a family. If you will do this, I can assure you that what has transpired here today will not be brought up against you, and you will never hear any more about it unless *sometime* in *later life* you should *get into politics.*"

[J. Street Brewer, *The State*, 1 January 1970.]

'Peal Her

Judge Albion Dunn is a prominent attorney in Greenville. Several years ago he had a client, an old farmer by the name of Woolard, who had been arrested for reckless driving while drunk. The case came up in the recorder's court and the recorder slapped a fine of $50.00 against Mr. Woolard.

" 'Peal her," he advised Albion. "Go ahead an 'peal her!"

So Albion gave notice of appeal and in due course of time the case came up in the Superior Court. It hadn't gone very far before the trial judge began talking about a 30-day road sentence. Soon as he heard that, Mr. Woolard tugged at Albion's sleeve and hoarsely whispered: " 'Peal her back, Albion! 'Peal her back to the recorder's court."

[Carl Goerch, *Characters . . . Always Characters* (Raleigh: Edwards and Broughton Co., 1945).]

The Legal Scene

Asked once to speak on constitutional law, [Senator Samuel J. Ervin, Jr.] said his inadequacy reminded him of the parson who had been responsible for the jailing of Job Hicks. The parson was trained at bricklaying, rather than pulpit exhortation, and his sermons were the worst that had been heard in decades.

Job, having partaken freely of the jug one Sunday, happened into the bricklayer's church. After listening awhile, he dragged the parson from the pulpit and threw him out of the church. In court the judge suggested that he had been so intoxicated he did not know what he was doing.

"Well, Judge," Job admitted, "I did have several drinks, but I wouldn't want you to think I was so drunk I could stand by and see the word of the Lord mummicked up like that without doing something about it."

In a recent committee hearing where an attorney was having trouble finding law to support his client's stand, Senator Ervin was reminded of the advice given by an old lawyer to a young one.

"The old lawyer said: 'If the evidence is against you, talk about the law. If the law is against you, talk about the evidence.'

"The young lawyer asked: 'But what do you do when both the law and the evidence are against you?'

" 'In that case,' replied the old lawyer, 'give somebody hell. That'll distract the judge and the jury from the weakness of your case.' "

Last year, while a witness before the Permanent Investigations Subcommittee was seeking to minimize his role in a flagrant graft operation, Senator Ervin was reminded of "Jim." He told the witness:

"Jim had been killed accidentally and his administrator was trying to hold a railroad responsible for the death on circumstantial evidence. He called a witness who testified that while walking the railroad track just after a train passed, he had seen Jim's severed head lying on one side of the rail and the remainder of Jim on the other.

The lawyer snapped, 'What did you do after discovering these gruesome relics?'

" 'Well,' replied the witness, 'I said to myself, something serious must have happened to him.' "

[Russell Baker, "A New Raconteur Reigns in Senate," *The New York Times* 13 May 1956. © 1956 by The New York Times Company. Reprinted by permission.]

Magnanimous Defendant

In a Charlotte domestic relations court, the judge listened intently to both sides in a case against an elderly man who was charged by his wife with nonsupport. After all the evidence was in, the judge told the defendant: "You haven't taken proper care of this good woman and I'm going to give her $25 a month."

The defendant beamed with pleasure. "That's mighty nice of your Honor," he said, "and I'll give her a dollar or two from time to time myself."

[Associated Press, *Fun Fare: A Treasury of Reader's Digest Wit and Humor* (Pleasantville, N.Y.: Reader's Digest Association, 1949).]

Zeb Vance

One of the many reasons that Zebulon Baird Vance (1830-94)—lawyer, governor, senator—was so much beloved by the people of North Carolina was that he possessed, in the words of one of his biographers, an "exhaustless flow of merriment and anecdote." Vance was a mountain man from Buncombe County with the personal attractiveness and rugged wit of most mountain men. Fortunately, dozens of his stories and humorous concoctions, some of them quite earthy, have been preserved. Among them are a few that were written down or used in speeches. Regrettably the authenticity of those of a spontaneous nature, which have been recalled by gleeful admirers who claim to have heard the words spoken by Vance, must always be questioned. In any case, they are good stories. Much of Vance's humor turns on the clever, unexpected retort.

Toads: His First School Composition

You told me to tell you what I know about toads. Well, toads is like frogs, but more dignity, and when you come to think of it frogs is wetter. The warts which toades is noted for cant be cured, for they is cronick but if I couldn't get well I'd stay in the house. My Grandfather knew a toad that some lady had trained till it was like folks, wen its  master whissled it would come for flies. They cetches 'em with their tong which is some like a long red worm but more like litenin only litenin hasint got no gum onto it. The fli will be a standing a rubbin its hind legs together and a thinking what a fine fat fli it is and the toad a sittin some distance away like it was asleep. While you see this fli as plane as you ever see anything all at once it aint there—

then the toad looks up at you solum out of his eyes like he said. What become of that fli? but you know he et it. Thats what I know about toads.

[*Charlotte Observer*, about 1889, found in a scrapbook in Wadesboro.]

The Black Book

Zebulon was about six years of age when he entered the school of M. Woodson, Esq. The school building was on Flat Creek, and was a preaching place for Rev. Stephen Morgan. . . . Zeb boarded with Nehemiah Blackstock, Esq., who resided on the Burnsville road, 13 miles north of Asheville. The squire was fond of telling anecdotes on Zebulon, many of which have been preserved in that section of country.

Among others, was one in connection with a blank book the squire kept for certain uses. He told Zeb that when he did anything wrong a black spot would come in the book. Squire's son Bob had a pony called "Pomp," and when Zeb did not behave at school as Bob desired he should, he would go home a near way on "Pomp," and inform his father.

Zeb fought with one of the boys one day, and when he got to the mansion that evening he saw the squire looking into the book. He shrunk back at first, but after a while he ventured to go into the room where the squire was sitting.

"It's there, is it, Uncle Miah?" said Zeb.

"Yes," said the squire; "it is very large and black today. What have you done?"

"I whipped ———today," said the boy.

"What for, Zeb?"

"Well, Uncle Miah, he was so cussed ugly that I could not help it."

[Clement Dowd, *Life of Zebulon B. Vance* (Charlotte: Observer Printing and Publishing House, 1897).]

Mouse-Hole

He was given, in his extreme boyhood, to profanity, learned, probably, from the young colored men on the farm. While at school his teacher, Mathew Woodson, Esq., long since gone to rest, undertook the laudable task of breaking Zeb of the habit. He placed the boy at a mouse-hole, with a pair of tongs in his hands, and told him not to open his mouth until he caught the mouse. Zeb took his place at the hole, and the work of the school went on. Finally the time for "spelling by heart" came round, and in the excitement of the contest everybody forgot Zeb. All at once he startled the school by shouting out: "Damned if I haven't got him!" and sure enough, he had the mouse gripped with the tongs.

[Clement Dowd, *Life of Zebulon B. Vance* (Charlotte: Observer Printing and Publishing House, 1897).]

About Being Born

Vance went on with the practice of law until he was called upon to run for the Legislature. A highly respected gentleman, a good deal older than Vance, was his competitor, who objected, among other points, to young Vance's age. The courtroom was crowded when this occurred. Zeb apologized for his youth, and declared that he would have cheerfully been born at an earlier date if it had been in his power; that his father and mother gave him no chance whatever about the matter, and he humbly begged pardon, and said he would try and do better next time. The uproar in the courthouse was tremendous, so much so that his competitor got angry and said he liked to see a smart boy, but this one was entirely too smart. Then the boys yelled, whooped and cheered like mad men, and that day's work, beyond question, secured Zeb's election to the General Assembly.

[Clement Dowd, *Life of Zebulon B. Vance* (Charlotte: Observer Printing and Publishing House, 1897).]

Caldwell County 'Possum

"My opponent charged that I would be snowed under [said Vance following a political campaign in 1858], but was vice versa. I remind myself of the Caldwell County 'possum, which an indignant mountaineer told me about. Said he, I stretched that 'possum's neck tell I thought he was dead; I skinned him and biled him for three hours, but don't you think when I took the lid off'n the pot, the cussed little devil was settin' up there on its hind legs, and had licked up the gravy."

[Kemp Plummer Battle's Scrapbook of North Carolina History, University of North Carolina Library, Chapel Hill.]

Shifting of the Wind

Late one autumn evening Vance was out hunting with some friends. The weather became very cold, and they stopped at a cabin to warm up. An old Negro woman greeted them and asked them to enter.

"Blow up the fire for us," said Vance.

She blew so hard on the fire that she fainted.

Vance turned to his friends. "The wind sure does shift mighty quick in these parts."

[Traditional.]

First-Class Style

While I am speaking of Governor Vance, I will relate a story he told on himself during the canvass he made for his second term as Governor. It is known, of course, that he was elected the first time while Colonel of the 26th Regiment, and in active service in the Army of Northern Virginia. And it is also known that his men almost idolized him; and, of course, the name of Vance was a household word in every home from which a member of his regiment went. The mothers, wives, sisters and sweethearts who had heard, from their many friends in the army, so many praises of Zeb Vance, naturally wanted to see him; and so, when the Governor made a canvass of the State, all the women, in certain counties from which the companies making up his regiment were drawn, went out to see him. I do not remember in what county the incident occurred; but, as the story was told, the Governor and several of his political friends were walking in the direction of the place of speaking one day, while on either side of the street hundreds of women, with a sprinkling of men, were waiting to see the "Old Colonel."

As they were going along, one woman was heard to say: "I've

come ten miles this morning just to see Zeb Vance. Bless his soul, I love him good enough to hug and kiss him." The Governor was about opposite the woman speaking, and turning toward her, he said: "God bless you, madam, come to my arms!" And the Governor said as he laughingly told the story to a parcel of gentlemen in this city afterwards: "The woman and I gave each other a good hugging.

"Yes," said the Governor, "her husband was one of my men, and a good soldier, and he seemed to take a delight in coming to my tent and listening to me and other officers, and that accounts, I suppose, for his wife's desire to see me. I don't know why she wanted to hug and kiss me, unless it was because her husband had told her what a good-looking fellow I was."

"Did you really hug and kiss her, Governor?" a bystander asked.

"I will give you her name, and you can write and ask her about it. I think she'll tell you that the old man never gave her a better squeezing than I gave her."

"Was she good-looking, Governor?" someone asked.

"I don't know; I never stand on looks in an engagement of that kind. The thing had to be did, and I did it in first-class style."

[Richard Harper Whitaker, *Whitaker's Reminiscences, Incidents and Anecdotes* (Raleigh: Edwards and Broughton Co., 1905).]

Wartime Hardships

"Public sentiment rigidly forbade the cultivation of any but limited crops of cotton and tobacco, and the distillation of grain was forbidden by law. Though, perhaps, mere *brutum fulmen,* in view of their constitutionality, these laws were cheerfully sustained by a patriotic public voice and were generally obeyed. The fields everywhere were green and golden with the corn and wheat. Old men and women, in many cases, guided the plough whilst children followed with the hoe in the gaping furrows. The most serious conditions of life are oftentimes fruitful of amusement to those who have philosophy sufficient to grasp it; and the sufferings of those dark days were frequently illumined by the ludicrous. The prohibition upon distilling was regarded by many as a peculiar hardship.

Old Rye grew to be worth its weight in silver, and Mountain Dew became as the nectar of the gods. Even New Dip became precious, and was rolled as a sweet morsel under our rebel tongues. Yet, true to their character of the most law-abiding people on the continent, all respected the act of Assembly. Many thirsting souls, however, fancied that I was invested with that illegal power, the exercise of which lost James II his crown, of dispensing with laws, and petitioned me accordingly for a dispensation. The excuses given were various. One had much sickness in his family, and would I permit him to make a small run for medicine? Another wanted to make just enough to go in camphor; and still another gave it as his solemn opinion that it was going to be a terrible bad season for snakes, and they must have a little on hand in case of bites! Finally, one man wrote me, with an implied slander on my appetite, shocking to think of even now, that he only wanted to make ten gallons, and if I would give the permission he would send me a quart! I replied in all seriousness, that I could not think of violating my official oath for less than a gallon. That broke the trade."

[Address, 1875, *Southern Historical Society Papers,* XIV, 1886.]

Capture at End of War

A great many reports as to Vance's capture obtained currency subsequently, and among them a statement from General Kilpatrick, of such an annoying character as to draw from Governor Vance the following caustic letter:

Charlotte, October 13th, 1868

To the Editor of the New York World:
I see by the public prints that General Kilpatrick has decorated me with his disapprobation before the people of Pennsylvania. He informs them, substantially, that he tamed me by capturing me and riding me two hundred miles on a bareback mule. I will do him the justice to say that he knew that was a lie when he uttered it.

I surrendered to General Schofield at Greensboro, N.C., on the 2d of May, 1865, who told me to go to my home and remain there, saying if he got any orders to arrest me he would send there for me. Accordingly, I went home and there remained until I was arrested on 13th of May, by a detachment of 300 cavalry, under Major

Porter, of Harrisburg, from whom I received nothing but kindness and courtesy. I came in a buggy to Salisbury, where we took the cars.

I saw no mule on the trip, yet I thought I saw an ass at the general's headquarters; this impression has since been confirmed.

Respectfully yours,

Z. B. Vance.

[Clement Dowd, *Life of Zebulon B. Vance* (Charlotte: Observer Printing and Publishing House, 1897).]

Vance in a Washington Prison

The prison seems to have been about as public as Pennsylvania Avenue, with persons coming and going in sufficient numbers that a small crowd would gather around Vance's cell to pass comments with him. These Northern curiosity seekers must have annoyed him at times, which is the only explanation for the conundrum he expounded.

"No boys," he said. "I am too sad to tell you funny tales. But I can give you a riddle. Why is the Southern Confederacy like the Biblical character Lazarus?"

"Because it is poor," someone answered.

"No, that's not the reason," said Zeb.

"We give up," said another. "You tell us why."

"Because," Vance said, looking them over, "it was licked by a set of dogs."

[Glenn Tucker, *Zeb Vance: Champion of Personal Freedom* (Indianapolis: Bobbs-Merrill Co., 1965). Copyright © by Glenn Tucker. Reprinted by permission of the publisher, The Bobbs-Merrill Company, Inc.]

Political Speech, 1868

Just go for Grant and—lo!!—you are loyal. I could make a loyal man out of myself in a few seconds by simply telegraphing that I would support the Grant and Colfax ticket. My sins would be forgiven and they would tell me to "depart in peace"—like a Buncombe magistrate of my town. The other day, a couple presented themselves before him to be married. He was a pompous sort of ignoramus and was smartly bothered "how to do it"—as a crowd of town boys had collected to see the fun. After he had battle-whanged them through and tied them as man and wife, there was a kind of pause. The couple didn't know it was all over. So straightening himself up, one arm akimbo, "My friends," said he, "depart in peace and sin no more.". . .

My friends, old-line Whigs, I like you. I used to believe the old Whigs were the salt of the earth, and I'm sorter of that notion yet. But the party is dead and buried and the tombstone placed over it, and I don't care about spending the balance of my days mourning at its grave. A sincere old Whig, when his party died—if he was true to his principles or his prejudices—would inquire for a party nearest like it. Which is that party? Is it Bill Holden at the head of 75,000 Negroes? A Negro boy once caught a large-sized catfish and, sticking it in the bank, passed up the creek. Another Negro, coming along that way and having a smaller-sized fish on his string, swapped cats. After a bit Jake returned for his fish and pulling it out exclaimed, "De great Lord, is dis my cat? Yes, here's whar I stuck him, *but ain't he swunk!*" If Henry Clay could rise from the dead and sound the bugle to summon up his party and then look at Holden and a few, halt, whipped, mangy-looking fellows at the head of 75,000 Negroes as they cry out, "Here's your Whig party, Henry Clay!"—"Great God!" would exclaim that statesman, "how the Whig Party has shrunk!"

[*Milton Chronicle*, 17 September 1868, Vance Papers, XVIII, State Archives, Raleigh.]

Governor Holden's Impeachment

The trial began February 2 and the final vote was taken March 22, 1871. One hundred and seventy witnesses were called, 57 by the House managers and 113 by Holden. The Governor was found guilty on six of the eight charges. When the result was announced, the Senate adopted a resolution adjudging that William W. Holden "be removed from the office of governor and disqualified to hold any office of honor, trust, or profit under the State of North Carolina." Lieutenant-Governor Tod R. Caldwell became governor, serving out the remainder of Holden's term. In referring to the impeachment trial, Vance remarked: "It was the longest hunt after the poorest hide I ever saw."

[Hugh Talmage Lefler, ed., *North Carolina History Told by Contemporaries* (Chapel Hill: University of North Carolina Press, 1956).]

Presbyterians

One day having some business with an old colored man, he asked his brother in black, "Uncle, do you belong to the Church?"

The man replied, "Yes, Boss, thank the Lord."

"What Church do you belong to?"

"To the Presbyterian Church," replied the darkey.

"Uncle, do you believe in election?"

"O, yes, Boss. I believes in election."

"Well, Uncle, do you think you are elected?" said Vance.

"Yes, Boss, thank the Lord, I thinks I am," said the darkey.

"Well, Uncle, do you think I'm elected?" inquired Vance.

"I'd never heerd, Boss, as how you was a candidate," replied the colored brother candidly.

[Clement Dowd, *Life of Zebulon B. Vance* (Charlotte: Observer Printing and Publishing House, 1897).]

Character

While he lived at Charlotte, an old gentleman from the country came to his office to see him. He said, "Governor, I have come several miles jist o' purpose to see you and git acquainted with you. I have heerd of you for many years and have wanted to see you mighty bad. I'll die better satisfied because I've got to see you. I've heeerd a good deal of your brother Bob, too, and I've always heerd he had the best character of the two."

[Clement Dowd, *Life of Zebulon B. Vance* (Charlotte: Observer Printing and Publishing House, 1897).]

Campaigning for the Senate

In another county, [Judge Thomas] Settle [who was campaigning against Vance in 1876] had a very large following of Negroes and scallawags while Vance had very few supporters at this meeting. Settle thought he would tease Vance about his (Settle's) number of supporters, and asked Vance how he felt being among so many of Settle's friends and followers.

Vance replied, "I feel just like a big, fat, plump grain of wheat in a box of rat droppings."

[Charles A. Reap, *A Story is Told* (Albemarle: p.p., 1968.]

In One Ear

Being a senator involved considerable humdrum and dullness for one of Vance's volatile humor and active nature. He was forced to listen to much dross in the sluggish dissertations on the floor. "I heard your speech," a colleague remarked tauntingly one day, "but it went in one ear and out the other."

"Nothing to stop it," was Vance's quick reply.

[Glenn Tucker, *Zeb Vance: Champion of Personal Freedom* (Indianapolis: Bobbs-Merrill Co., 1965). Copyright © 1965 by Glenn Tucker. Reprinted by permission of the publisher, the Bobbs-Merrill Company, Inc.]

Republicans

"If I thought the Republican party were standing upon the brink of a precipice [said Vance in the Senate in 1880], beneath which seethed those cold waters of oblivion, instead of warning them, I pledge you my word I would try to induce them to step over the edge; in fact, I might lend them a push. [Laughter] At least, I should feel as indifferent about it as the lodger at an inn did, who was awakened in the night when the meteors were falling, and told that the day of judgment had come. 'Well,' he said, testily, 'tel the landlord about it; I am only a boarder.' [Laughter]"

[Clement Dowd, *Life of Zebulon B. Vance* (Charlotte: Observer Printing and Publishing House, 1897).]

At Chesapeake Bay

Some of the senators, their wives and other ladies went on an outing in Chesapeake Bay. They had to climb the ladder to board the vessel. Zeb happened to glance up just as the lady ahead of him looked down and saw that he had a view beneath her skirts.

"Senator," she admonished, "I can see that you are no gentleman."

"I beg your pardon, madam," Zeb replied quickly, "but I can see that you are not, either."

[Glenn Tucker, *Zeb Vance: Champion of Personal Freedom* (Indianapolis: Bobbs-Merrill Co., 1965). Copyright © 1965 by Glenn Tucker. Reprinted by permission of the publisher, The Bobbs-Merrill Company, Inc.]

In Wilmington

At a Wilmington reception in his honor, Senator Vance was approached by a full-bosomed New Hanover lady who wasted no time telling the Senator what was on her mind.

"I have a goose to pick with you, Senator Vance. Not at all do I agree with you in the way you plan to go about dredging the Cape Fear River. And I plan to give you tit for tat!"

Said the joyous Senator mildly: "Tat."

[Traditional, related by Frances Gray Patton, Durham, 1971.]

R. S. V. P.

Senator Vance, when arguing a case in the Supreme Court of the United States, received a note with R. S. V. P. in the corner. The interruption annoyed him, but he scribbled off a short reply with S. B. N. in the corner. His friend, on meeting him, asked what S. B. N. stood for. Vance, affecting to be ignorant, said, "Pray, tell me first what R. S. V. P. stands for." His friend replied, "Why, Governor, I thought every educated man knew that they are the initials of a French phrase which means answer requested now. What does S. B. N. stand for?" "Why," said Vance, winking at the crowd, "I thought every educated gentleman knew that they are the initials of an English phrase which means, 'sent by a nigger.'"

[Z. V. Walser, *Flashes of Wit and Humor of the North Carolina Bench and Bar: An Address at the Annual Meeting of the North Carolina Bar Association, at Morehead City, July 2d, 1908* (n.p., n.d.).]

Chestnuts

In and around Sylva, a story is told of Uncle Ira Barker, who sold chestnuts to passengers on the railroad cars running west of Asheville.

On one occasion, Vance was on the train and bought some chestnuts from Uncle Ira.

"You know, Senator," said Uncle Ira, "what those chestnuts will do to you, don't you?"

"Yes," said Vance, "and every time I fart, I'll think of you."

[Traditional.]

General Lee

Zeb . . . turned the tables on the Yankees when he went to Massachusetts to deliver a lecture. The Bay Staters, knowing his droll manner and practical jokes, baited him by hanging Robert E. Lee's picture in the men's outhouse. When Vance returned from it he disappointed them by remaining silent. Finally, they were compelled to query him.

"Senator, did you see General Lee's picture hanging in the privy?" someone asked.

"Yes," Vance replied indifferently.

"Well, what did you think of it?" they prodded.

"I thought it was very appropriate," he responded. "That is a good place for General Lee's picture. If ever a man lived who could scare the dung out of the Yankees, that man was Robert E. Lee!"

[Glenn Tucker, *Zeb Vance: Champion of Personal Freedom* (Indianapolis: Bobbs-Merrill Co., 1965). Copyright © 1965 by Glenn Tucker. Reprinted by permission of the publisher, The Bobbs-Merrill Company, Inc.

Joining the Church

. . . In a newspaper of that day there is an account of [Bill] Nye's meeting with Zeb Vance. A banquet was given for Nye in Asheville, and among the guests was Vance.

Vance said he was glad to welcome Nye to North Carolina, and hoped "he would be received into fellowship—not like the servant girl who joined the church, and when asked by her employer if she had joined, replied, 'Not plumb jined—they just took me in on suspicion.'"

[Edward Garner, *Asheville Citizen-Times*, 17 April 1955.]

The Beautiful French Broad

Again, when the Senate was considering an appropriation for his own French Broad River, the stream of his boyhood, which rises near the South Carolina border and meanders northward and westward, cleaving through high mountains on either side and bounding over boulders and shelvings until it joins the Tennessee River opposite Knoxville, he became annoyed at Yankee criticism. The obstacle to the dredging appropriation was a Senator from Rhode Island, who, according to the version which reached the North Carolina mountains, made the mistake of belittling the beautiful French Broad, the pride of every western North Carolinian. It was a small stream indeed alongside such navigable rivers as the Hudson and the Delaware, but scarcely the trickle the New Englander claimed when he said he could stand on one bank and spit halfway across it. Vance in truth had not favored the appropriation, or others of the pork barrel type. It had been introduced in the House by his brother Robert, a Congressman representing the western North Carolina district. But Zeb was unwilling to have his beloved French Broad degraded by anyone and went to its defense. He rose half in drollery, but with a touch of irritation, to take advantage of the opening.

"The gentleman who makes that remark about the French Broad comes from the puny little state of Rhode Island," he declared. "Why, I could stand on one border of Rhode Island and piss halfway across that state!"

"Order! Order!" shouted the presiding officer. "The gentleman from North Carolina is out of order!"

"Yes," Vance blandly continued, "and if I wasn't out of order I could piss clear across the whole durned state!"

[Glenn Tucker, *Zeb Vance: Champion of Personal Freedom* (Indianapolis: Bobbs-Merrill Co., 1965). Copyright © 1965 by Glenn Tucker. Reprinted by permission of the publisher, The Bobbs-Merrill Company, Inc.]

Bill Nye

By 1886, when he bought a home at Buck Shoals near Skyland in Buncombe County, Edgar Wilson Nye (1850-96) was fast becoming "one of the chief public figures of the American scene." A native of Maine, he had risen to fame in Wyoming and journeyed throughout the country by way of the lecture platform with another humorist, James Whitcomb Riley. Nye's straight-faced humor generally depended on casual, mannered nonsense and exaggeration that readers of his day found pleasantly comical. A number of his sketches have to do with North Carolina. Nye is buried in the Cavalry Episcopal Church cemetery at Fletcher.

Weather Report

Asheville, December 6.—I write these lines from the South. I came here in order to evade the severe winters of the North. . . .

I thought before I came here that I would find the oriole flitting through the soughing boughs of the magnolia and the mockingbird cooing to its mate, but as I write the snow is nearly two feet deep on a level, trains are not expected for six days and the snow is still falling.

Imagine a slight, almost girlish, figure like my own, clad in a crinkled seersucker, a Mackinaw hat and a fire-shovel battling with the elements and digging holes through the virgin snow in order to get to the grocery store.

"Yet, once I was pure as the beautiful snow." It wasn't over twelve or thirteen years ago at the outside.

I had thought that the odor of the orange blossom and the mint julep would float along upon the gentle brow of the soft and voluptuous air. I had pictured to myself a land of gentle suns and soughing breezes, instead of which I seem to be the principal sougherer myself.

I was fool enough to imagine this a broad and beautiful green State, with here and there a dark red isothermal line across it, but

107

the whole surface of the earth is covered knee-deep with the same kind of snow that people select up in Manitoba when they decide to perish and want something in which to do up their remains.

People here say that this is an unusual winter, and that is why I am bitterly disappointed. I've been in Utah, Colorado, Wyoming, Minnesota, Wisconsin, Iowa, Maine, Oregon, Montana, Washington Territory, Pennsylvania, Michigan, Ohio, Indiana and Chicago in winter, but in each one of these localities I was so unfortunate as to strike an unusual winter. For thirty-five years and in various parts of the United States I have been the victim of unusual winters. I came here to evade this very thing. I said to my family last fall: "It looks now as though we are going to have another of those unusual winters here. We will go South just as soon as we can and see how it will be there."

The result is that old-timers say they never had such an unusual winter since they have been here, although the winters have been growing more and more unusual for ten years.

I thought that here I would sit on the vine-embowered porch all the livelong day and smoke a cob pipe, while drowsy influences and enervating sloth would soothe my troubled breast. So far it has been different. The houses are made to resist the mild cold of what may be termed a usual winter, but, greatly to the surprise of every one, there hasn't been a winter of that kind since before the war.

Therefore the raw and chilling blast comes stealing up through the shrunken floors and socks out the Northern gentleman who has left his winter underwear at home in his trunk.

I am trying to tell the everlasting truth, for I know that I shall be criticized, but there is as much winter right here today, with less preparation to resist it and the prospect of more actual suffering among the poor and improvident, of which classes there are a great many, than anywhere in the North where I have been.

What I reproach the Southern builder for is his absolute failure to build houses that will protect people from the cold. Last winter people ate their breakfasts clothed in fur overcoats and mittens in Florida, and here comes a little flurry of snow, lasting three days already, and still falling, while three tobacco warehouses have already fallen in with the weight of snow on their roofs; but the houses that will be erected here next summer will be thrown together in the same wild and reckless manner by carpenters who yet fondly hope to witness a winter that will fit their perforated style of architecture.

If you will excuse me I will cease writing in order to nail a bed quilt up to the window where too much climate is now gently stealing in and freezing some of my children.

[*New York World*, 12 December 1886.]

The Tar-Heel Cow

There is no place in the United States, so far as I know, where the cow is more versatile or ambidextrous, if I may be allowed the use of a term that is far above my station in life, than here in the mountains of North Carolina, where the obese 'possum and the anonymous distiller have their homes.

Not only is the Tar-heel cow the author of a pale but athletic style of butter, but in her leisure hours she aids in tilling the perpendicular farm on the hillside, or draws the products to market. In this way she contrives to put in her time to the best advantage, and when she dies, it casts a gloom over the community in which she has resided.

The life of a North Carolina cow is indeed fraught with various changes and saturated with a zeal which is praiseworthy in the extreme. From the sunny days when she gambols through the beautiful valleys, inserting her black retrousse and perspiration-dotted nose into the blue grass from ear to ear, until at life's close, when every part and portion of her overworked system is turned into food, raiment or overcoat buttons, the life of a Tar-heel cow is one of intense activity.

Her girlhood is short, and almost before we have deemed her emancipated from calfhood herself we find her in the capacity of a mother. With the cares of maternity other demands are quickly made upon her. She is obliged to ostracize herself from society, and enter into the prosaic details of producing small, pallid globules of butter, the very pallor of which so thoroughly belies its lusty strength.

The butter she turns out rapidly until it begins to be worth something, when she suddenly suspends publication and begins to haul wood to market. In this great work she is assisted by the pearl-gray or ecru-colored jackass of the tepid South. This animal has been referred to in the newspapers throughout the country, and yet he never ceases to be an object of the greatest interest.

Jackasses in the South are of two kinds, viz., male and female. Much as has been said of the jackass pro and con, I do not remember ever to have seen the above statement in print before, and yet it is as trite as it is incontrovertible. In the Rocky mountains we call this animal the burro. There he packs bacon, flour and salt to the miners. The miners eat the bacon and flour, and with the salt they are enabled to successfully salt the mines.

The burro has a low, contralto voice which ought to have some machine oil on it. The voice of this animal is not unpleasant if he would pull some of the pathos out of it and make it more joyous.

Here the jackass at times becomes a co-worker with the cow in hauling tobacco and other necessaries of life into town, but he goes no further in the matter of assistance. He compels her to tread the cheese press alone and contributes nothing whatever in the way of assistance for the butter industry.

The North Carolina cow is frequently seen here driven double or single by means of a small rope line attached to a tall, emaciated gentleman, who is generally clothed with the divine right of suffrage, to which he adds a small pair of ear-bobs during the holidays.

The cow is attached to each shaft and a small singletree, or swingletree, by means of a broad strap harness. She also wears a breeching, in which respect she frequently has the advantage of her escort.

I think I have never witnessed a sadder sight than that of a new milch cow, torn away from home and friends and kindred dear, descending a steep, mountain road at a rapid rate and striving in her poor, weak manner to keep out of the way of a small Jackson Democratic wagon loaded with a big hogshead full of tobacco. It seems to me so totally foreign to the nature of the cow to enter into the tobacco traffic, a line of business for which she can have no sympathy and in which she certainly can feel very little interest.

Tobacco of the very finest kind is produced here, and is used mainly for smoking purposes. It is the highest-priced tobacco produced in this country. A tobacco broker here yesterday showed me a large quantity of what he called export tobacco. It looks very much like other tobacco while growing.

He says that foreigners use a great deal of this kind. I am

learning all about the tobacco industry while here, and as fast as I get hold of any new facts I will communicate them to the press. The newspapers of this country have done much for me, not only by publishing many pleasant things about me, but by refraining from publishing other things about me, and so I am glad to be able, now and then, to repay this kindness by furnishing information and facts for which I have no use myself, but which may be of incalculable value to the press.

As I write these lines I am informed that the snow is twenty-six inches deep here and four feet deep at High Point in this State. People who did not bring in their pomegranates last evening are bitterly bewailing their thoughtlessness today.

A great many people come here from various parts of the world, for the climate. When they have remained here for one winter, however, they decide to leave it where it is.

It is said that the climate here is very much like that of Turin. But I did not intend to go to Turin even before I heard about that.

Please send my paper to the same address, and if some one who knows a good remedy for chilblains will contribute it to these columns, I shall watch for it with great interest.

Yours as here 2 4.
Bill Nye

P. S.—I should have said, relative to the cows of this State, that if the owners would work their butter more and their cows less, they would confer a great boon on the consumer of both.

[Edgar Wilson Nye and James Whitcomb Riley, *Nye and Riley's Wit and Humor* (Chicago: Thompson & Thomas, [c. 1900], a reissue of *Railroad Guide*, 1888. Among its many reprintings, "The Tar-heel Cow" is sometimes entitled "In the South."]

Rural Retreat

Buncombe County—which may also properly be spelled Bunkum—is a large and beautiful county on the French Broad and Swannanoa rivers, with Asheville as the county seat. The name itself first gave rise to the expression "Talking for Buncombe," which is now a classic, towards the close of the famous debate on the "Missouri question" in the Sixteenth Congress. It was used at that time, according to history, by Felix Walker, an old mountaineer of the cute, quaint and curious variety so common and so delightful in the hills of Western North Carolina and Eastern Tennessee. He lived, I am told, at Waynesville, in Haywood County, on the borders of Buncombe, which was also one of the counties of his district.

The old man arose to speak in the midst of a stormy howl for the "question," and, it is said, when an hour or two only remained of the session. He rambled on in an aimless sort of way, which is so exasperating to bright young Congressmen whose heads are yet big with their first unuttered speech. Felix could not talk for sour apples, it was said, but as yet he had not himself made a speech, and he felt that he could not look the voters of Hickory township and Sandy Mush in the face if he yielded to others and went home without brightening up the pages of the *Congressional Record*. When the forensic sprouts of the Sixteenth Congress, therefore, came to him and offered him their bright new Congressional jack-knives if he would quit, he simply shut his lips a little closer and stated, as the gavel fell, that he was talking only for Buncombe.

Buncombe County has an area of 450 square miles and is bounded on the east by the Blue Ridge. It is very mountainous, but fertile, with an all-purpose climate that cannot be beaten in the world. Cattle, grain, tobacco and wool are among the products.

Skyland is where I am at as this letter is being written. It is a small but growing place, containing thirty-seven inhabitants and eight head of horses. It is quiet here at present, of course, owing to shrinkage in values at the large money centers, but this, it is thought by our best minds down at the store, cannot last long.

My house is rather a heavy set cottage and is made from the trees which grew where the house now stands. It faces towards a little brawling stream called Croup Creek. I call my place the Skyland Thought Works. I am some like the gentleman in the foreground of the almanac—I let my works show for themselves. Skyland has an inexhaustible water supply, consisting of Croup Creek and a couple of patent wooden pails on which bonds have been issued bearing a low rate of interest.

The works are in charge of my coachman and I also control the bonds. As the town grows we propose to put in another bucket service.

George Vanderbilt's extensive new grounds command a fine

view of my place. I was over there yesterday to see how the work was progressing. It is a beautiful site. One can see from the foundations of his prospective mansion for miles up the beautiful French Broad River, and the smoky tops of the soft, blue mountains make a magnificent picture of gentleness and repose.

It is a pleasant sight to drive over there on a quiet morning, when the thrush is singing in the persimmon branches and the pawpaw is soughing in the mountain zephyr, to see Mr. Vanderbilt, with a little leather bootleg bag of shingle nails tied around his waist, laying shingles on an outbuilding which he proposes to use as a chicken-house, or, possibly, wearing a pair of lime-spattered boots and finishing out a chimney as he cheerily calls for "More mort." He likes to be busy, he says. "Duty done is the soul's fireside," he remarked to me yesterday, as he put a lot of nice fresh liniment on his thumb and showed me where a pretty little pink nail was sprouting over the ruins of the other one.

Mr. Vanderbilt will have one of the most extensive and beautiful if not the most extensive, expensive and beautiful home in the world when it is completed. One reason I have not yet finished up my place is that I want first to see what George does, and thus get the advantage of his experience. He does not mind that, he says. His house will be bigger than Charlie Kuster's hotel at Laramie City, and will have hot and cold water and gas in every room.

The servants will occupy rooms entirely apart from the family. Mr. Vanderbilt will keep help the year round. He has set out his pieplant already and yesterday ordered a span of horseradish plants.

A railroad running from Biltmore, on the main line, to Mr. Vanderbilt's place is owned by him, and is used solely for conveying building material and salaries to the men. It is called the Vanderbilt system; $20,000 per month is the sum paid at present to men working on the grounds, aside from those who are building. And yet my grounds, especially on Monday, present, I think, a more cheerful appearance than his'n does. I often tell him that when our folks are rinsing out their white clothes in the second water, and placing my new parboiled shirts on the lawn to bleach, I know of no landscape gardener who can begin to get such effects as we do.

Mr. Vanderbilt is very popular here, especially on Saturday evenings but he is not loved alone for his vast wealth. Here, as on

Staten Island or in the city, he is known as a quiet, studious, thorough gentleman and scholar, as well as a good judge of the native wines made here in the mountain fastnesses of the State out of the grains and cereals of Carolina, and used to shorten the long stage waits formerly so painful when the Governors of the two Carolinas were thrown together.

The richest of gold mines known, prior to the acquisition of California, was found in North Carolina, and yielded $500 to the bushel. Possibly the reader thinks that I am trying to be facetious, but that was the rate—$500 to the bushel of earth—for it was a placer mine—or $3,000,000 while the mine was being worked. Then it suddenly became flooded, and I believe it is still a little moist as this letter goes to press.

Diamonds of fine water, and from one-half to two carats in weight, have been found in the State, but not in sufficient quantities to interfere with agriculture. Fine detached crystals of zircon, garnets and graphite occur in Franklin, Lincoln and Mecklenburg Counties. North Carolina is also headquarters for granular or crystalline corundum, or emery. Arsenic, antimony, bismuth, cobalt and nickel are also met up with here, but not in the gneissoid rocks.

The climate of North Carolina, especially of Buncombe County, is really its chief charm. It is, in fact, why both me and Vanderbilt came here. We said to ourselves: "Staten Island is beautiful beyond description, especially at times, but is not suitable for the entire year. One should go up into the hills at least for a part of the year that the ozone may dawdle through one's whiskers. Change is a good thing, and the climate of North Carolina has its good points."

Once I came here along with a fall of two feet of snow and a mean temperature. I had nothing to do with it, but even yet (and that was better than five years ago) the people of Buncombe County, whenever a frost strikes the valley, as they profanely hunt in the bottom of the rag barrel for their ear muffs, murmur to themselves and begin to look at the depot for baggage with my name on it.

At night, or in the shade, it is always cool here, especially during the holidays. But take the year around, facts, figures and poorly patronized cemeteries show that this county can easily give points to the field and carry off the blue satin ribbon.

Relatively, the larger part of the State is very near as the

Creator left it in the sun to dry. Virgin forests are still that way after the lapse of millions of years, and I have had them pointed out to me with pride on that account by old-timers here. There are thousands and thousands of acres everywhere, and nowhere will you see thereon where an effort has been made at clearing up the land, save the unsatisfactory one, it seems to me, of trying to clear a farm by cutting down a tree every two weeks in order to get a 'possum that is concealed in it. From the oranges of the coast to the buckwheat pancakes of the Blue Ridge, from the terrapin of her tropical shores to the maple syrup of the mountains, North Carolina has almost everything on earth that is good to eat; and, in the language of Daniel Webster, her skies shed health and vigor. I do not just remember for sure whether Webster said that or whether I quote from myself, but it is good and true.

To this point comes the worn and weary capitalist, with his household and his hemorrhages, his income and his insomnia. He comes to swap his scudi for a few stolen afternoons this side the non-dividend-declaring grave. It is a good place for that, but better still for those who have been wiser and who came earlier.

The tar vineyards of this State are well known everywhere, and rank with those of Europe as to adhesive qualities and bouquet. The mule also flourishes here, and it is well to take a day off while he is doing so. The mule is rarely found associated with his own kind here, but is often hitched up with a highly mortified horse, or sometimes a budding heifer of two or three summers.

The North Carolina mule has never been entirely satisfied with the terms of surrender at Appomattox, and it has embittered him a good deal, so that instead of taking up the duties and obligations of life and winning success for himself he strikes one as being rather morbid and unhappy. He seems also prone to comment harshly on the lack of congeniality among his parents, and to be constantly asking himself, "Is marriage a failure?"

On the train, day before yesterday, I saw a newsboy get a very severe rebuke from an old gentleman here. He was a clerical looking old gentleman, with a clear blue eye of intense beauty and purity. The newsboy, with that keen sense of the eternal fitness of things which prompts him to fill my car seat full of lives of the Younger brothers, and novels of a highly hectic shade, left a work in the old gentleman's lap which I judge by the title was the biography of a

man named Cameron, by some rising young author named Boccac-
cio. The old gentleman glared at it a while, and then he said:
"Young man, I do not care for that book. Remove it at once. It is
not such a book as I would care to read on a train or anywhere else.
The print is too small."

[*New York World,* 7 June 1891.]

Folk Shenanigans

In spite of the writings of literary wits and sophisticated urban dwellers, indigenous American humor has been for the most part a folk humor flourishing among the denizens of countryside and small town. In such areas, the repeated oral transmission of spontaneous quips, of inspired coups and manueuvers, permitted a recitation to be expanded and perfected. A mere mosquito, with each storytelling, grew and grew until the insect was picking its teeth with a cow's horn. In earlier days, the lives of the folk centered around the home, the fields and woods, the country store, the courthouse, the church. The sheriff and the preacher were the visible potentates of the realm. While only the bravest man would make fun of the sheriff, the preacher was more vulnerable. Tall tales, hunting yarns, outrageous stupidities, monstrous exaggerations, and comic stories of witches and ghosts, of sheriffs and preachers are narrated here with an infectious and intoxicated joie de vivre.

Poison

There's an old story of a woman who mixed such a potent poison for her husband that it killed him, a pack of wolves that ate his body, her hogs which ate the wolves, and herself who ate a chicken that had eaten a part of the hog. Some poison! Thank heaven her recipe has been lost.

[Mary Hicks Hamilton, *News and Observer* (Raleigh), undated clipping. Mrs. Hamilton, an avid collector of folklore, is co-author of *Animal Tales from the Old North State.*]

Luck with Potatoes

My brother over in Yancey County had some mighty good luck with 'taters oncet. They was planted on a steep hillside and when he dug under the row one of the big ones rolled down the hillside and a great slew o' dirt followed after. The dirt dammed up a good-sized stream and made a fifty-acre lake, bored a hole through a little mountain where the railroad company was fixin' to dig a tunnel, and went on down a half mile further and dammed up a stream where a company was plannin' to build a power plant.

With the money he got for his lake, and what the railroad paid him for the tunnel, and with what he got from the power company for saving them the price of a dam, he was sure settin' on top o' the world.

He didn't always have such good luck. I mind the time he couldn't buy a hen and chickens. He got so down and out he tried to kill hisse'f. He had a old pistol, but he was afraid it wouldn't work, so he went down to the store and bought him a gallon o' kerosene, a piece o' strong rope, and some rat poison. Then he went down to the river and got in a boat and rowed down to where some trees hung way out over the water.

He tied the rope around his neck and to the limb of a tree, soaked hisse'f in kerosene, et the rat poison, and set his clothes afire, figgerin' on shootin' hisse'f just as he kicked the boat from under.

Well, he kicked the boat away and the pistol went off and shot the rope in two, he fell in the water and that put out the fire in his clothes, and he got to chokin' and stranglin' when he went under— and throwed up the poison. He figgered his luck had changed, so he swum over to the bank and announced hisse'f as candidate for the legislater. Got elected, too.

[Lee Morris, as told to Dudley W. Crawford, in Benjamin Albert Botkin, ed., *A Treasury of Southern Folklore* (New York: Crown Publishers, 1949).]

Four Folk Yarns

THE GIRL WHO NEVER LAUGHED—Once a farmer had a daughter who had never laughed in her life. He offered a big reward to the person who could make her laugh. A boy came an' told the farmer he could make her laugh. He asked for a hog an' a gallon of buttermilk. He fed the buttermilk to the hog, an' then set a monkey to chasing the hog around the house. The monkey caught the hog by the tail, but the hog kept on running, an' the buttermilk began to fly out of its rear end. When the girl saw the hog running round an' round, and the buttermilk flying out of its rear end an' in the monkey's face, and the monkey hanging onto the hog's tail with one paw an' wiping the buttermilk out of his eyes with the other, she laughed heartily.

[From Buncombe County.]

THE BOY WHO HAD NEVER SEEN WOMEN—Once a man raised his boy without ever letting him see a woman. When the boy was twenty-one years old, his father took him to town, and on the street they saw three women. The boy asked his father what they were, an' his father told him they were geese (or devils). That night when they got home, the boy said, "Dad, I'd like to go back an' see that tallest goose agin."

[From Buncombe County.]

THE FARMER'S DAUGHTER—One night a man came to a house an' asked for shelter. "We're a little crowded," said the farmer, "but you can sleep with the baby or in the shuckpen." The

man didn' like the idea of sleepin' with a baby, so he slept in the shuckpen.

The next mornin' he went out to the well, an' met a very pretty young girl. "Who are you?" he asked.

They call me the Baby. An' who are you?"

"I'm the damned fool that slept in the shuckpen."

[From Edgecombe County.]

THE WITCHBALL—Once there was a poor boy who wanted to marry a girl, but her folks didn' want him. His grandma was a witch, an' she said she'd fix it up. She made a horsehair witchball, an' put it under the girl's doorstep. The girl come outside, passin' over the witchball, an' went back in the house. She started to say somethin' to her mother, an' ripped out [*crepitus ventris*], an' every time she spoke a word, she'd rip out. Her mother told her to stop that or she'd lick her. Then the mother went out for somethin', an' when she came back in, she broke wind, too, every time she spoke.

The father come in an' he did the same thing. He thought somethin' was the matter, so he called the doctor, an' when the doctor come in over the doorstep, he started to poop with every word he said, and they were all atalkin' an' apoopin' when the ole witch come in, an' told 'em God had probably sent that on them as a curse because they wouldn' allow their daughter to marry the poor boy. They told her to run an' git the boy, 'cause he could marry their girl right away, if God would only take that curse offa them. The ole witch went an' got the boy, an' on her way out, she slipped the witchball out from under the doorstep. The boy an' girl got married an' lived happy ever after.

[From Clay County.]

[Ralph Steele Boggs, "North Carolina White Folktales and Riddles," *Journal of American Folklore* 47 (October-December, 1934). Boggs was active in folklore studies while a professor of Spanish at The University of North Carolina at Chapel Hill, 1929-50.]

Sketch of a North Carolina Joker

In my last, I promised to give you some account of our neighbors, of whom there are only two who need mention. They are brothers, but of entirely different characteristics, the one being generous and intelligent, though of no education, and the other quite the reverse. It is the former with whom I have the most to deal. At an early age he left the farm (which they have since jointly inherited from their father), to look about the world and learn something, as this place is fifty years behind the age. He went to sea, and has seen the elephant to some advantage, as it will take a "Right smart man" to "get ahead of his time." You can tell him nothing he didn't "know before"; no man has seen the strange sights, but he has seen stranger. A rare fish or bird that puzzles others, he has caught and shot quantities of. In short, we find in him a perfect Munchausen, and he is so fruitful a subject we will call him a Lemon, not that he is sour, though he is ever ready to *peel* in a conflict of wit, and though he has never been squeezed, he is always *dry*, in every sense of the word.

He called this morning, and at an invitation to "take something," replied, "Well, I don't keer if I du, seein' it's you—here's *ter ye,* gentlemen!'' and that is his stereotyped reception.

One of our party was speaking of a four-legged chicken he had seen, when Lemon immediately averred that that chicken was not near so peculiar as a duck he had seen in his youth, of whom a certain Captain Morgan was the fortunate possessor, for it not only has two pairs of legs, but that "one pair growed from his back." It would be impossible for me to repeat his own words, but his story was that this duck, chasing grasshoppers, after getting tired with running on one pair of legs, would turn over and continue his feeding.

This story rather nonplussed one of the party, who suggested that it was impossible for the duck to have fed, with his bill pointing upward.

"Oh!" says Lemon, "his neck turned on a swivel!"

"But how about the wings, Lemon?"

"Well, to tell you the truth, them shifted!"

In speaking of mosquitoes of large size, seen by one of our party in a Southern state, Lemon, who was a seafaring man many years, remarked, "Well there, Surinam is the *darndest* place for skeeters I ever seed. Last time I went for a load of Merlasses, my cousin driv me aeout to a plantation and 'mong other things on the farm I seed one of the prettiest yoke of cattle I ever laid my eyes on. Naeou—I'm tellin' the truth, you needn't larf—when I come back where them cattle was fust, one ox was missin', or there was nothin' of him left but skin and bone, anyway—and, if you'll believe me, I squinted up tu a tree, and there was the cussedest big skeeter I ever seed, a-pickin' his teeth with one of the horns!"

[Signed "Tog" from Shanty, *Spirit of the Times* (New York), 1 September 1855.]

Ain't All They Done

It took Sandy Martin, of Marven Township, to tell about [Sherman's Bummers]. Sandy was a great orator. He had been to Chapel Hill and could talk with the professors there, and the Presbyterian pastor and the Episcopal rector at Wadesboro, no holds barred. But when he made speeches to the folks he talked like folks. He loved to make speeches at Confederate reunions, and especially on Memorial Day (Confederate, not Yankee, Memorial Day). But he talked everywhere, at the drop of a hat. And like a famous old Roman spellbinder he had just one end to his speech, no matter what he had been talking about. It went like this.

"Our brave boys whupped old Sherman out of Mississippi, Alabama, and Georgia into South Carolina. By the time they got to South Carolina they was mad and on the run. They was getting clost to the center of things. And you know the way it is with a Yankee: Shoot at him and he gets all the madder. Well, he and his boys bummed their way to the Pee Dee River. And this is what happened.

"They crossed the Pee Dee by the light of burnin' ginhouses. *And that ain't all they done.*

"They blowed up the courthouse and burnt down the churches in Wadesboro. *And that ain't all they done.*

"They called Colonel Jim Bennett out on his piazzy and shot him dead. *And that ain't all they done.*

"They drove the mules and the horses and the cows and calves and hogs to the swamps and shooed the guinea hens and the pea-fowls and the geese over the tall timber. *And that ain't all they done.*

"They throwed dead mules into widow-women's wells and split open feather-beds and scattered them over the houseyard. *And that ain't all they done.*

"They stabled their horses in Miziz Judge Marshall's parlor and fed 'em in Miss Minnie Minervy's peeanner box. *And that ain't all they done.*

"They caught Little Billy Barrett with a busted old rifle gun and hung him to the oak tree by the Four-Mile Board. *And that ain't all they done.*

"Ladies and gentlemen, *that ain't all they done.* You know *that ain't all they done.* That wasn't the worst they done.

"Ladies and gentlemen, here I pause to expectorate, spit, and squirt forth ambeer on their tracks and in the direction of where they lie buried in dishonor.

That wasn't all they done.

"They sneaked up to Jim Swink's house, tolled out Ring and Jerry, and shot the two best damned coon dogs in Anson County."

[Hermine Caraway, *North Carolina Folklore*, July 1955. Miss Caraway is on the faculty of East Carolina University.]

Preacher in the Haunted House

One time I was on trip. . .and I got so out of money, and it was in the fall of the year. And it was raining and very cool on my tramp, too. So I begin to hunt for a place to rest for the night. And on the roadside I come to big white house. And so I goes up to this house and knocks on door. And a man come to the door. And I explain to him my condition. I told him I were a long ways from home, and I wanted to know if he would let me stay for the night in dog-house or barn or sumpin'.

So the man looked at me and says he had house up on the hill an' I could stay there for the night. He told me I would find wood to make fire and bed to sleep in but no one was livin' there now. So now I felt satisfied. So I thanks him and tells him good night and off I goes up to that house on the hill.

I opens the door and goes in. Everything looks well and fine. So I strikes match and lit lamp. And also makes fire in fireplace. And I set down an' begin to dry and rest with ease, ease, my Lawd, settin' in the Kingdom jes' like John. Until all at once I heard someone say upstairs, "I'm comin' down, I'm comin' down."

And just 'bout that time I look and there he was dress all in white between me an' the door, yes sir, Lawd, Lawd, between me an' the door. So out the window I had business.

I run 'bout seven miles down road and I met a preacher and he halt me and I stop. He said, "Young man, where are you going in such hurry?" I told him if he had seen what I had seen, he would be in a hurry too. So I explain to him what I had seen.

So he said, "My Brother, it is nothing to that."

I told him, "You don't tell me!"

So he says, "Listen, my friend, I'll prove that you are wrong."

I asks him, "How?"

He says then, "I'll go with you to the house." So then I asks him who was going to be with us, an' he said the good Lord.

So off we went, I and he side by side. We kep' walkin' an' after so long time we come to the house. The light was still lit and fire was in fine shape. So he opens door and walks in. So I raises window, and he sets down and opens his Bible an' begins to read. So I heard a voice sayin', "I'm comin' down, I'm comin' down." So there he was again. The preacher look at me and I look at him an' he look at me.

So 'bout that time out the window I goes again, preacher in behind me. So after little ways we were side by side, 'cause he sho' wus runnin' for the Lord. So after we had run 'bout ten miles, I asks old preacher if good Lord is with us now.

And preacher, he says, "Well, if He is, I be-dam' if He ain't traveling some!"

[Howard W. Odum, *Cold Blue Moon: Black Ulysses Afar Off* (Indianapolis: Bobbs-Merrill Co., 1931). Professor Odum (1884-1954), noted sociologist at The University of North Carolina at Chapel Hill, wrote five books on the folklore of the Negro.]

In Sampson County Long Ago

Folks did a lot of praying during prayer meetings at Persimmon College too. Some prayers were short, and some were long. I reckon you could say some were just middling. At prayer, as elsewhere, neither old Brother Clute Sampson nor Uncle Nath Ward would be outdone by anybody else. Brother Clute prayed as loud as he sang, and one night just before his "Amen" he lifted both his voice and his hands to heaven: "And now, O Lord," he pled, "wash away all our sins an' make us white as the crimson snow!"

Praying for an ailing member of the congregation, another evening Uncle Nath Ward petitioned the Almighty: "Let your healing hand touch the body of Sister Marthie, Heavenly Father, an' bless all her relatives too—white an' black!"

Some prayer meetings were devoted to special problems, such as a needed rain. Let two or three weeks pass without rain, and the folks at Persimmon College would meet to do something about it. That was the way the situation stood one night when Brother Clute bombarded the firmament with this petition: "Open the floodgates of heaven, blessed God, an' send us a gully washer!"

Uncle Ely James, who was easily upset when anything threatened to get out of hand, decided it was time to amend that request. His faith was pretty steady anyway, and more than once he warned his neighbors first to decide what they wanted and then to ask for it.

"We all know how good an' powerful you are, dear Lord," he

prayed calmly. "Brother Clute there knows too; he's jest likely to overdo it a mite. So please, Lord, don't send us no gully washer. What we're really asking for is jest an all-night drib-drab."

Now and then outsiders did settle in Persimmon College—not many, but enough to cause trouble. Karl Baum bought a farm and was soon growing the best tobacco in the neighborhood. Some folks admired him and some envied him. To everyone he was suspect, however, when he began to appear regularly at prayer meeting. You might say they were right, for he did suggest changes. The first notion he tried out was to increase the congregation by bringing in people who lived in a near-by swamp. Karl sent his own wagon to haul them; then he himself assumed responsibility for reviewing the fundamentals of religion on their behalf.

To one of the women, Karl posed this question: "Sister, don't you know who died for you?"

"Course I do," she snapped. "Old Dyce Jacobs dyed fer me up till last fall. Seeing how she's passed away though, now I ain't sure who in the devil I'll git."

Somewhat taken aback, Karl changed the subject: "Where is your husband tonight, sister?"

"Dang'd if I know where the ole loafer is tonight nor any other time, now that fishing season is here."

"Do you and your husband stand in fear of the Lord?" Karl asked.

"God knows I don't," she laughed. "But John must. Last time I seen him, he was headed 'cross the lowgrounds carrying a doubled-barreled shotgun."

Karl dropped the catechism right then and there. "Maybe it's better to start from scratch," he said. So he began relating stories from the Bible. He did his best to keep the stories so simple that nobody could get mixed up; still, when he paused, up rose a swamp man: "Come again, preacher," he demanded. "Which un did you say died fer us—the ole man, or his son?"

The last of Karl's preachers was another northerner. He made his way to Persimmon College all right, but didn't stay around long enough to do any damage. One laugh at his expense was all he could handle. He got that at a country store, where most of the farmers around Persimmon College had stopped to blow during the noon heat. The individual closest to him was an old slave-woman.

"Good morning, lady," said the preacher. "Could you give me a little information?"

She threw up her hands and grinned. "Lawdy, no suh! I'z done an' got too ole foh dat bizness, specially wid white folks!"

[Joseph T. McCullen, Jr., *Publications of the Texas Folklore Society*, 1961. Professor McCullen, at Texas Tech, in Lubbock, is a native North Carolinian, a Shakespeare scholar, and a folklorist.]

Circumstances Alter Cases

There was a man in Nash County who hadn't walked for years. He had had his son push him in a wheel chair every time he went out of the house.

Near their house was a cemetery. One day two boys who had been fishing took their fish under the shade trees in the cemetery to divide them. They left the two biggest ones at the gate.

The boy came along pushing his father in the wheel chair. It was just at twilight, and the voices issuing from the cemetery had a ghostly quality. "You take this one and I'll take that one."

The other voice protested. "But yours is bigger than mine." So it went.

The boy heard, paused, whispered harshly, "The Lord and the devil are dividing the souls."

The father said, "Stop for a minute, I want to listen."

Just then the voice inside the cemetery said, "There's two at the gate. You can have one of them and I'll take the other."

The boy could stand no more. He fled, leaving the old paralytic sitting there. He ran home and dashed into the house crying, "Oh, Ma, I left Pa at the cemetery and the Lord and the devil are in there dividing our souls. They'll get Pa sure."

His mother answered, "Don't you worry none about Pa, son. He beat you here by a full minute, but somebody has got to go back after his chair. You know your Pa can't walk a step."

[Mary Hicks Hamilton, *News and Observer* (Raleigh), 15 April 1951.]

The Laziest Man

He was the laziest man in the country. They said he was so lazy that he wouldn't feed his family. Some of the neighbors got so disgusted that they decided to pull a trick on him. One day they drove up to his house with wagon and team, seized him, and bound him in the vehicle. They told him that if he didn't promise to go to work they would bury him alive.

The wagon moved out of the yard and headed for a cemetery nearby. Neighbors along the way decided that the joke had gone too far, and rushed out saying that they would give the man a bushel of corn or two if his captors would only not bury him alive.

The captive, hearing this charitable offer, rose up from the floor of the wagon and asked, "Is it shelled?" The neighbors shook their heads. "Well, drive on, boys," said Lazybones.

[Mary Louise Medley, *North Carolina Folklore,* July 1957. Miss Medley is a Wadesboro journalist, poet, and historian.]

Tall Tales from Wilkes County

FLUSHING A COVEY.—Did I ever tell you about that old bird dog I used to own? I guess he's about the best old dog that anybody ever hunted after. I know one time I had 'im out goin' out through the field with 'im, and I had an old single-barreled gun and he went into a briar patch and he pointed a covey of birds. I told him to flush 'em, and out come one bird and I killed it, and loaded my gun back, and when I got it loaded out come another bird. And after I'd killed about five or six birds I got to wonderin' how he's a-lettin' one bird fly at a time, how he's a-flushin' one instead of the whole covey. So I got to lookin', and he'd pointed 'em in a stump hole and ever' time I'd load my gun he'd pull his foot off and let a bird fly out, and then he'd slap his foot back over the hole till I loaded my gun back.

SKELETON DOG.—I finally lost 'im though. I took him out a-huntin' one day and he got gone, and I hunted and hunted and hunted and I never did find my dog. I knew he was a good dog. He wouldn't break a point if he ever pointed a covey of birds. He'd just stand and hold 'em until I came and told 'im to flush 'em. And the next year I went back and I found his bones where he's standing at full point and he had nine piles of potteridge bones in front of him. He'd pointed a covey of birds and stood there and held them till they all starved to death, and he starved to death, too.

COON DOG.—Did I ever tell you about the coon dog I had a few year ago? I believe he was the best that I've ever been in the woods with, and I've owned several good coon dogs. I know I went one night, settin' up on a ridge and there was a big chestnut tree over there on the side of the ridge there, right below me. And that old dog, when he run a coon that went inside of a den in a holler tree, he'd bark different than he did when it was on the outside of the tree, so I'd just call 'im, and he'd leave. Well, I set up on that ridge that night, and he just kept strikin' a coon, and he'd run it, and it'd make a big circle around over the mountain, and come back and go in that one holler chestnut. I don't know how many coons he did run there that night, and the next mornin' about daylight he treed in that old holler chestnut, and I went over there and he had so many coons in that tree that, ever' time the coons would draw their breath in, the crack in the chestnut would spread four inches and when they'd let it out, it'd go back together. I don't know how many they was; I didn't keep count of 'em, but they was several coons in that tree.

HOISTING A MILL ROCK.—My Grandpa, when he got up about eighty-five years old, he had 'im a big mill rock, oh, it was about six foot across and about eight inches through. He'd always, ever' Christmas, he'd get him a gallon of apple brandy and he'd go out and pick that mill rock up and stick it up over his head. He'd done that ever' Christmas ever since he got married, so one Christmas he's about eighty-seven he got him a gallon of brandy, and he'd always wait till after dinner before he'd go out and stick the mill rock up. He got him a gallon of brandy, and he took 'im two or three drinks, and he eat dinner, and took 'im another drink or two, and he decided to go out and put the mill rock up over his head. And it'd been awful cold there for about six weeks, just real freezin' weather and the ground hadn't thawed nor nothin', and he went out there and he got down and he got a-hold of that mill rock and he couldn't even shake it. So he goes back in and drinks a little more brandy, and goes out and tries it again, and he couldn't move it again. He goes back and he sets down, and he looked awful bad. Granny said to him, "Grandpa," said, "What's the matter with you?" said, "What are you so down and out about?" He said, "I'm a-gettin' old and old fast, woman," said. "Last year that rock wadn't even heavy, and this year I can't even move it." He sat and studied a while and took in two or three more drinks of brandy, and went out and he got down on his knees and he got a-hold of that rock, and he grunted and groaned a time or two and give a heave and stuck it up over his head and he had nine acres of topsoil froze to it.

HUNTING OUT OF SEASON.—Did I ever tell you about the cold winter we had when I was a boy? I know one winter, sound was even froze. It was so cold everything just froze; you didn't hear a sound all winter. I know I had a pack of dogs and I got out there one day a-rabbit-huntin'. They jumped a rabbit and run away round the mountain and backwards and forewards for about an hour; and I noticed I couldn't hear 'em bark but I didn't think much about it, I'd got so used to not hearing no racket. Rabbit run by me and I killed it, and thought no more about it till the next spring. And it turned warm up in the spring after the game law had closed, and there wasn't no open season on rabbit, and the game warden happened to be a-passin' through and heard them dogs runnin' that rabbit around the mountain and the gun go off and shot it. And he come and arrested me for huntin' out of season.

HOME-LOVING CAT.—I know when I was a kid we had an old cat and wanted to get rid of 'im. My Daddy he hauled him off to town. It was ten miles to town. We was ridin' in a wagon. We took 'im down to town and turned him loose. We carried him across the

Yadkin River and over to the North Wilkesboro side and turned his loose. Well, when we got back home, the blame cat was settin' at home on the porch. And Dad said, "I will fix him," so he got him a sack and put him in it the next time he went to town, and he got him some big rocks, and he put the rocks in the sack, and tied the old cat up in the sack, and throwed him in the river. And when we got home, he's a-settin' on the porch, as wet as he could be, and I don't know how he got out of that sack. Dad told me, he said, "Well, you've got to see if you can't get rid of that cat." And I said, "Why, I can get rid of him easy." So I took the old cat way down in the woods. There's a big stump down there, and I took my axe with me. I just laid him down on that stump and chopped his head off. Went on back to the house, and in about an hour we's settin' there on the porch talkin', and I looked out the road and there come that cat, come out of the woods and was trottin' out the road with his head in his mouth.

[John E. Joines, as told to his son Jerry D. Joines, *North Carolina Folklore,* March 1972. The elder Joines was born in 1914 in the Brushy Mountains section of Wilkes County.]

Religion at Masonboro Sound

White baptisings were usually held at Elijah Hewlett's landing. One of the local fishermen, upon being baptised in the creek, happened to see a mullet jump. Before he could think where he was and of the solemnity of the occasion, he called out: "By Jesus, there's a mullet!" It almost broke up the baptising.

In the early days, anyone who had a strong voice and a Bible could become a Baptist preacher. One of the local swains announced one day that he had felt called to preach and that he had heard the voice of the Lord. "That wasn't the Lord," Henry Kirkum promptly told him. "That was old man Jim Hollis calling his hogs."

One time Myles [Walton] was preaching way out in the country. He did not know there was a man in the congregation by the name of Abraham. Waxing quite eloquent, he quoted from a passage of scripture in which the Lord called out: "Abraham, Abraham, what has thou in thy bosom?" The fellow in the congregation turned red and stammered: "An apple dumpling."

[Crockette W. Hewlett, *Between the Creeks* (Wilmington: p.p., 1971). Mrs. Hewlett moved to Masonboro Sound near Wilmington after her marriage to Addison Hewlett, Jr.]

Gathering at a Country Store

About that time, John Russell, who lives on the road up toward Healing Springs [in Davidson County], drove up, got slowly out of his old car, and ambled over to us. Claude looked up and said: "John, you're late. What kept you?"

"What makes you think I'm late?" John asked. "You didn't even know I was coming."

"You always come after it rains, and we've been waiting for you to show up," Claude said.

"Well, I would've got here sooner, but I stopped to help Will Thompson. You know that stubborn, balky old mule he keeps. He'd laid down in the barnlot and wouldn't get up. Will did everything he could think of to make him get up, but he wouldn't move. He coaxed him, pulled at the bridle, prodded him with a stick, and kicked him, but the mule wouldn't budge. By cracky, I got him up."

"How'd you do it?" Jim asked.

"I got some unslaked lime and put a lot of it around and under him, and then I got a bucketful of water and wet it."

"What did the mule do?" Claude asked.

"By golly, he riz."

[A. C. Reid, *Tales from Cabin Creek* (Raleigh: p.p., 1967). For forty-six years, Dr. Reid, who grew up in Davidson County, was chairman of the Department of Philosophy at Wake Forest.]

The Durnedest Fellow for Hard Luck

"Well, I have been lookin' for my luck to change, but I done give up. I ain't got a chancet. You see, I got this little ole place that use to bring in purty good stuff, but here lately somethin's always happenin'. I didn't git my corn worked at the right time and the crabgrass taken it. I always raises a lot o' beans but this year the beetles et 'em up. My wife she run off with one o' them sawmill fellers from over on North Fork and that fine fox dog o' mine up and died the other day. And there's that oldest gal o' mine. Durned if she ain't turned out to be a schoolteacher. Have a drink?"

I had one. I sorta begun to want to talk some myself. "Too bad about that grass takin' your crop," I said.

"Oh, that's all right. It'll give me the finest hay crop in the country."

"Well, it sure is too bad about you wife leavin' you thataway."

"Now, I don't know as that's so. I'll be a long time forgittin' the way she rung a skillet over my head and I had to go to the blacksmith to git the rim filed off my neck."

"Well, it's awful about the beetles gittin' your beans."

"Aw no, not a-tall. Them beetles is the finest feed in the world for guinea. My guinea hens is layin' mo' aigs than I know what to do with. I has a nice fat guinea ever' Sunday for dinner."

"Well, I know you hated to lose that fine fox dog, didn't you?"

"In a way, yes. But she had just dropped seven o' the finest pups you ever see. They're gonna be the finest pack o' fox dogs in this state."

"Is that so! Well, at least it must be nice to have a schoolteacher in the family."

"Nope. That gal has got the walls o' this cabin papered with the awfullest lookin' pictures I ever seen. Drawin's and photygraphs o' human chitlin's bein' devoured by alcohol. I can't hardly go inside, they's so ugly. Yep, I am the durnedest feller for hard luck that ever was."

[Lee Morris, as told to Dudley W. Crawford. Benjamin Albert Botkin, ed., *A Treasury of Southern Folklore* (New York: Crown Publishers, 1949).]

The Sheriff and the Moonshiner

Sheriff [Lane of Craven County] had been tipped off that a moonshine still was operating out in the county, and he slipped through the woods in an effort to find it. He suddenly came upon a clearing where he found a man busily engaged in building a fire under a small copper kettle. The distiller, apparently thinking the visitor was a neighbor or some sportsman, didn't bother to turn around and look, but kept on with his job.

"Making liquor?" the sheriff asked in a matter-of-fact tone.

"Ain't making water," replied the man.

"Going to sell it?" the sheriff continued.

"Ain't gonna give it away," airily replied the moonshiner.

Then he turned around, and his eyes popped as he recognized the visitor. "Fore God!" he exclaimed. "Hit's the sheriff!"

"It ain't the preacher," Sheriff Lane answered.

"Gonna take me to jail?" quavered the culprit.

"Ain't taking you to church!"

[Billy Arthur, *The State*, 1 December 1967. Now a Chapel Hill resident, Arthur has had a varied career in journalism, politics, and business.]

The Mountain Man and the Motorcycle

Right over there to the left on the side of the road lookin' over yo' right shoulder, in that li'l cabin up on the mountainside, was where my grandma's half-brother used to live. He was real handy with a shotgun and took a shot at everything he saw.

One evenin' just before sunset when it just was beginnin' to get dark, grandma's brother an' his wife was settin' out on a bench in front of the cabin when they looked up an' saw a man ridin' down the road on a motorcycle. They had never laid eyes on a motorcycle before; so they thought that it was some kind of animal from the noise it made and the way it looked. As soon as grandma's brother saw it, he grabbed up his shotgun that he had layin' on the ground next to the cabin steps and fired at the motorcycle. The buckshot hit the motorcycle and made it turn 'round and 'round on the ground, causing the man to fall off it.

When the motorcyle fell to the ground, grandma's brother's wife said, "Did you kill it?"

"No, I didn't kill it," he replied, "but I sho made it turn that man loose."

[J. Mason Brewer, *Worser Days and Better Times: The Folklore of the North Carolina Negro* (Chicago: Quandrangle Books, 1965). A leading Negro folklorist, Brewer taught at Livingstone College in Salisbury for a decade, 1959-69.]

On the Outer Banks

RODANTHE HONESTY—I heard of the islanders' extraordinary honesty. Until the recent coming of the road, no door on Hatteras was ever locked, whether the time was daylight or dark.

"These people in Rodanthe's so honest if they tell a lie you can see it going down their throat, like a egg a snake's swallowing," said a jovial, heavy-set figure sitting on a stool at the counter beside me. "They're so honest it pretty near kills 'em. While ago a fisherman named Black Luke had a wife that got tired of him and said she wanted to marry another fisherman named Charley. Well, she wasn't much good, so Black Luke said it was all right with him, and he'd let her go if Charley gave him something to trade for her. Charley said all right, he'd give two good fishing nets, and he brought 'em over to Black Luke that night. Black Luke took 'em, but he couldn't get to sleep worrying. And soon as it got daylight, he knocked on Charley's door. When Charley opened up, Luke handed him a net! 'You give me two nets for her yesterday,' he said. 'I don't want to cheat you so I brought this net back. She ain't worth but one.' "

THE BIGGEST TOBACCO CHEWER ON OCRACOKE— "Got some characters around here, though," volunteered a middle-aged man chipping at a cork float with his pocketknife. "Like Old Marty, that was the biggest tobacco chewer on the island. Marty's wife got mad at him and said she'd never talk to him again. Marty thought a while how he'd make her talk, and then he took out the false teeth he was wearing, and tied a long string to 'em, and went out in front of his house and began dragging 'em all around the grass, just like he was walking a dog. His old woman waited for a long time without saying anything, and then she couldn't hold in any longer. 'You stop that foolishness right away,' she burst out. 'Look at them people standing in the street, come from all over town just to watch you. What you dragging them teeth for? You going crazy?'

"Marty kept on pulling the string, and walking up and down nice and easy. 'I ain't crazy no-ways,' he told her. 'I just lost my plug of tobacco in the grass and this here's the best way to find it. If them teeth get near that plug they know it so good they'll snap onto it quicker than a rat onto cheese.' "

[Ben Lucien Burman, *It's a Big Country* (New York: Reynal & Company, 1956). Burman is a prominent American reporter, novelist, and travel writer.]

Shepherd M. Dugger

In Queer Books *(1928), Edmund Pearson wrote that Shepherd M. Dugger (1854-1938) was "one of the most delightful authors and one of the most charming, though unconscious, humorists in America." Dugger's noted production,* The Balsam Groves of the Grandfather Mountain: A Tale of the Western North Carolina Mountains, Together with Information Relating to the Section and Its Hotels, Also a Table Showing the Height of Important Mountains, Etc., *is a combined novel and guidebook that has never lost popularity since its first publication in 1892 at Banner Elk, where Dugger lived a long life as educator, writer, and business-man. In later books, he unfortunately abjured the periphrasis and purple patches so delightful in his first one, but he did not lose his cheerfulness and enthusiasm. He could always, in the words of Philips Russell, "swing the English language around his head."*

The Heroine

The beautiful young lady, Miss Lidie Meaks, was one of the faculty of St. Mary's School, in the city of Raleigh. She was medium-sized, elegant figure, wearing a neatly fitted traveling dress of black alpaca. Her raven-black hair, copious both in length and volume and figured like a deep river rippled by the wind, was parted in the center and combed smoothly down, ornamenting her pink temples with a flowing tracery that passed round to its modillion windings on a graceful crown. Her mouth was set with pearls adorned with elastic rubies and tuned with minstrel lays, while her nose gracefully concealed its own umbrage, and her eyes imparted a radiant glow to the azure of the sky. Jewels of plain gold were about her ears and her tapering strawberry hands, and a golden chain, attached to a timekeeper of the same material, sparkled on an elegantly rounded bosom that was destined to be pushed forward by sighs, as the reader will in due time observe. Modest, benevolent, and mild in manners, she was probably the fairest of North Carolina's daughters.

[Shepherd M. Dugger, *The Balsam Groves of the Grandfather Mountain* (Banner Elk: Printed by J. B. Lippincott, Co., 1892).]

The Proposal

When Clippersteel observed that those in front were about to advance, he said: "Miss Lidie, I offer you my hand, as in the days of yore, to help you up the rocks and steps of a path which, my guide informs me, leads through flowery beds and mossy dales like these."

"I accept your offer with thanks, Mr. Charlie; but you are not ready to go: you have not drunk the health you promised," she said, handing him the concave bark with a smile.

"Pardon me, my friend," said he; "it cost me four years in a foreign land to travel to the frigid zone of my heart, where the snows that ended the summer of love were lighted only by the flitting meteors of the borealis race. But your unexpected presence here today, which I could not avoid, has placed that icy region again under the burning sun of the tropics. Already the snows have gone, and their place is occupied by the water lily, perfumed with the spices and the cloves and spreading its sweet petals upon my bosom. How can you drive such love as mine from its mortal habitation and leave my bosom empty with all but wondering pain? My heart is thirsty, and you are its living fountain. Let me drink and water a desert that will soon flourish with the green bay tree and the balm of Gilead."

"O God," she cried, "pardon the weakness of woman," and burying her face in his bosom, her lachrymal lakes overflowed and anointed his garments with drops that were to him the myrrh of the soul. "It is pursuit," she said, "and not possession, that man enjoys, and now therefore the tender regard you have for me is ready to be cremated upon the pyre of my broken spirit, and nothing but an urn of ashes left to its memory."

"Never," replied Charlie, "never until God himself is buried, and the dark marble of oblivion erected for his tombstone, shall my person or my angel forsake fair Lidie Meaks."

When Clippersteel had thus vowed his eternal love and his lady had confessed her devotion, their friends had gone far out of sight up the mountain.

[Shepherd M. Dugger, *The Balsam Groves of the Grandfather Mountain* (Banner Elk: Printed by J. B. Lippincott Co., 1892).]

Wedding at the Waterfall

The country gentlemen, having leaned their rifles against the cliff, stood with their women folks, anxiously awaiting the expected event. In due time the bride and groom, attended by Colonel and Mrs. Salmer, were arrayed for marriage.

Their backs were in the neighborhood of the guns, while their faces were towards the great pouring column, whose white wings and boiling pedestal sent forth a breeze that set all the near flora and other equally movable objects in motion,—bush, weed, and flower, as well as ribbons, tresses, whiskers, and moustaches, and even the leaves of the minister's book were all dancing to the wind of the falls. As Mr. Skiles composed the fluttering pages beneath his thumbs, he drew so near and spoke so loud, in order to be heard above the roar of the waters, that his manner, elsewhere, would have been suitable only to those who were partially deaf. The charming bride, with dovelike eyes, looked steadily upon the minister; and, as he proceeded with the beautiful Episcopal service, there never was a bliss more wild and warm and boundless than that which thrilled her heart. "If any man," said the clergyman, "can show just cause why they may not lawfully be joined together, let him now speak or else hereafter forever hold his peace."

To the great surprise of all present, a sneering voice, on a different key from the thundering of the falls, was heard to say, "I object." This came from none other than Leathershine, who had resolved to avenge his defeat by vexing the occasion with this obnoxious objection, based, as we shall see, upon an odious falsehood; and, the better to accomplish his design, he had concealed himself in the green of the steeps, so as to appear at a time when the groom could not contravene his purpose nor do him violence.

"What is the ground of your objection?" inquired the minister.
"She is engaged to me" was the reply.

No one can describe the trembling pallor that seized the person of poor Lidie Meaks. With eyes full of overflowing fondness, she looked upon him she loved, as if to say, "I am innocent."

Her chin dropped upon the flowers that adorned her bosom; every nerve and muscle of her frame lost its energy, and she sank at the feet of the groom, not in the fashion of one who falls under the influence of excessive excitement, but like a pure woman borne down by the weight of a calumny perpetrated upon a warm life that no sin had ever tarnished.

The copious pool, so near the fainting bride, was yet so far that not a drop of its pellucid contents could be had with which to bathe her brow.

But the groom quickly produced from his pocket a little bottle of brandy, which he carried, as a precaution, in case of accidents, and spreading a portion of its contents over her pallid face, the signs of restoration soon became apparent. The country folks had gathered round like the people of a city rushing to the scene of an accident, when those at disadvantage look over the shoulders of those in front to get a view of the within.

By this time Leathershine had run down the lake, and was ascending the heights at a point below, when Clippersteel, darting through the crowd, snatched a rifle from its leaning-place, and was aiming a shot that would have despatched the retreating coward, had not Mr. Clark grabbed the muzzle of the gun and borne it downward until he had gone out of sight.

A few minutes later, the infamous dude mounted his horse, and, riding directly to Valle Crucis, packed his trunk and fled before Mr. Skiles had returned.

The tumult was now ended; the bride was able to sit upon a shawl which had been offered by a good mountain matron; and an hour later the marriage service was closed.

[Shepherd M. Dugger, *The Balsam Groves of the Grandfather Mountain* (Banner Elk: Printed by J. B. Lippincott Co., 1892).]

Banner Elk

Here are not hotels, but at the farmhouse of Mrs. Patsey H. Whitmore, the combined storehouse and dwelling of R. L. Lowe,

Esq., and at the author's Shonnyhaw cottage, tourists are invited to spring beds, and to tables heavily laden with such food as roasted mutton, yeast bread, biscuits and corn bread, unskimmed sweet milk, and sour milk just from the churn, coffee, fried or boiled swine's ham, buckwheat cakes and maple syrup, fresh butter, chicken and eggs, vegetables, honey, jellies, jams, preserves, pickles, speckled trout, and last of all, turnip salad, of which the Irishman said that he had come "all the way from 'Auld Ireland,' just to eat broad grass like a cow."

For board on Banner Elk the terms are one dollar a day, six dollars a week, and twenty dollars a month.

[Shepherd M. Dugger, *The Balsam Groves of the Grandfather Mountain* (Banner Elk: Printed by J. B. Lippincott Co., 1892).]

Valle Crucis

The very best rural board can be had at Valle Crucis, at reasonable country prices, with D. F. Baird, Sheriff of Watauga County, who lives in a commodious white house, where the air without blossoms with the odor of plenty's horn, and the within is adorned with a cheerful wife and three rose-lipped daughters of joy.

[Shepherd M. Dugger, *The Balsam Groves of the Grandfather Mountain* (Banner Elk: Printed by J. B. Lippincott Co., 1892).]

Weather at Linville

In winter, the snowfall at Linville is lighter and more gentle, and the climate less cold and damp, than that of the Northern States; in spring, the blooming dogwood and service trees hang out their white curtains as flags of truce in a green tasselled army of innumerable trees; in summer, leagues of the most beautiful leafage that ever waved to Aeolian breezes stretch across and far beyond the company's broad estate, and in autumn, the monarch of gentle decay walks through the land with a many-colored garment, robbing the leaves of their verdure and painting on them a thousand tints more brilliant than the Tyrian dye; while to these beauties of nature the company have added all art and enterprise in order to induce pleasure- and health-seekers to purchase homes of peace and gladness within their beautiful domain.

[Shepherd M. Dugger, *The Balsam Groves of the Grandfather Mountain* (Banner Elk: Printed by J. B. Lippincott Co., 1892).]

Eseeola Inn, Linville

But the most commodious building in the town is Eseeola Inn, a chimney-topped, shingle-gabled, and verandad edifice, where the summer nights are rendered comfortable by the blazing logs of many open fireplaces, and the days are cheerful with a health-giving tide of sweet air that floats through the balanced windows and gives "back the invalid the rose to his cheek." Opposite the office on the first floor is a large music-room, which is beautifully finished in native hardwoods, lighted with brilliant chandeliers, ornamented with a sweet-toned piano, and, having a floor as hard as lignumvitae and as slick as a peeled onion, furnishes the finest facilities for tripping the fantastic toe.

When your feet have grown tired of waltzing, Morpheus folds you in his peaceful arms and lays you where the ease of spring-beds and the soft touches of downy pillows give the weary rest.

Three thousand years ago Solomon said: "There is nothing new under the sun": but if he could come back to this world and engage board at Eseeola Inn, he would find that something new has been invented; for he could hollow "halloo" in the a telephone and receive an answer from a social-minded fellow in the telephone office over at Cranberry, and he could chalk his cue and try his luck on a billiard ball, like which no rotary object ever revolutionized across a rectangular game-table in the city of Jerusalem.

This splendid building has hot and cold baths, smoking and reception rooms, broad stairways of easy ascent, carpeted rooms and hallways, marble-topped office counters, extensive piazzas for promenades, and a beautiful dining room, whose sumptuary in-gatherings are guaranteed by the proprietors to be equal, if not superior, to those of any other house in the mountains of North Carolina.

Such is the variety and flavor of the food that, when you place your foot on the threshold of the masticating department, your nasal proboscis is greeted with the aroma of roasted mutton or beef, and the alimentary pupils of your orbicular instruments are fixed upon large slabs of comb honey, consisting of the gathered sweets from mountain flowers, and rivalling in delicacy the nectar of the gods.

Among the delicious dishes of Eseeola's tables is pure maple syrup, manufactured from maple orchards on the Company's lands, and those popular mountain batter-cakes, made from that peculiarly shaped grain, about which a lady recently interrogated a gentleman, as follows:

"Kind sir," said she, "do you know how buckwheat came into this country?"

"No, madam," replied the man; "but I will thank you for any information you may give me on that point."

"Well, sir," said the lady, "I will tell you. It came into this country three-cornered."

[Shepherd M. Dugger, *The Balsam Groves of the Grandfather Mountain* (Banner Elk: Printed by J. B. Lippincott Co., 1892).]

Kissing

On a Saturday evening I went to see my little sweetheart; the parents sat up late, and failing to get rid of me, went to bed looking savage; the mother lay in front with the cover drawn diagonally across one eye, and the other half buried in the pillow pretending to snore, but indeed was wide awake and keeping close watch on the courtship. My girl, who had a double name, complained of having toothache.

I whispered, "My dear Mary Malitha Matilda Hulda Jane, if you will let me kiss your cheek directly over that cruel tooth it will get well."

She refused, but I insisted. I whispered again, "My dear Mary Malitha Matilda Hulda Jane, if you will but allow me to kiss that rosy cheek directly over that savage tooth I will guarantee a cure in one minute."

Here the old lady with acute ears spoke out and said, "Let him kiss you, my daughter, let him kiss you, and if it cures you then I will get him to kiss that boil on my back—he'd as well do something for me as you."

[Shepherd M. Dugger, *The War Trails of the Blue Ridge* (Banner Elk: p.p., 1932).]

Reading

It reminded me of the story wherein a widower who could not read visited a widow who handed him a late paper for entertainment and went out. Returning, she said: "Do you find anything of interest?"

"Oh, yes! There's been a great storm at sea—the ships are all turned bottom upward."

"Why, sir, you've got the paper upside down."

"I knew that but I learned to read left-handed."

[Shepherd M. Dugger, *The War Trails of the Blue Ridge* (Banner Elk: p.p., 1932).]

Divers Anecdotes

Surely no county, city, or town in North Carolina today is without its rightful number of raconteurs. Faced with the sheer impossibility of chasing them all down and wresting their best anecdotes from them, one must be content with samples from a few experts—such experts as Tom Henderson, John G. Bragaw, Bill Sharpe, Billy Graham, Edmund Harding, Albert Coates, T. H. Pearce, Charles Craven, and A. C. Snow. One can only be grateful that they and others who are similarly gifted have recorded their best stories and that they can be enjoyed again in this collection.

Two Scotchmen

There is a current story that two Scotchmen made a wager of 25 cents each as to which one could stay under the water longer. The wager was never paid as both of them drowned.

[John A. Oates, *The Story of Fayetteville and the Upper Cape Fear* (Fayetteville: p.p., 1950). Oates (1870-1958) was a Fayetteville lawyer and historian.]

Not a Beehive

A young couple went on their honeymoon and stopped at a hotel. He went downstairs to smoke. He came back in a dreamy, sentimental mood and, opening a door, looked into dark space.

"Honey," said he.

There was no reply.

"Honey," he cried again.

Silence.

"Honey," he said in a louder voice.

Then—

A bass voice from the blackness, saying: "This ain't no beehive, you damn fool. It's a bathroom."

[Isaac Erwin Avery, *Idle Comments* (Charlotte: Avery Publishing Co., 1905).]

Two from Burlington

FAITH IN THE WORD.—There was an old preacher once who told some boys of the Bible lesson he was going to read in the morning. The boys, finding the place, glued together the connecting pages. The next morning he read on the bottom of one page: "When Noah was one hundred and twenty years old he took unto himself a wife who was"—then turning the page—"one hundred and forty cubits long, forty cubits wide, built of gopher-wood, and covered with pitch inside and out." He was naturally puzzled at this. He read it again, verified it, and then said: "My friends, this is the first time I ever met this in the Bible, but I accept it as an evidence of the assertion that we are fearfully and wonderfully made."

HE COULDN'T VERY WELL.—A husband was being arraigned in court in a suit brought by his wife for cruelty.

"I understand, sir," said the judge, addressing the husband, "that one of the indignities you have showered upon your wife is that you have not spoken to her for three years. Is that so?"

"It is, your honor," quickly answered the husband.

"Well, sir," thundered the judge, "why didn't you speak to her, may I ask?"

"Simply," replied the husband, "because I didn't want to interrupt her."

[Judge Buxton Robertson, ed., *Gems of Truth in Stories of Life* (Burlington: p.p., 1932). Robertson (1875-1940), native of Alamance County, was a public school administrator.]

Dr. Frank Gave Him an F

Dr. Frank Graham recalled that he once flunked U.N.C. football player Monk McDonald, '23, in history.

"Why did you give me an F?" McDonald came to him to ask.

"Because there was nothing lower," the teacher replied.

Dr. Frank was always very careful to add that McDonald took the course again and did very well on it.

[*The University Report,* April 1972.]

From up around Newton

I heard a preacher telling about one of his members whose business was buying and selling cattle. On one occasion the preacher was taking a collection and said, "Who will give $10.00?" This cattle buyer, who was asleep, suddenly woke up and thought he was attending a cattle auction. "I will give fifteen if she's fat."

[George Franks Ivey, *Humor and Humanity* (Hickory: Southern Publishing Co., 1945). Ivey (1870-1952) was a Hickory industrialist.]

Quips from Yanceyville

TEMPERATURED LIPS.—In the Bank of Yanceyville sometime ago, I shook hands with a mighty pretty married lady, and I commented on the warmth of her hands.

"Yes," she replied in acknowledging the compliment, "and I also have a warm heart and temperatured lips."

I was caught off my guard, but I recovered my timidity sufficiently to daringly say, forgetful of a good wife who knows my weaknesses and hasn't as much confidence in me as she ought to have:

"Young lady, you are married and your husband is bigger than me, but I warn you that no pretty girl has ever yet puckered her lips at me without me puckering back."

[Thomas Johnston Henderson, *Honeysuckles and Bramblebriars* (Yanceyville: p.p., 1943).]

KEEP YOUR MOUTH SHUT.—Rural carriers come in close contact with the lifeblood of a nation. They become the friends of and personal confidants of friends all along their routes. Carrier Sink, of Lexington, told me this story while we were over at Reidsville some years ago attending a banquet of the Ladies' Auxiliary of the North Carolina Rural Carriers' Association, toastmastered by its then stately and gracious president, Mrs. J. Hester Foulkes, of Pelham.

A maiden lady of splendid character and attractive personality appealed to Sink for advice in a highly delicate matter. She was in love with and anxiously desirous of marrying a man of recent acquaintance, who had already proposed and been gladly accepted. She said in her appeal: "My sweetheart is forever praising my beautiful teeth, and they're the only part of my anatomy which elicits his passionate compliments. I fear to tell him that these beautiful white teeth are false, lest his love for me grow cold; and I hesitate to deceive him and marry him, lest he afterwards hate me and perhaps leave me. What shall I do?"

"Mary," replied Carrier Sink in fatherly tones, "for heaven's sake go on and marry the boy—and keep your durn mouth shut!"

[Thomas Johnston Henderson, *Homespun Yarns* (Yanceyville: p.p., 1943).]

BAD NEWS.—One of North Carolina's "gentlemen wanderers" once absented himself from the state for some twenty years, and the report came back home that he was dead. But one summer morning he shuffled up the steps of the portico of his brother's fine home, where his brother sat, reading a newspaper, and proudly announced: "The dead has come to life!"

The brother recognized his footsteps and the voice, but he never looked up. Keeping his eyes glued on the newspaper, he ungraciously said: "I'm damned sorry to hear it."

[Thomas Johnston Henderson, *Plain Tales from the Country* (Yanceyville: p.p., 1943).]

THE PERFECT HUSBAND.—Candidate Melville Broughton, now Governor, in apologizing for some of the possible mistakes of the New Deal, told a story which to my sense of humor suggests that it may have a truer significance and deeper application than he intended to signify or imply. One wife was bragging to another wife about the impeccable qualities and habits of her husband. Said she:

"He doesn't drink, he doesn't chew, he doesn't smoke, he doesn't go out nights, and he doesn't chase around after pretty skirts."

"My, my," said the other wife, "you must have the perfect husband. What's the matter with him, anyhow?"

The bragging wife admitted to a crippling cause of her husband's perfection when she answered:

"He's paralyzed."

[Thomas Johnston Henderson, *Plain Tales from the Country* (Yanceyville: p.p., 1943). Thomas Johnston Henderson (1883-1959) was a Yanceyville farmer, editor, and local historian.]

Down at Little Washington

TYPESETTER TROUBLES.—A wholesale concern was happy over the arrival of a shipment of nuts and raisins, since the local retail supply was getting low, and they rushed a classified ad down to the paper. The typesetter, tired and hurried, picked up an "a" instead of "u," reversed its position with "n," and the ad came out:

Fresh arrival of ants and raisins at
The Fruit Store
Send your orders quick.

Something worse happened to a classified ad the late H. B. Thompson, seed dealer of Washington, inserted in the daily paper some years ago. It was oat-planting time and he received a carload of seed oats, but the ad read:

Carload of Rust Proof Cats Just Received
Get'em While They Last.

COLLARDS.—Emma, one day just after Christmas, was engaged in taking down the mistletoe which had been hung on the chandelier. Mrs. Pickles called her from the next room. "All right, Mis' Ellen, I be dere soon as I gits dese collards outen de lamp."

[John G. Bragaw, *Random Shots* (Raleigh: Edwards and Broughton Co., 1945). Bragaw (1879-1960) was a Washington, N.C., columnist and insurance man.]

At Charlotte and Elsewhere

CHARLOTTE WEDDING.—At a wedding reception in Charlotte, a friend of the groom decided to find out whether anyone in the receiving line knew what the hundreds of people filing past were saying. As he moved along, he purred, "My grandmother just died today."

"How nice!" "Thank you so much!" "How sweet of you to say so!"—were the responses to his announcement. No one had the slightest idea what he said, least of all the groom, who exclaimed jovially, "It's about time you took the same step, old man!"

[Una Taylor]

THE UNDERTAKER.—State College alumni attending a dinner in Raleigh were asked to name their professions. One shy young undertaker, fearing the derision of the crowd when he told his calling, answered smoothly, "I'm a southern planter."

[Betty C. Waite]

HIGH WAYS.—As I stood by the curb in Selma, I observed a young man mopping his brow and peering nervously up the street. At that moment an old Ford convertible came slowly around the corner, a girl of about twenty gripping the steering wheel and gazing fixedly ahead. As she approached us, the young man gestured frantically and yelled, "Keep more to the right! Shift into high!Don't forget the clutch or you'll strip your gears!"

The car passed out of sight and he relaxed momentarily, then began peering up the street again. Soon the Ford rounded the corner once more, sputtering and jerking even worse than before. "Choke 'er!" he shouted.

The car leaped forward. "Brake down and shift to second at the corner," he called as the car passed.

Turning to me he explained, "It's my wife learning to drive."

"But couldn't you teach her better if you were in the car?"

"Maybe," he replied. "But the car's insured, and my life ain't!"

[W. Howard Rambeau]

[Associated Press, *Fun Fare: A Treasury of Reader's Digest Wit and Humor* (Pleasantville, N.Y.: Reader's Digest Association, 1949).]

Wedding Chambers

At the turn of the century, a lad from the upper reaches of Chatham County managed to persuade a gawky girl to marry him, and off they went to Washington on a honeymoon. The clerk at the hotel immediately recognized the couple as newlyweds and inquired, "You'll want bridal chambers, won't you?"

"Well," replied the rustic fellow, "we'll rent one for my wife, but I'll wet out the window like I do at home."

[Traditional.]

Ambition

John [Harden] tells a story about the Cherry administration. On one occasion, a highway commissioner died, and the news of his death had hardly reached the public before Cherry got a telegram from an ambitious Tar Heel. "I would like to take the place of Joe Blank," the telegram implored,

Governor Cherry wired back: "It's all right with me if you can make arrangements with the undertaker."

[Bill Sharpe, *The State*, 1 June 1967. Sharpe (1903-71) was editor of *State* magazine from 1951 until his death.]

Recommended

Jonathan Daniels . . . recently told this story about the late Governor Gregg Cherry:

Governor Cherry was in an elevator in his home town of Gastonia when a timid little lady, visiting in the city, asked him who was the best lawyer in Gastonia. He replied promptly:

"Gregg Cherry—when he's sober."

Dismayed, she asked who was the second best lawyer in Gastonia.

"Gregg Cherry—when he's drunk."

[Curtis Russ, *The State*, 15 May 1969.]

Senator Sam J. Ervin: Contexts

The Senator's gift for the illustrative yarn first drew attention in the debate over the censure of Senator Joseph R. McCarthy. The Wisconsin Republican had attacked Mr. Ervin before the latter took the floor. The attack was based on a quotation taken out of context and attributed to Senator Ervin.

Mr. McCarthy's habit of lifting statements out of context, Senator Ervin said, reminded him of the nineteenth-century Carolina preacher who became enraged at the female habit of wearing the hair in gaudy top knots. The preacher decided to invoke the gospel against this vice. Gathering all the ladies to church, he delivered a mighty sermon on the text, "Top Knot Come Down."

After the sermon, an angry woman declared the sermon a fraud and challenged the preacher to find any such text in the Bible. The preacher opened the book and pointed to the seventeenth verse of the twenty-fourth chapter of Matthew. It read:

"Let him which is on the housetop not come down to take anything out of his house."

[Russell Baker, "A New Raconteur Reigns in Senate," *The New York Times*, 13 May 1956. © 1956 by The New York Times Company. Reprinted by permission.]

Briefly

All reporters write too much.

It drives editors crazy.

You can say a whole lot in a few words.

I believe it was in Governor William Umstead's administration that a man on Death Row in Raleigh sat down and wrote to the governor. He probably was tempted to write a whole book.

He couldn't have said much more than he did.

The letter:

"Dear Governor: They are going to execute me on Friday. This is Monday. Sincerely yours. . . ."

[Roy Thompson, *The State*, 1 February 1970. Thompson is a special writer for the *Winston-Salem Journal*.]

Wit and Religion

I heard about a man some time ago who had a watermelon patch, and some young rascals in the community were stealing him blind.

So he said, "All right, I'll get 'em." So he put up a sign in his watermelon patch that said, "One of these melons is poison."

He went to bed and got up the next morning, and sure enough they hadn't stolen a watermelon. Everything was the same, except the sign had been changed. It now read, "Two of these watermelons is poison."

[Ninth Sermon, Charlotte Crusade, 1958.]

I heard about a man who was supposed to preach for twenty minutes and he spoke for thirty and forty and fifty; an hour and twenty minutes later he was still speaking. The man who introduced him couldn't stand it any longer and he picked up a gavel and threw it at the speaker. It missed the speaker and hit a man in the front row, and as the man in the front row was going into subconsciousness, he said, "Hit me again, I can still hear him."

["Youth of Today Searching for Security," Houston Crusade, 1965.]

I heard about one preacher one day, and he was preaching, and he said, "Has anybody ever heard of a perfect man?" He didn't expect anybody to stand up. Finally there was one spineless little fellow stood up in the back—little, weak, weasel-faced fellow. And he stood up sort of hesitatingly. And the preacher said, "You know of a perfect man?"

And he said, "Uh, yes, sir, I do."

And he said, "Well, who?"

And he said, "Well, my wife's first husband was perfect."

["Problems of the American Home," Dallas, Texas, 23 June 1951.]

Well, I heard about a man who had read a book review on Bridie Murphy and the transmigration of souls. He was helping his wife with the dishes and he asked his wife, "Does that mean if I die I will come back to this world in another form."

"Yes, that's what it means," his wife said.

"Do you believe if I were to die, for example, I would come back as a worm?"

"Sweetheart," she replied, "you are never the same twice."

[Twenty-second Sermon, Charlotte Crusade, 1958.]

I heard about a fellow sometime ago who was talking to a friend of his and he said, "Boy, my wife is an angel."

My friend said, "You're lucky, my wife is still living."
[Twenty-second Sermon, Charlotte Crusade, 1958.]

[Bill Adler, ed., *The Wit and Wisdom of Billy Graham* (New York: Random House, 1967). William Franklin Graham, born in Charlotte in 1918, is an evangelist who is known worldwide.]

The Sad, Sad Tale of Horace the Mule

Mrs. George Wood, now deceased, of Chowan County, had a mule who was named Horace. One evening she called up Dr. Satterfield in Edenton and said to him, "Doctor, Horace is sick, and I wish you would come and take a look at him."

Dr. Satterfield said, "Oh, Fannie Lamb, it's after six o'clock, and I'm eating supper. Give him a dose of mineral oil, and if he isn't all right in the morning, phone me, and I'll come and take a look at him."

"How'll I give it to him?" she inquired.

"Through a funnel."

"But he might bite me," she protested.

"Oh, Fannie Lamb—you're a farm woman and you know about these things. Give it to him through the other end."

So Fannie Lamb went out to the barn, and there stood Horace, with his head held down, and moaning and groaning.

She looked around for a funnel but the nearest thing she could see to one was her Uncle Bill's fox-hunting horn hanging on the wall. A beautiful gold-plated instrument with gold tassels hanging from it.

She took the horn and affixed it properly. Horace paid no attention.

Then she reached up on the shelf where medicines for the farm animals were kept. But instead of picking up the mineral oil, she picked up a bottle of turpentine instead, and she poured a liberal dose of it into the horn.

Horace raised his head with a sudden jerk. He let out a yell that could have been heard a mile away. He reared up on his hind legs, brought his front legs down, knocked out the side of the barn, jumped a five-foot fence, and started down the road at a mad gallop.

Now Horace was in pain, so every few jumps he made, that horn would blow.

All the dogs in the neighborhood knew that when that horn was blowing, it meant that Uncle Bill was going fox hunting. So out on the highway they went, close behind Horace.

It was a marvelous sight. First, Horace running at top speed, the hunting horn in a most unusual position, the mellow notes issuing therefrom, the tassels waving, and the dogs barking joyously.

They passed by the home of Old Man Harvey Hogan, who was sitting on his front porch. He hadn't drawn a sober breath in fifteen years, and he gazed in fascinated amazement at the sight that unfolded itself before his eyes. He couldn't believe what he was seeing. . . .

By this time it was good and dark. Horace and the dogs were approaching the Inland Waterway. The bridge tender heard the horn blowing and figured that a boat was approaching. So he hurriedly went out and uncranked the bridge. Horace went overboard and was drowned. The dogs also went into the water, but they swam out without very much difficulty.

Now it so happened that the bridge tender was running for the office of sheriff of Chowan County, but he managed to poll only seven votes.

The people figured that any man who didn't know the difference between a mule with a horn up his rear and a boat coming down the Inland Waterway wasn't fit to hold any public office in Chowan County.

[Edmund Harding, in Vernon Sechrist's column, "Relax," *Rocky Mount Telegram,* reprinted in *The Carolina Journal of Pharmacy,* September 1971. Harding (1890-1970), of Washington, N.C., won fame throughout the United States as a platform humorist.]

People, People

BURYING EXPENSES—A big real estate operator's widow told the undertaker that she wanted him planted with all the trimmings, the best of everything. She got a bill for $4,700. She was outraged.

"But madam," reminded the undertaker, "you said the best."

"Yes," she fumed, "for $300 more I could have buried him in a Cadillac!"

AT THE GOVERNOR'S MANSION—A creviced but durable dowager, who for an unaccountable number of years has been prominent in the most rarefied of the social spheres in our city, was in a downtown office recently and spied a photograph of U.S. Senator [W. Kerr] Scott who formerly was Governor. With shrill-voiced hauteur, she disclosed: "He was the only governor I was not intimate with in the Mansion for twenty-five years."

COURTROOM SCENE—The defendant approached Solictor Lester C. Chalmers, Jr., and said, "I want to thank you. You have just put me on my feet."

He had just been convicted of drunken driving, his driver's license automatically revoked.

[Charles Craven, *Charles Craven's Kind of People* (Chapel Hill: Colonial Press, 1956). Craven is a Raleigh columnist and newspaper reporter.]

She Wasn't Sure

[Henry] Belk [of Goldsboro] tells the story of a funeral at which the deceased was richly eulogized. One worthy at the casket described the departed as now "walking the milkyway." After listening intently, the widow said to one of her sons: "Go up there and see if that's your daddy in there."

[Charles Craven, *News and Observer* (Raleigh), 31 October 1968.]

Baptism

A minister was about to baptize a young girl in a North Carolina river.

"Now, Veronica," the pastor said, "I'm going to wash all your sins away."

"My goodness," giggled Veronica, "in that 'itty bitty li'l ol' crick?"

[Earl Wilson, syndicated column, "It Happened Last Night," *News and Observer* (Raleigh), 25 April 1966. Reproduced by courtesy of Publishers-Hall Syndicate.]

Anything Can Happen in Chapel Hill

We've read the story in several newspapers, but until we read Pete Hulth's column in the Smithfield *Herald* we never realized that it had happened to someone in Chapel Hill.

The way Pete tells it a man and his wife and fourteen-year-old daughter from Chapel Hill took a small camp trailer with them as they attended Expo 67 and toured New England.

When they got within forty-five miles of home, the husband said he was tired. He had driven every mile since the family had left home. Since his wife knew the remainder of the route home, he got in the camp trailer to relax for the rest of the trip.

It was hot and stuffy in the camper, so he kicked off his shoes, then stripped down to his underwear.

About the time he fell asleep, there was a loud crash, and the trailer came to an abrupt halt. Thinking his wife has struck another vehicle, he jumped out of the trailer to investigate. As it happened, his wife has just applied the power brakes and made a sudden stop, while there was a rear-end collision in the next lane.

As the man stood there in his underwear, the light changed, and his wife pulled away. He waved frantically, but she had her eyes on the road ahead. He even ran to a service station to ask the attendants to rush him to the departing car. They thought he was crazy and would pay no attention to him.

He finally convinced a taxi driver to take him to Chapel Hill, where he obtained a check and pen, cashed the check, and paid the taxi driver in cash.

The taxi driver took a short cut to the residence, and the man beat his wife and daughter home.

As he sat on the front steps awaiting the rest of the family, he thought to himself, "It could have been worse."

Then his wife and daughter drove up. His wife was so surprised to see him sitting on the front steps, and in his underwear, that she drove through the carport and knocked down the tool shed!

[*Chapel Hill Weekly,* reprinted in *Raleigh Times,* 28 September 1967.]

Resourcefulness and Other Matters

RESOURCEFULNESS—The other day I talked to an unlettered farmer in Orange County. He had shown considerable initiative and resourcefulness in handling a difficult situation, and I had congratulated him. Here was his reply: "Well, I'll tell you, Mr. Coates, when you ain't got no education you got to use your head."

GETTING TO HEAVEN—I recalled the question asked of the Episcopal bishop after his doctrinal sermon: "Is there any other way to get to heaven than through the Episcopal Church?"

"Yes," said the bishop, "there are other ways, but no gentleman would take them."

SENSITIVE HANDS—I told them of my wife's experience buying lamb chops after we were married. The butcher was a frail, Shelley-like person, who would skin the lamb chops for her. But on this particular morning he had difficulty, which he explained in this way: His girl was a beauty parlor operator. She would give him a manicure on Friday nights when he went to see her. The night before, she had cut his nails so short he couldn't skin the lamb chops! My wife was looking at the meats on display and casually observed: "Your girl must be sensitive to hands."

A silence followed, and my wife looked up at a rather startled expression on the butcher's face, as he confided: "Well, you know, she is right toucheous!"

WATER INTO WINE—Not long ago a law-enforcing friend told me he had just caught a bootlegger who had eluded him for months. That morning he had come on him with fruit jars covering the floor of his station wagon and asked him what he had in them. "Water" was the answer.

"Let me taste it," said the officer, and turning up a jar started drinking and kept on drinking. When he put it down, he wiped his mouth and said: "It tastes like wine to me."

"Lord, Lord," the old bootlegger answered, "Jesus has done it again!"

[Albert Coates, *What the University of North Carolina Meant to Me* (Richmond: p.p., 1969). Coates, born in Johnston County in 1896, is best known as the founder of the Institute of Government at Chapel Hill.]

Official State Mammal

North Carolina's General Assembly made the gray squirrel the official state mammal. But it wasn't a snap.

When the bill came up in the House, Rep. Basil D. Barr, the sponsor, told his colleagues: "The gray squirrel is thrifty. He buries nuts."

And Rep. Henry Boshamer commented: "Any animal that buries nuts would be dangerous to this General Assembly."

[William J. Conway, *Raleigh Times,* 21 August 1969.]

Morganton Citizen

A good doctor used to tell of the time he was called to treat a man for snake bite, only to find his patient happily inebriated from drinking a large potion of denatured alcohol.

"Don't you know that stuff will kill you?" angrily demanded the doctor.

"Well, ole snake done bit me an' gonna die anyhow," said his happy patient.

When the same man was cautioned by the druggist once before and informed that to continue drinking wood alcohol might cause blindness, he replied, "Why, Morganton ain't so big and I done seed all they wuz to see anyhow."

[J. Alex Mull, *The State,* 1 September 1966. Mull, born in 1909 in Morganton, is a real estate broker.]

Duck-Hunting

A duck-hunting old-timer was bragging about his ability to kill ducks. "Why," he said, "if I ever missed one of the critturs, I don't rightly remember it."

Pressed by one listener to prove his boast, the old-timer agreed. And the next morning found them both in a duck blind.

Along came a duck and the old-timer whispered: "Sit tight, son, and I'll show you how it's done."

With that he blasted away. Naturally, the duck flew on.

Carefully lowering his gun, the old-timer looked at his companion. "Well, son," he said, "you're witnessin' a miracle. Yonder goes a dead duck—flying'."

[Frank A. Montgomery, Jr., *The State,* 15 January 1968.]

Over at Louisburg

FIFTY-CENT BET.—Folks will bet on almost anything. Take one night down at the Firehouse. Mayor Tommy Peoples and some others were sitting around discussing, of all things, how rapidly they could dress or undress. Finally it boiled down to the mayor and one other. This one fellow claimed that he could get undressed faster than anyone in the world. The mayor, leading him on, said, "O.K. I'll bet you fifty cents that I can get my clothes off faster than you can."

"O.K., that's a bet."

"You go around back of the firetruck," said the mayor, "and I'll stay around here. Then when Joe gives the signal we both start and first one undressed wins the money."

The signal was given and all the bystanders stood there with the mayor, trying to hold back their laughter as the butt of the joke rushed his undressing.

In a few seconds the winner came rushing around the firetruck, stark naked, to roars of laughter. "Well," said the fully dressed mayor, "you win. Here's your money," and handed over fifty cents.

BLOWING TAPS.—Funerals are not funny, particularly for those involved [such] as family, friends and loved ones, but occasionally things happen on such tragic occasions that are sources of amusement to many who are not closely involved.

For example, a few years back, two county brothers met their deaths in the service of their country and were brought back to the county for burial with full military honors. It was a sad occasion for their families and a large crowd gathered at the little family burying ground, consisting of all possible members of their family, many friends, and a goodly number of the curious who always turn out for such affairs. Then there was the military guard of honor and squad of riflemen to fire the last salute to the gallant pair.

It was a trying and sad occasion, several women in the family just about broke down, but finally it was coming to a close. Taps was blown by an Army bugler and the guard of honor fired the final salute. This proved too much for an elderly lady in the family, and she keeled over in a dead faint, almost at the exact moment the riflemen fired their salute.

There was almost complete silence, broken by a small boy's voice that carried clearly to the entire crowd as he almost screamed, "Damn, they shot Grandma."

[Thilbert H. Pearce, *How to Sell a Dead Mule* (Freeman, S.D.: Pine Hill Press, 1971). Thilbert Pearce is a Franklin County photographer, historian, and free-lance writer.]

Sno' Foolin' in Raleigh

FARM SCENE.—Raleigh's Tom Bremson was riding through eastern North Carolina this week when he noticed a man in a field unloading baskets of collards from a truck.

Tom stopped and ambled out to the farmer.

"Say, Mister, would you mind selling me a mess of those good-looking collards?" he asked.

"Where you from?" asked the farmer.

"Raleigh."

"What's your business?" drawled the farmer.

"I'm a diamond man," answered Tom.

"Well, I shore hope you know a helluva lot more about diamonds than you do about collards, 'cause these are tobacco plants," grunted the tobacco grower.

[A. C. Snow, *Raleigh Times*, 14 May 1966. Snow, born in 1924 in Dobson, is a Raleigh columnist and newspaperman.]

FOOTBALL TROUBLE.—Dr. Buck Menius, dean of N.C. State's School of Physical Science and Applied Math, was speaking recently to the Engineering Foundation, when he told the story about a young athlete who believed in following instructions.

The third-string quarterback hadn't played all season until the final game came up. The first-string quarterback was injured; the second-string signal caller was at home in bed with the flu.

Third-stringer Jones was told to go in with the home team trailing by only six points but in the waning moments of the game.

The bench warmer was told by the coach: "Now Jones, do exactly as I tell you. Run three off-tackle plays and then kick the ball."

In went Jones. On the first off-tackle play, he ran fourteen yards; on the second, he gained twenty-four; on the third, he racked up another fifteen yards. On the fourth down he kicked.

The coach throttled Jones as he came off the field.

"Man," he ranted. "What on earth were you thinking about when you kicked the ball?"

"Sir," sobbed Jones in frustration. "I was thinking I've got the stupidest coach in the whole world!"

[A. C. Snow, *Raleigh Times*, 7 March 1969.]

PINCH-PENNY.—"Don't be fooled," said the ad in the morning paper; and it said that the airport money, if authorized, will put "an unjust tax burden on your children and grandchildren."

"Ye gods!" said my pinch-penny friend. "I had planned to vote against this thing, but if my children and grandchildren are going to pay for it, I believe I'll be able to afford it."

[A. C. Snow, *Raleigh Times*, 30 October 1968.]

BIRTHDAY PRESENT.—And then I heard about a visiting N.C. State professor from Hong Kong. He said concubines are what he misses most in the American culture.

"My father gave me a concubine for my twenty-first birthday," he sighed.

"Would you like a concubine for your twenty-first birthday?" I asked a young friend of twenty years.

"I never really thought about that!" he said with a new light in his eyes. "I've been wanting a Mustang."

[A. C. Snow, *Raleigh Times*, 15 August 1969.]

IN A HURRY.—Billy Arthur tells about the lady who called the Intimate Bookshop in Chapel Hill and asked if they had *The Power of Sexual Surrender.*

They didn't and asked if they could order it for her.

"No," she sighed. "I've got to have it by tonight."

[A. C. Snow, *Raleigh Times*, 29 June 1971.]

WEATHER BUREAU.—The tale is still told about the young man who was transferred to the Raleigh-Durham airport weather bureau from a Big City in the north and a farmer called to inquire:

"Do you think it will be cold enough to kill hogs today?"

"No, I don't think it will be cold enough to hurt them at all," he was told.

[A. C. Snow, *Raleigh Times,* 25 September 1969.]

WHAT'S NEXT.—Don't you believe it, but a real estate friend likes to tell about the time he was showing a prospect of Swedish origin around a new home.

"And now that we've seen the living room and dining room, we'll look at the bedroom and den."

"And den what?" she asked indignantly.

[A. C. Snow, *Raleigh Times,* 24 March 1970.]

GOVERNORS LEAVING TOWN.—Governor Bob Scott helped kickoff Co-op Week with a little joke on himself when he spoke at ceremonies in the NCSU Faculty Club this week.

He and Mrs. Scott recently were recalling how friends gave the Governor's father, W. Kerr Scott, a Ford when the elder Scott left Raleigh.

"Governor Hodges rode out of town in a Thunderbird and Terry Sanford rode out in an Oldsmobile," Scott said. "Friends gave Governor Moore a Cadillac. I wonder if my friends will give me anything."

"You don't have to worry," said Mrs. Scott. "At the rate you're going, they'll ride you out of town on a rail."

[A. C. Snow, *Raleigh Times,* 4 October 1969.]

Last Book?

Marse Grant, editor of the *Biblical Recorder* and author (*Whiskey at the Wheel*), relays this story about Brooks Hays of Winston-Salem, recently named chairman of the state Good Neighbor Council. Someone asked Hays' father if he had read his son's last book. "I hope so," the father replied.

[*News and Observer* (Raleigh), 8 February 1970.]

Just Killing Times

Nick Carrington and I were reviewing the human condition, as we are wont around here at slack moments, and the subject got around to a person's acceptance of a terminal illness. I said I would give some thought to doing myself in, and the talk moved to ways to do it. Carbon monoxide seems simple enough, I said, but what do you do while you're just sitting there in the car waiting for eternity?

"Well," Nick said, "you could listen to the radio."

[Len Sullivan, *Mooresville Tribune*, reprinted in *The State*, 15 August 1970.]

Poetic Outlook

A University of North Carolina English instructor introduced to his class what he termed "one of the finest, most elegant lines of poetry in the English language." He had duly recorded it in all of his notebooks as a constant reminder of its beauty. "Walk with light!" he quoted, and then repeated softly and blissfully to himself, "Walk with light . . . now isn't that a wonderful thing to say to someone?" The class agreed, of course, and wished to know the author.

"I suppose it's anonymous," said the instructor. "It's written on a sign at an intersection of Franklin Street."

[Associated Press, *Reader's Digest*, August 1971.]

In Shelby

Pete McKnight told the story about Charlie Keel . . . and the time President Roosevelt came to Shelby. The crowds first lined Marion Street to await FDR's arrival, then rushed to Warren Street when a rumor got out. The rumors about which street the President was coming down kept changing, and the crowd kept moving.

As it turned out, most of the people missed the President when he came down the street they had just left.

Said a thoroughly disgusted Keel, "Dern a town with two streets."

[Bill Sharpe, *The State*, 1 June 1969.]

Thomas Wolfe

First readers of Look Homeward, Angel *have been so caught up in its unforgettable, intense lyricism that they have tended to overlook the author's sense of humor and, thereafter, to even deny that he had one. On the contrary, Thomas Wolfe (1900-1938) was a meticulous craftsman who knew that poetic emotionalism required a light-hearted balance. He was born in Asheville and was only fifteen when he entered The University of North Carolina at Chapel Hill, where he dreamed of becoming a playwright. After graduation he attended Harvard and eventually taught at New York University. Disappointed that his plays were not accepted for production, Wolfe turned to fiction. He early developed a bent for satire, parody, and caricature, and he was ever aware that comic value lies just beneath the surface of the most serious action. During the year before his death, he infused* The Hills Beyond *with racy hyperbole and a masculine folk wit that reflects the jokes and breezy tales of Zeb Vance, who was from the same mountain county of Buncombe.*

Dawn at the Greasy Spoon

Nacreous pearl light swam faintly about the hem of the lilac darkness; the edges of light and darkness were stitched upon the hills. Morning moved like a pearl-gray tide across the fields and up the hillflanks, flowing rapidly down into the soluble dark.

At the curb now, young Dr. Jefferson Spaugh brought his Buick roadster to a halt, and got out, foppishly drawing off his gloves and flicking the silk lapels of his dinner jacket. His face, whisky-red, was highboned and handsome; his mouth was straight-lipped, cruel, and sensual. An inherited aura of mountain-cornfield sweat hung scentlessly but telepathically about him; he was a smartened-up mountaineer with country-club and University of Pennsylvania glossings. Four years in Philly change a man.

Thrusting his gloves carelessly into his coat, he entered. McGuire slid bearishly off his stool and gazed him into focus. Then he made beckoning round-arm gestures with his fat hands.

"Look at it, will you," he said. "Does any one know what it is?"

"It's Percy," said Coker. "You know Percy Van der Gould, don't you?"

"I've been dancing all night at the Hilliards," said Spaugh elegantly. "Damn! These new patent-leather pumps have ruined my feet." He sat upon a stool, and elegantly displayed his large country feet, indecently broad and angular in the shoes.

"What's he been doing?" said McGuire doubtfully, turning to Coker for enlightenment.

"He's been dawncing all night at the Hilliards," said Coker in a mincing voice.

McGuire shielded his bloated face coyly with his hand.

"O crush me!" he said, "I'm a grape! Dancing at the Hilliards, were you, you damned Mountain Grill. You've been on a Poon-Tang Picnic in Niggertown. You can't load that bunk on us."

Bull-lunged, their laughter filled the nacreous dawn.

"Patent-leather pumps!" said McGuire. "Hurt his feet. By God, Coker, the first time he came to town ten years ago he'd never been curried above the knees. They had to throw him down to put shoes on him."

Ben laughed thinly to the Angel.

"A couple of slices of buttered toast, if you please, not too brown," said Spaugh delicately to the counterman.

"A mess of hog chitlings and sorghum, you mean, you bastard. You were brought up on salt pork and cornbread."

"We're getting too low and coarse for him, Hugh," said Coker. "Now that he's got drunk with some of the best families, he's in great demand socially. He's so highly thought of that he's become the official midwife to all pregnant virgins."

"Yes," said McGuire, "he's their friend. He helps them out. He not only helps them out, he helps them in again."

"What's wrong with that?" said Spaugh. "We ought to keep it in the family, oughtn't we?"

Their laughter howled out into the tender dawn.

"This conversation is getting too rough for me," said Horse Hines banteringly as he got off his stool.

"Shake hands with Coker before you go, Horse," said

McGuire. "He's the best friend you've ever had. You ought to give him royalties."

The light that filled the world now was soft and otherworldly like the light that fills the sea-floors of Catalina where the great fish swim. Flat-footedly, with kidney-aching back, Patrolman Leslie Roberts all unbuttoned slouched through the submarine pearl light and paused, gently agitating his club behind him, as he turned his hollow liverish face toward the open door.

"Here's your patient," said Coker softly, "the Constipated Cop."

Aloud, with great cordiality, they all said: "How are you, Les?"

"Oh, tolable, tolable," said the policeman mournfully. As draggled as his mustaches, he passed on, hocking into the gutter a slimy gob of phlegm.

"Well, good morning, gentlemen," said Horse Hines, making to go.

"Remember what I told you, Horse. Be good to Coker, your best friend." McGuire jerked a thumb toward Coker.

Beneath his thin joviality Horse Hines was hurt.

"I do remember," said the undertaker gravely. "We are both members of honorable professions: in the hour of death when the storm-tossed ship puts into its haven of rest, we are the trustees of the Almighty."

"Why, Horse!" Coker exclaimed, "this is eloquence!"

"The sacred rites of closing the eyes, of composing the limbs, and of preparing for burial the lifeless repository of the departed soul is our holy mission; it is for us, the living, to pour balm upon the broken heart of Grief, to soothe the widow's ache, to brush away the orphan's tears; it is for us, the living, to highly resolve that—"

"—Government of the people, for the people, and by the people," said Hugh McGuire.

"Yes, Horse," said Coker, "you are right. I'm touched. And what's more, we do it all for nothing. At least," he added virtuously, "I never charge for soothing the widow's ache."

"What about embalming the broken heart of Grief?" asked McGuire.

"I said *balm*," Horse Hines remarked coldly.

"Say, Horse," said Harry Tugman, who had listened with great interest, "didn't you make a speech with all that in it last summer at the Undertakers' Convention?"

"What's true then is true now," said Horse Hines bitterly, as he left the place.

The Younger Set

As Jeff Spaugh roared off Harry Tugman said jealously: "Look at that bastard. Mr. Vanderbilt. He thinks he's hell, don't he? A big pile of bull. Ben, do you reckon he was really out at the Hilliards to-night?"

"Oh for God's sake," said Ben irritably, "how the hell should I know! What difference does it make?" he added furiously.

"I guess Little Maudie will fill up the column to-morrow with some of her crap," said Harry Tugman. " 'The Younger Set,' she calls it! Christ! It goes all the way from every little bitch old enough to wear drawers, to Old Man Redmond. If Saul Gudger belongs to the Younger Set, Ben, you and I are still in the third grade. Why, hell, yes," he said with an air of conviction to the grinning counter-man, "he was bald as a pig's knuckle when the Spanish American War broke out."

The counterman laughed.

Foaming with brilliant slapdash improvisation Harry Tugman declaimed:

"Members of the Younger Set were charmingly entertained last night at a dinner dance given at Snotwood, the beautiful residence of Mr. and Mrs. Clarence Firkins, in honor of their youngest daughter, Gladys, who made her debutt this season. Mr. and Mrs. Firkins, accompanied by their daughter, greeted each of the arriving guests at the threshhold in a manner reviving the finest old traditions of Southern aristocracy, while Mrs. Firkins' accomplished sister, Miss Catherine Hipkiss, affectionately known to members of the local younger set as Roaring Kate, supervised the checking of overcoats, evening wraps, jock-straps, and jewelry.

"Dinner was served promptly at eight o'clock, followed by coffee and Pluto Water at eight forty-five. A delicious nine-course collation had been prepared by Artaxerxes Papadopolos, the well-known confectioner and caterer, and proprietor of the Bijou Café for Ladies and Gents.

"After first-aid and a thorough medical examination by Dr. Jefferson Reginald Alfonso Spaugh, the popular *gin*-ecologist, the guests adjourned to the Ball Room where dance music was provided by Zeke Buckner's Upper Hominy Stringed Quartette, Mr. Buckner himself officiating at the trap drum and tambourine.

"Among those dancing were the Misses Aline Titsworth, Lena Ginster, Ophelia Legg, Gladys Firkins, Beatrice Slutsky, Mary Whitesides, Helen Shockett, and Lofta Barnes.

"Also the Messrs. I. C. Bottom, U. B. Freely, R. U. Reddy, O. I. Lovett, Cummings Strong, Samson Horney, Preston Updyke, Dows Wicket, Pettigrew Biggs, Otis Goode, and J. Broad Stern."

Ben laughed noiselessly, and bent his pointed face into the mug again. Then, he stretched his thin arms out, extending his body sensually upward, and forcing out in a wide yawn the nighttime accumulation of weariness, boredom, and disgust.

"Oh-h-h-h my God!"

[Thomas Wolfe, *Look Homeward, Angel* (New York: Charles Scribner's Sons, 1929). Copyright © 1929 Charles Scribner's Sons. Reprinted by permission of Charles Scribner's Sons.]

Tombstone for a Prostitute

[*Altamont's leading madame arrives at W. O. Gant's stone-cutting shop.*]

"How are all the girls, Elizabeth?" he asked kindly.

Her face grew sad. She began to pull her gloves off.

"That's what I came in to see you about," she said. "I lost one of them last week."

"Yes," said Gant gravely, "I was sorry to hear of that."

"She was the best girl I had," said Elizabeth. "I'd have done anything in the world for her. We did everything we could," she added. "I've no regrets on that score. I had a doctor and two trained nurses by her all the time."

She opened her black leather handbag, thrust her gloves into it, and pulling out a small bluebordered handkerchief, began to weep quietly.

"Huh-huh-huh-huh-huh," said Gant, shaking his head. "Too bad, too bad, too bad. Come back to my office," he said. They went back and sat down. Elizabeth dried her eyes.

"What was her name?" he asked.

"We called her Lily—her full name was Lillian Reed."

"Why, I knew that girl," he exclaimed. "I spoke to her not over two weeks ago."

"Yes," said Elizabeth, "she went like that—one hemorrhage right after another, down here." She tapped her abdomen. "Nobody ever knew she was sick until last Wednesday. Friday she was gone." She wept again.

"T-t-t-t-t," he clucked regretfully. "Too bad, too bad. She was pretty as a picture."

"I couldn't have loved her more, Mr. Gant," said Elizabeth, "if she had been my own daughter."

"How old was she?" he asked.

"Twenty-two," said Elizabeth, beginning to weep again.

"What a pity! What a pity!" he agreed. "Did she have any people?"

"No one who would do anything for her," Elizabeth said. "Her mother died when she was thirteen—she was born out here on the Beetree Fork—and her father," she added indignantly, "is a mean old bastard who's never done anything for her or any one else. He didn't even come to her funeral."

"He will be punished," said Gant darkly.

"As sure as there's a God in heaven," Elizabeth agreed, "he'll get what's coming to him in hell. The old bastard!" she continued virtuously, "I hope he rots!"

"You can depend upon it," he said grimly. "He will. Ah, Lord." He was silent a moment while he shook his head with slow regret.

"A pity, a pity," he muttered. "So young." He had the moment of triumph all men have when they hear some one has died. A moment, too, of grisly fear. Sixty-four.

"I couldn't have loved her more," said Elizabeth, "if she'd been one of my own. A young girl like that, with all her life before her."

"It's pretty sad when you come to think of it," he said. "By God, it is."

"And she was such a fine girl, Mr. Gant," said Elizabeth, weeping softly. "She had such a bright future before her. She had more opportunities than I ever had, and I suppose you know"—she spoke modestly—"what I've done.". . .

They had always known each other—since first they met. They had no excuses, no questions, no replies. The world fell away from them. In the silence they heard the pulsing slap of the fountain, the high laughter of bawdry in the Square. He took a book of models from the desk, and began to turn its slick pages. They showed modest blocks of Georgia marble and Vermont granite.

"I don't want any of those," she said impatiently. "I've already made up my mind. I know what I want."

He looked up surprised. "What is it?"

"I want the angel out front.". . .

He was silent, thinking for a moment of the place where the angel stood. He knew he had nothing to cover or obliterate that place—it left a barren crater in his heart.

"All right," he said. "You can have it for what I paid for it—$420."

She took a thick sheaf of banknotes from her purse and counted the money out for him. He pushed it back.

"No. Pay me when the job's finished and it has been set up. You want some sort of inscription, don't you?"

"Yes. There's her full name, age, place of birth, and so on," she said, giving him a scrawled envelope. "I want some poetry, too—something that suits a young girl taken off like this."

He pulled his tattered little book of inscriptions from a pigeonhole, and thumbed its pages, reading her a quatrain here and there. To each she shook her head. Finally, he said:

"How's this one, Elizabeth?" He read:

She went away in beauty's flower,
Before her youth was spent;
Ere life and love had lived their hour
God called her, and she went.

Yet whispers Faith upon the wind:
No grief to her was given.
She left *your* love and went to find
A greater one in heaven.

"Oh, that's lovely—lovely," she said. "I want that one."
"Yes," he agreed, "I think that's the best one.". . .

[Thomas Wolfe, *Look Homeward, Angel* (New York: Charles Scribner's Sons, 1929). Copyright © 1929 Charles Scribner's Sons. Reprinted by permission of Charles Scribner's Sons.]

After the Crap Game

Tugman: . . .Boys, I've been in a crap game and I took 'em for a hundred and fifty bucks.

Willis: Which means you're a dollar and a quarter to the good, I suppose. (*Quietly, viciously*) A hundred and fifty bucks—why God-damn your drunken soul, you never saw that much at one time in your whole life.

A. P. Man: How much of it you got left, Tug?

Tugman: Not a lousy cent. They took me to the cleaners afterwards. Tell you how it was, boys. We was down at Chakales Pig. When I picked up the loot I looked around and counted up the house and decided it was safe to buy a round of drinks, seein' as there was only five guys there. (*His manner grows more riotously extravagant as with coarse but eloquent improvisation he builds up the farce.*) Well, I goes up to the bar, thinkin' I'm safe, and says: 'Step right up, gentlemen. This one's on me.' And you know what happens? (*He pauses a moment for dramatic effect.*) Well, boys, I ain't hardly got the words out of my mouth when there is a terrific crash of splintered glass and eighteen booze hounds bust in from the sidewalk, six more spring through the back windows, and the trap doors of the cellar come flyin' open and thirty-seven more swarm up like rats out of the lower depths. By that time the place is jammed. Then I hear the sireens goin' in the street, and before I know it the village fire department comes plungin' in, followed by two-thirds of the local constabulary. I tries to crawl out between the legs of One-eye McGloon and Silk McCarthy, bŭt they have me cornered before I gets as far as the nearest spittoon. Well, to make a long story short, they rolled me for every nickel I had. Somebody got my socks and B.V.D.'s, and when I finally crawled to safety Chakales had my shirt and told me he was holdin' it as security until I came through with the six bits I still owed him for the drinks.

[Thomas Wolfe, "Gentlemen of the Press" in *The Hills Beyond* (New York: Harper & Brothers, 1941). Reprinted by permission of Harper & Row Publishers, Inc.]

The Sons of Bear Joyner

In examining the history of that great man [Zachariah Joyner], we have collected more than eight hundred stories, anecdotes, and jokes that are told of him, and of this number at least six hundred have the unmistakable ring—or *smack*—of truth. If they did not happen—they *should* have! They belong to him: they fit him like an old shoe.

"But," the pendants cunningly inquire, "*did* they happen? Now, really, *did* they? Ah, yes, they *sound* like him—he *might* have said them—but that's not the point! *Did* he?"

Well, we are not wholly unprepared for these objections. Of the six hundred stories which have the smack of truth, we have actually verified three hundred as authentic beyond the shadow of a doubt, and are ready to cite them by the book—place, time, occasion, evidence—to anyone who may inquire. In these stories there is a strength, a humor, a coarseness, and a native originality that belonged to the man and marked his every utterance. They come straight out of his own earth.

As a result of our researches, we can state unequivocally that there is no foundation in fact for the story that one time, in answer to a lady's wish, he called out to a Negro urchin at a station curb, who had a donkey wagon and a load of peanuts:

"Boy! Back your ———— over here and show this lady your ————!"

But he certainly did make the speech in the United States Senate (in rejoinder to the Honorable Barnaby Bulwinkle) that is generally accredited to him, even though there is no account of it in the *Congressional Record*:

"Mr. President, sir, we are asked by the honorable gentleman to appropriate two hundred thousand dollars of the taxpayer's money for the purpose of building a bridge across Coon Creek in the honorable gentleman's district—a stream, sir, which I have seen, and which, sir, I assure you, I could ——— halfway across."

The Vice-President (pounding with his gavel): "The Senator is out of order."

Senator Joyner: "Mr. President, sir, you are right. If I was *in* order, sir, I could ——— the whole way across it!"

The last story that is told of Zachariah Joyner is that in his final days of illness (and, like King Charles, in dying, he was "an unconscionable time") he was aroused from coma one afternoon by the sound of rapid hoofs and wheels, and, looking wearily out of the window of his room, he saw the spare figure of his brother Rufus hastening toward the house. Even in his last extremity his humor did not forsake him, for he is said to have smiled wanly and feebly croaked:

"My God! I reckon it's all up with me! For here comes Rufe!"

People told the story later and, despite the grimness of the joke, they laughed at it; for the family trait to which it pointed was well known.

Bear Joyner, in his later years, after he had moved to Libya Hill, when told of the death of one of his sons in Zebulon by his second marriage, is known to have said:

"Well, I reckon some of the children will attend the funeral." Here he considered seriously a moment, then nodded his head with an air of confirmation. "Hit's—hit's no more than right!" And after another pause he added virtuously: "If I was thar, *I'd go myself!*" And with these words, he wagged his head quite solemnly, in such a way as to leave no doubt about the seriousness of his intent.

Zachariah is reported, when asked the number of his kin, to have replied: "Hell, I don't know! You can't throw a rock in Zebulon without hitting one of them!" He reflected on his metaphor a moment, and then said: "However, let him that is without sin among you throw the first stone. I can't!" And with these words he turned virtuously away, scratching himself vigorously in the behind.

Again, when he responded to the greeting of a member of the audience after a political rally at which he had made a speech, he is reported to have said:

"My friend, your face looks familiar to me. Haven't I seen you somewhere before?"

To which the person so addressed replied: "Yes, sir. I think you have. I was yore pappy's ninth child by his second marriage, and you was his fourth 'un by his first. So I reckon you might say that you and me was both half-brothers, distantly removed."

The grimmest story in the whole Joyner catalogue, perhaps, is that old Bear Joyner, when reproached one time for a seeming neglect of his own brood, is reputed to have said to his inquisitor:

"My God Almighty! A man can plant the seed, but he cain't make the weather! I sowed 'em—now, goddamn 'em, let 'em grow!". . .

Meanwhile he [Rufus Joyner] lived in his father's old house on College Street. Eventually his lusty, gusty, old-maid sister, Hattie, came from Zebulon to keep house for him. But not all the wit and savor, the irrepressible spirits and joy of living that animated the sprightly figure of Miss Hattie Joyner could ever deflect Rufus from his grim purpose. Even in his youth his stinginess was proverbial, and in his old age his brother, Zachariah, then also hale and sere, had no hesitation in proclaiming it:

"Why, he's so mean," Zach roared, "he wouldn't ——— down a preacher's throat if his guts were on fire! If you fell down and broke your leg he wouldn't come across the street to help you because of the shoe leather he'd use up. He stops the clocks at night to keep the cogs from wearing out, and when he goes to church he puts a two-cent stamp in the collection plate and takes back a penny's change!"

Hattie, who was more like Zachariah in her ribald humor than any of the others, and who outlived all of them, would cackle gleefully and say: "Just wait till that old skinflint dies! I'll beat him yet—even if I have to live to be a hundred. When he's gone I'm goin' to open up the purse strings and let the moths fly out! I tell you, I'm just waitin' till he dies *to cut loose and raise hell!*. . .

"I have heard," Zachariah would say in later years, warming up to his subject and assuming the ponderously solemn air that always filled his circle of cronies with delighted anticipation of what was to come—"I have heard that fools rush in where angels fear to tread, but in the case of my brother Theodore, it would be more accurate to say that he *leaps* in where God Almighty crawls! . . . I have seen a good many remarkable examples of military chaos," he continued, "particularly at the outset of the war, when they were trying to teach farm hands and mountain boys the rudiments of the soldier's art in two weeks' time. But I have never seen anything so remarkable as the spectacle of Theodore, assisted by a knock-kneed fellow with the itch, tripping over his sword and falling on his belly every time he tried to instruct twenty-seven pimply boys in the intricacies of squads right."

That was unfair. Not *all*, assuredly, were pimply, and there were more than twenty-seven.

"Theodore," Zack went on with the extravagance that characterized these lapses into humorous loquacity—"Theodore was so short that every time he ———— he blew dust in his eyes; and the knock-kneed fellow with the itch was so tall that he had to lay down on his belly to let the moon go by. And somehow they had got their uniforms mixed up, so that Theodore had the one that was meant for the knock-kneed tall fellow, and the knock-kneed tall fellow had on Theodore's. The trousers Theodore was wearing were so baggy at the knees they looked as if a nest of kangaroos had spent the last six months in them, and the knock-kneed fellow's pants were stretched so tight that he looked like a couple of long sausages. In addition to all this, Theodore had a head shaped like a balloon— and about the size of one. The knock-kneed fellow had a peanut for a head. And whoever had mixed up their uniforms had also got their hats exchanged. So every time Theodore reared back and bawled out a command, that small hat he was wearing would pop right off his head into the air, as if it had been shot out of a gun. And when the knock-kneed fellow would repeat the order, the big hat he had on would fall down over his ears and eyes as if someone had thrown a bushel basket over his head, and he would come clawing his way out of it with a bewildered expression on his face, as if to say, 'Where the hell am I, anyway?' . . . They had a devil of a time getting those twenty-seven pimply boys straightened up as straight as they could get—which is to say, about as straight as a row of crooked radishes. Then, when they were all lined up at attention, ready to go, the knock-kneed fellow would be taken with the itch.

He'd shudder up and down, and all over, as if someone had dropped a cold worm down his back; he'd twitch and wiggle, and suddenly he'd begin to scratch himself in the behind." . . .

It is true that Theodore's slogan occasioned a good deal of mirth at his expense when it was repeated all over town with Zachariah's running commentary upon it. The father of a student at the school was one of Zack's most intimate friends; this man had attended the convocation, and he told Zack all about it afterwards.

"Theodore," this friend reported, "gave the boys a rousing new motto to live up to—earned, he said, by their predecessors on the glorious field of battle. Theodore made such a moving speech about it that he had all the mothers in tears. You never heard such a blubbering in your life. The chorus of snifflings and chokings and blowing of noses almost drowned Theodore out. It was most impressive."

"I don't doubt it," said Zack. "Theodore always did have an impressive manner. If he only had the gray matter that ought to go with it, he'd be a wonder. But what did he say? What was the motto?"

"First at Manassas—"

"First to eat, he means!" said Zachariah.

"—fightingest at Antietam Creek—"

"Yes, fightingest to see who could get back first across the creek!"

"—and by far the farthest in the Wilderness."

"By God, he's right!" shouted Zachariah. "Too far, in fact, to be of any use to anyone! They thrashed around all night long, bawling like a herd of cattle and taking pot-shots at one another in the belief that they had come upon a company of Grant's infantry. They had to be gathered together and withdrawn from the line in order to prevent their total self-destruction. My brother Theodore," Zachariah went on with obvious relish, "is the only officer of my acquaintance who performed the remarkable feat of getting completely lost in an open field, and ordering an attack upon his own position. . . . His wounds, of course, are honorable, as he himself will tell you on the slightest provocation—but he was shot in the behind. So far as I know, he is the only officer in the history of the Confederacy who possesses the distinction of having been shot in the seat of the pants by one of his own sharpshooters, while stealthily and craftily reconnoitering his own breastworks in search of any enemy who was at that time nine miles away and marching in the opposite direction!" . . .

Zachariah Joyner assured the stranger that he was coming to "the greatest country in the world," and enlarged upon the theme in the syllables of the ornate rhetoric of which he was a master. What Webber said is not on record, but it can be assumed from his character that his comment was bluntly noncommittal, quiet, to the point.

The talk then turned to travel and to railway journeys, which in those days were considerably more complicated and difficult than they are now. Webber remarked that he had come all the way from Baltimore, that the trip had been a long and wearing one, with many changes, and that he would be glad when it was over because he was pretty tired. Zachariah then told a story about "Greasy" Wray, a country lawyer out in Zebulon whom Joyner had appointed a Circuit Judge during his first term as Governor. Greasy Wray had never been anywhere, and when he received his first instructions to hold court in Harrington, a seacoast town four hundred miles away, he was delighted at the prospect of seeing so much of the world and proceeded at once to heed the call of civic duty. He set out on horseback to Libya Hill; then he went by stage to Millerton; then by the Exeter and West Catawba Railway to Exeter; then by the Belmont, Fletcher, and West Central to Sanderson; then by the Sanderson and Northeastern to Dover; then by the Dover and Mount Arthur to Redfern; then by the Redfern and Eastern Shore to Bellamy, where, all exhausted from his three-day journey, he arrived to find the boat waiting. Greasy Wray got on board at once and went to sleep, and woke up the next morning to find the boat docked at its destination. He saw a great crowd of Negroes on the wharf, went ashore and hired a hack, was driven to a hotel, and demanded of the astounded clerk that the sheriff be sent for right away. Fifteen minutes later he welcomed the no less astounded sheriff in his room and said: "I am Judge Way of Zebulon, and I have been sent here to open court in Harrington." The sheriff was speechless for a moment, then he replied: "Hell, man, this ain't Harrington. It's *Baltimore!*"

This story was one of Zachariah's favorites, and he told it with gusto. He was off to a good start now, and as the stage toiled up the mountainside the stories rolled from him in a swelling tide. Just before the stage reached Ridgepole Gap, on the last bend of the road as the team pulled toward the crest, the wheels lurched down into a heavy rut. The two women were almost tossed out of their seats. They screamed, and then, as the team pulled out of it again, one of the ladies turned to Zachariah and, giggling apprehensively, remarked:

"Oh, Senator! I do declare! It seems as if all the holes are on our side!"

"Yes, madam," Zachariah boomed out gallantly and without a moment's hesitation, "and all the roots on ours." . . .

[Thomas Wolfe, *The Hills Beyond* (New York: Harpers & Brothers, 1941). Reprinted by permission of Harper & Row Publishers, Inc. Zachariah Joyner is a fictional character partially based on Zeb Vance.]

Paul Green

The first folk plays Paul Green wrote were tragedies, but he soon discovered the old truth that, without comedy, life would be simply insufferable. Thereafter his plays, short stories, novels, and essays were touched with a humor that came directly from the fields and crossroads of Harnett County, where he was born in 1894. As an undergraduate at The University of North Carolina at Chapel Hill, he began his lifelong playwriting career, and he was awarded the Pulitzer Prize in 1927. Ten years later The Lost Colony *was produced, his first "symphonic drama," a term that he coined for a new kind of American play based on history which included music and sweeping movement. In* Words and Ways: Stories and Incidents from My Cape Fear Valley Folklore Collection, *published as an issue of* North Carolina Folklore, *December, 1968, he gathered together nondramatic material old and new, modest and ribald, real and imaginary. The following seven selections, all from* Words and Ways, *are indicative of the abundant humor to be found in Paul Green's many books.*

Future Life

 A folk-belief held by millions and millions of people in this world and the majority of people in the Valley—that when one dies, he will enter into eternal bliss if his life has been good, and into eternal woe if it has been bad. . . .

I heard about a man who died and went into the afterlife, and there he was given a beautiful room with the ladies waiting on him, beautiful girls they were, and anything he wished for he had it. Food, drink, wine, music, girls—anything—and immediately there it was. Finally, after a few days he began to get tired of this, because he could not wish for anything that it didn't instantly come to him. So, finally, he asked a long-faced neighbor of his, "Say, is this the way it's to be forevermore, to have everything you want? I didn't

179

know heaven was like this. I knew it was supposed to be perfect, but this is too perfect. It's already beginning to get boring." Then his neighbor looked at him and said, "Where do you think you are?"

[Paul Green, *North Carolina Folklore,* December 1968.]

Gallinipper

A huge mosquito that inhabits the Cape Fear Valley, its size usually depending on the imagination of the person describing it.

We boys used to hear many mosquito stories told along the Cape Fear River. A popular little one was about two Irishmen, Pat and Mike. These two sons of Erin had joined a labor gang canalizing the Cape Fear River there below Lillington a few miles. Early in the first night they were badly bothered by mosquitos and they moved several times wrapping themselves up in their blankets. Finally Pat looked out and saw the whole swamp winking with little lights—lights of fireflies. "Faith me Christ, Mike," said Pat. "Let's leave out of here. Them dom mosquitos are coming after us now with lanterns." And so they fled the job.

[Paul Green, *North Carolina Folklore,* December 1968.]

Frog

There is one common superstition about frogs and that is that if they make water on you, you are sure to have warts. And, of course, there are all sorts of cures for warts.

A tiny little boy was asking his Valley mother one day where babies came from, and she told him that they sprouted like seeds in the garden and they came up—which to me was a better account than the old Valley common folk answer, "The doctor finds them in old hollow stumps." Nothing would do but the little boy had to plant himself some seeds to see if he could get some babies of his own. So she, indulging him, let him plant some beans, and he packed the dirt on them and put a board over the ground to keep it damp. And during the night he dreamed about his babies that might come. The next morning early he was up to see what had happened. He pulled the plank off, and there sat a little toad frog. He ran yelling into the house to his mother in tears and frantic, "Mama, mama, I've already got a baby, and he's so ugly I feel like killing him!"

[Paul Green, *North Carolina Folklore*, December 1968.]

Martin

A fabulous Valley cat, whether big or little, or dangerous or gentle, no one knows, for this Martin has never been seen, his presence continuing in the Valley only in a folk tale from which the local proverb derives—"Can't do nothing till Martin comes," this being often said when one is waiting for someone else to show up who has more authority or power than any of those present.

"Massa Landlord bet one of his Negro slaves five dollars that he wouldn't dare spend one night alone in an old empty cabin down by the river which was supposed to be ha'nted. The slave was a preacher and sort of a holy fellow and said he was not skeered of anything above the earth, on the earth, or below the earth, and he needed five dollars, and the Holy Book would protect him. So he said he would take up his master on the bet.

"The next night the Reverend got his Bible and went to spend the night in the haunted cabin. He built himself a fire and got out his Bible and sat there reading it. While he was reading he heard a little wind blowing in the trees outside. He listened an instant and then went on with his reading. 'I will fear no evil, for thou art with me an—' At this moment the old door creaked on its hinges as it opened, and in came a great black cat. The preacher looked at the cat and said nothing, holding only the tighter to his Bible. The cat went over to the fireplace, gobbled up a mouthful of red hot coals, spat out the sparks and then went over to the side of the hearth and sat down and looked at the preacher with his narrow cat eyes.

" 'We can't do nothing till Martin comes,' he said in a high fine voice. The preacher trembled and began reading away again, 'Verily I say unto you—' The door squeaked once more and in came another cat, much bigger than the first, big as a dog. This cat likewise went over to the fireplace, got a great mouthful of red-hot coals, spat out the sparks, and went over and sat down by the first cat. 'We can't do nothing till Martin comes,' he said in a middle-sized voice.

"The preacher shivered and shook but held onto his Bible. '—The Lord is my helper, I will not fear—'

"The old door squeaked again and in came a third great black cat, this time as big as a calf. He went over, stuck his head in the fireplace, got a great mouthful of red-hot coals, chewed them, spat out the sparks, swallowed the coals and then took his place by the other two cats. And in a great bass voice that made the weather-boarding rattle he said, 'We can't do nothing till Martin comes.' The preacher slammed his Bible into his pocket and said,

" 'Well, you gentlemen tell Martin when he do come that I done been called away!' And with that he dived through the windowpanes, carrying the sash and framing with him."

[Paul Green, *North Carolina Folklore*, December 1968.]

Black-Eyed Peas

A popular garden crop in the South. If cooked with hogjowl and eaten on New Year's Day these peas are supposed to bring financial good luck for the coming twelve months. It is common talk around in the Valley that a person will have as many dollars then as peas he eats on New Year's Day. I was told so when a boy, and I ate away manfully enough for two or three occasions, counting the number of peas spoonful by spoonful as I ate them. But when no betterment came in my poor finances, I lost my taste for peas, if I ever had had any. To tell the truth, to my way of thinking they are mighty poor eating at best. But I heard of one fellow who loved them even to gluttony.

"It was a pow'ful rainy night and as dark as the inside of a grave with the wind blowing," said Lonnie Cofield, "and this fellow was travelling down the river road toward Fayetteville, hoping to find a place to stay. The country weren't settled in them days the way it is now, and a man out at night had to shift for sleeping quarters the best he could. On and on he went. Now why he was out in such a night I don't know. I reckon he was some sort of drummer and had been trying to make a late sale and so got caught in the storm earlier than he had thought for. Anyhow, the way I've always heard it was that he kept pushing right on. Well, finally he saw a dim red firelight ahead of him, and he hurried on fast as he could and come to a little cabin by the roadside. He whammed and hammered on the door and finally it was opened by a rough sort of farmer man. The young fellow asked if he could come inside from the storm, and the farmer let him in.

"A good lightwood fire was going in the fireplace and the fellow was mighty glad to see it, for he was wet slam through to the skin. The farmer had a young wife and she was mighty polite and hospitable at once to the young fellow and helped him off with his wet coat and hung it on a chair to dry and brung him a towel to wipe his face and hair and scurried about for this and that to make him comfortable.

" 'You're mighty kind,' the fellow said to her, 'and soon's I get dry and the storm lets up I'll be on my way toward Fayetteville.'

" 'Seems like the storm's getting worse,' she said.

"The farmer was a kind-hearted fellow and he told the stranger that they'd be glad to offer him some of their poor fare. 'We were just about to set down to a late supper, such as it is,' he said.

" 'I'm sure anything would taste good to me,' said the young fellow, 'for I ain't et since breakfast.'

" 'We ain't got nothing but a big pot of black-eyed peas,' said the farmer. 'Everything's mighty short with us this year.'

" 'Black-eyed peas!' said the young fellow all quick-like. 'Nothing I love better than black-eyed peas.'

"By this time he was getting dry and the young wife set out another plate and brung the big pot of peas from the stove and put it on the table. And they all went to it. That fellow sure did prove the truth of his words. He soon cleaned up his first big helping and held out his plate for more, and the young wife was quick to oblige him. The farmer looked at him and said, 'Like you said, you really like black-eyed peas!"

" 'True, true,' said the young fellow as he gobbled away. 'And whoever cooked these peas knew how to do it.'

" 'I cooked 'em,' said the young wife, pleased and looking across at him.

"When she had helped the fellow to a third fill, the farmer got up, lifted the pot and took it over and put it firmly back on the stove. 'We'll need some in the house for tomorrow,' he said.

"The storm raged and roared outside and the young wife said it looked like too bad a night for anybody to be out in.

" 'Yes, I reckon it really is,' said the farmer, who as I said was at heart a good sort of fellow. And he went on, 'As you see we ain't got but one room to our house and only one bed, but we'll accommodate you as best as I can.'

" 'Thank you most kindly,' said the young man, 'you mustn't disfurnish yourself. I'll sleep anywhere—lie down on the floor here till day comes.'

" 'You might catch your death of cold doing that,' said the young wife.

" 'So you might,' said the good man. 'Well, seeing the night's the way it is and you a wayfaring stranger and the Good Book advising us to be neighborly one with another, I tell you what—we'll share our bed with you. My wife can sleep next the wall, I'll lie in the middle and you next to me, and no harm done.'

"And so it was. And there they lay side by side while the rain poured and the wind blew. Before long the good farmer was sleeping away, and his snores began to sound in the room. But the young wife wasn't sleeping. And maybe the stranger wasn't sleeping either. Soon the storm began to subside. The young wife all of a sudden punched her husband in the side, 'Wake up, wake up,' she cried out. 'Wake up!' He grunted and squirmed and finally wanted to know what the trouble was. 'Why, can't you hear it? Can't you!' she called.

" 'Hear what?' he mumbled.

" 'Hear the pony down in the stable kicking away? He's kicking that calf, that's what he is, about to kill it. Get up and go down there and stop it! Quick, hurry! Oh, oh, my poor little calf!'

"Growling and grumbling, the good husband finally crawled out of bed, pulled on his shoes and made his way out of the house and on down to the barn. The young wife turned quickly toward the young fellow and whispered in his ear, 'Now's your chance.'

"You know what that fellow done then, Paul?" said Lonnie.

"No, I don't, Lonnie, but I know what I—"

"Why, he got up and et the rest of them black-eyed peas. Hah, hah!"

[Paul Green, *North Carolina Folklore*, December 1968.]

Don't Mix Medicine and Religion

"Ashe," he said, "you better be careful how you mix your medicine and your Lord. They're like oil and water. You ain't old enough, but I remember the case of Tatum Baker, the liquor-head. He woke up one morning with his back bent like a jacknife. Some said a spell had been put on him, others that he slept without a sheet and had caught the cramps. Anyhow, he went for months like that. He tried all kinds of quack doctors, plasters, pills and even took a case or two of female disorder medicine, but nothing seemed to help him. Finally he gave in to his wife's pleading and went down to the Holiness meeting at Falcon to be prayed over.

"And the sisters and brothers prayed all right—for a night and the whole of next day they did. About sundown of the second day, the misery left Tatum, and he straightened up and went to shouting. Not only that, but he happy-danced off a piece up and down the aisle, and let loose a great bellowing of unknown tongues. Yessir, he was healed and healed good. He thought he was. But old Moster was only playing with him. Later that night going home he felt so fine he couldn't be contained. He had to celebrate. He stopped there in Dunn and got himself a quart of liquor and drank it all as he walked on home. This time wouldn't count, he said, just the way all you liquor-heads say, and before long he was addled and drunk as he wobbled ahead.

"It was a hot night and a big thundercloud had come up. As he wandered up the lane at the Shovel place, a real cloudburst fell out of the sky. Now it happened that old Andrew Shovel himself was lying dead in his house. Some neighbors were there sitting up, and in front of his yard was a hearse with its two black-plumed horses tied to a tree. Tatum hurried along as fast as he could, and as he got near, in his disordered state of mind, he mistook the hearse for some sort of covered carriage. Since it was pouring such a heavy rain and thundering and lightning so, he opened the door and crawled in to keep dry.

"Now as everybody knows, a hearse don't have any handles on the inside, for the corpse has no need to open the door from within. Well, all of a sudden and blam! the lightning struck a tree in old Shovel's yard. The horses bucked and charged and broke loose, and away they went with hearse, Tatum and all. Lickety-split they went right down the lane back toward Dunn where they came from. As they went charging along, and the hearse leaning and blundering from side to side, Tatum's mind cleared up somewhat and he realized where he was. And then he set up a terrible yelling and screeching and praying to the Lord God Almighty—sort of the way you must have done the other day, Ashe, when you were trying to get saved at the mourner's bench—yeh, no doubt just the way you did.

"Other neighbors heard the hearse coming, and they rushed out on their porches as it went by. And in the flashes of lightning they could see the 'dead man' in there, squatted on his knees, throwing up his hands and bowing and praying. And they fled back inside and barred their doors. Finally the horses ran smack into the main avenue of Dunn, and there by the street lights the inhabitants visioned this strange flying contraption. And more than one of them bolted out of the house and took to the alleys and side streets and even fields. Right on through the town the horses ran. As they swerved around the curve going toward Clinton, the hearse turned over and threw Tatum out through the broken glass and hard against a ditch stump. This time he was really hurt. His back was cracked.

"From that day forth he walked exactly as he walked before—bent all over—and neither doctors nor preachers could ever heal him. They said he learned his lesson all right, but he learned it too late. For before long he died a lost soul from hardening of the liver and in great pain. No sir, it won't do to mix your medicine and your religion."

[Paul Green, excerpt from "White Swelling," *North Carolina Folklore*, December 1968.]

Goodly Works

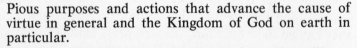

Pious purposes and actions that advance the cause of virtue in general and the Kingdom of God on earth in particular.

Archie and Angus McNeill were identical twins and as alike as two persimmon seeds in the same persimmon or two peas in a pod. Not only did they look exactly alike and dress alike, but they behaved alike. They had the same motions and gestures and talked alike, voice for voice, and often used the same expression. You want to remember that about the voice and expressions.

They were little men and supple and quick, and in their young days had the reputation of being fierce as bantam roosters and cocks of the walk in their manhood among the shady women along the Cape Fear River. One summer Reverend Sandy King held a three-week revival in the Little Bethel Church, and under the power of his preaching Archie and Angus both got converted good and hard from their sins, and they took the right hand of fellowship, were baptized good and deep in MacDonald's millpond, and so set their faces clear and shining to serve their Lord.

For a long time the people had been wanting and needing an organ there in Little Bethel Church. And Reverend McGregor, the regular pastor, felt that now since the congregation had been so much increased by Brother King's conversions, the time had come to get a good one and some new songbooks, too. Accordingly, the good members were called upon and exhorted to make pledges for the amount needed to buy the organ and the books. Under the spell of their new-found grace, and maybe because they had been such notorious sinners and wanted people to know they were a hundred percent on the Lord's side now, Archie and Angus stuck up their hands and promised the final fifty dollars toward the purchase. It was a rather rash promise considering how hard money was to come by in those days, as time well proved. But, the Lord willing, they said to themselves, they would make the pledge good in the fall when the crops were housed.

The fall came along and the crops everywhere in that section of the world that year were picayunish and small. First there had been too much wet weather and then too much dry. And that was a queer thing too—to think that the one year Archie and Angus had tried to serve their Lord, He or whatever stood for Him had sent them the worst crop they'd ever had. They took notice of that fact betwixt themselves but tried to make the best of the situation instead of complaining against this High Authority. At the first killing frost they hauled their little bitty mess of peas, potatoes and pork down to Fayetteville and sold them. But by the time they had paid the market and inspection charges and had their mule shod, they only had a dozen or so shillings left, as they called dimes in those days.

While they were sitting around in a cafe glum as sick herons and hungry enough in their bereft condition to eat the Lamb of God, as Bull Broadhuss used to put it, they heard a couple of half-drunk fellows laughing and talking a scandalous thing over in a corner. They were telling about a fast woman by the name of Mrs. Markham who ran a sort of fast house there in Fayetteville and had a standing bet that no man could outdo her in the bouts of love. Yes, she had a standing bet of fifty dollars for any man who could make her call for the calf rope from the Mount of Venus. The twins sat there taking it all in, and they heard the fellows say that no man had ever been able to collect that bet and no man ever would.

"You hear that, Archie?" said Angus, or maybe Archie said it to Angus. It didn't make any difference which, being as they were so identical in their feelings and thinking.

"Ah, the wickedness of creation!" said Archie.

"Worse'n Sodom and Gomorrah!" said Angus.

And then they looked at each other. The same idea was coming to them both.

"Like there's a sign in it," said Archie after a while.

"The Lord works in mysterious ways," said Angus.

"His wonders to perform," breathed Archie.

So of the same mind now, they wandered on up the street toward Mrs. Markham's place. It was night by this time and they finally stopped in front of the house, and there in the dark by the sidewalk hedges caucused a while, the way folks were wont to do at the Democratic Convention in Linneyville each campaign year. And so they made their plans.

"Certain to my soul 'twould be no sin!" said Angus.

"Seeing it's all for the cause anyhow," said Archie.

"And a service to righteousness," said Angus.

"And the wind and the weather bloweth where it listeth, as the Good Book says."

"And the Lord's rain falls on the just and unjust. And sometimes it don't fall at all!"

"Bless His name anyhow," said Archie humbly. "And the scriptures declare—be ye zealous in good works. Amen."

"Aye, lad, true, true—it do say in Hebrews ten that we should provoke unto love and do goodly works," said Angus.

So Angus took his courage in his hand, as you might say, and went into the house. Or it might have been Archie for all I know. It didn't make any difference which. And sure enough he found the lady waiting in her parlor. Angus said he was in bad need of a bed and comfort. And so, projicking and hinting around with the widow and saying he had money coming in the morning to match hers, the agreement was at last made and they started upstairs. She said she was willing to trust him but if his money wasn't there when she called for it she would have him where the hair was short and she meant short. Her determined and certain manner kind of shook him in his shoes and set back his confidence. So he put up a little silent prayer for help and guidance as she led him along the hall and into her room.

Well, some time later he told the lady to please excuse him a minute, he had to get up and go out to the garden house to—er —answer the call of nature. Outside Archie was waiting.

"Well?" asked Archie.

"It's an undertaking, and we're up against it," answered Angus solemnly. "It's do or die for us. It's your time now."

"Aye," said Archie, forlornlike. And he suddenly shook hands with Angus as if he were departing for foreign parts, which he was.

"And ye'd better keep a kind of little prayer going the while, Archie," said Angus. "I did—for a while."

"No, no, do pray tell!" said Archie hurriedly and alarmed.

"We've tackled several in our time, lad, but she's the wheel hoss!"

"I will then if I can, but I misdoubt I'll be able to keep my mind on religious matters," said Archie.

"This is a religious matter!" said Angus sternly. So Archie went in.

"You come and go mighty quick," said Mrs. Markham.

"Yea, I'm a brief man, and I move quick," said Archie. "And be not weary in well-doing, as the Scriptures put it."

"Lord have mercy, you ain't a preacher, are you?" asked the lady all shocked and aghast.

"No, Ma'am, no," said Archie. "But someday I hope to be a deacon in Little Bethel Church."

So he put in his licks and some extra for the cause. And then he said excuse him, he had to answer the call of nature but would be right back.

He met Angus waiting by the hedge. "Well?" Angus said, giving him a good look.

"Oom," said Archie, "make no mistake about it, we've got our hands full."

"Our calling and our election's got to come from above," said Angus, "though we do all we can below!"

"Aye," said Archie. So Angus went in again.

And it kept up like that pretty much till daybreak, this visiting the widow and going out to answer the call of nature and eating in between. And finally the woman, stout as she was, hollered "calf rope!—eenough!" And when she paid over the fifty dollars, she turned the lamp up good and strong, saying, "I want to see what manner of man you be—that's played such havoc here tonight and no doubt ruined my garden house."

"I'm little but loud," said Angus—or Archie, whichever one it was—as he stowed the money away in his pocket.

"Loud!" moaned the woman. "You're the loudest thing that's ever put head in this place. And if you was full grown you'd be a plumb bucket of adders. Get gone from my house, and stay gone!"

"Why, bless my soul, you ain't on the puny list, are ye, Miz Markham?" said Angus—or Archie, all gleeful-like. He felt like bragging a bit now that he had the money all safe and won.

"And close the door soft when you leave," she whimpered as she turned out the light, "for I want to sleep a week."

The next Sunday the Reverend McGregor stood up in Little Bethel Church and called for the pledges to be paid. And down the aisle marched Archie and Angus, proud as the two bantam roosters they were, their hair all slicked back and their faces and their collars shining with godliness. They laid the promised fifty dollars on the plate, and Reverend McGregor broke into jubilation. He called on the congregation to witness the deed of Brother Archie and Brother Angus.

"My friends," he said, "behold the goodly works of the Lord's true servants!"

"Amen," said Archie and Angus as they stood before the mercy seat, their eyes cast humbly down.

"Heavenly grace has blessed them mightily," said the preacher, "and their religion is where their pocketbook is."

Which is to say, the Reverend McGregor might be a good

preacher, but as a carpenter with a measuring rule he would have been a failure. He was off several inches.

You might wonder too what the church did when the story got out—as all stories finally do somehow, bless God! Well, it didn't do anything. For by that time Archie and Angus had been made deacons, and the organ was sounding mighty sweet when beautiful Belle Bethune played it Sundays, and the young and the old sang happily from their fine songbooks. So the people didn't make much of a to-do about it, except to tell the story on the sly—the way I'm telling it here—but with more of the details of goodly works in it no doubt.

And I hope it will keep on being told long after I am dead and gone, for it certainly was a thing.

[Paul Green, *North Carolina Folklore*, December 1968.]

Black Merriment

Though humor of the blacks appears elsewhere in this collection, especially in the sections entitled "Legal Wit," "Folk Shenanigans," and "Divers Anecdotes," the fact remains that it has always been considered a thing apart. Its separateness is attested by excellent anthologies of humor confined solely to that of the Negro. The line between white and black comedy may be thin, yet it is generally agreed that a distinction, although certainly difficult to define, does indeed exist. Particularly noticeable is the Negro's joy in "smart" answers, in big talk and verbal bombast. His natural, uncomplicated wisdom makes him contemptuous of circuity. Another difference can be observed in the narrator: if he is white, the humor is usually gentle, occasionally condescending; the black storyteller, on the other hand, gives no quarter. Although Negro dialect and the native wit of the old-time black man are no longer in fashion, a survey of North Carolina humor would, nevertheless, be incomplete without examples of both.

African Wit

Old *Cato* on his deathbed lying,
Worn out with work and almost dying,
With patience heard his friends propose
What Bearers for him they had chose.
There's Cuff and Caesar, Pomp and Plato,
Will they do? *"Bery well,"* quoth Cato.
And Bantum Phillips—now for t'other,
We must take Scipio, Bantum's brother.
"I no like Scip," old Cato cries;

"Scip rascal—tell about me lies,
And got me whipp'd."—Ki! 'tis all one—
Scip shall be Bearer—Scip or none.—
"Mind me," cries Cato, *"if dat cur,*
Dat Scip, come Bearer—I won't stir."
[*Edenton State Gazette*, 12 February 1789.]

Anecdote

An ignorant preacher, being one day about starting on the circuit, ordered his Negro servant to bring his horse to the door, and sent him upstairs for some corn to feed him. The Negro, being rather careless, scattered the corn along downstairs and outdoors where an old sow was feeding, who getting on the track of the corn, by degrees followed the trail upstairs. After a while, the preacher sent the Negro upstairs for his saddle.

By this time the old sow had found her way under the bed. The Negro, hearing the swinish grunt and not knowing the cause of it, ran down in a terrible fright, crying out, "Massa! Massa!—de debil be upstairs, Massa." The master in an angry tone sent him up again. The Negro, hearing the grunt of the sow repeated, ran down more scared than ever, saying, "Massa, de debil be upstairs sartin, for I hear him go *eh, eh* tree [sic] four time."

The master, being somewhat superstitious, concluded to venture up himself, but gave the Negro orders to pray for him while he was gone. No sooner had the knight of the black coat reached the head of the stairs than the old sow rushed from her covert, ran between his legs and carried him down backwards. All the prayer that the Negro could make was "Amen," which he pronounced very devoutly.

The preacher, no less terrified than his servant, cried out, "The devil has got me, Cuff. Why don't you pray?"

"Amen," says the Negro.

[*Elizabeth City Star and North Carolina Intelligencer*, 10 December 1831, reprinted in F. Roy Johnson, *Witches and Demons in History and Folklore* (Murfreesboro: Johnson Publishing Company, 1969). Since 1938, Johnson has been a resident of Murfreesboro, where he has been active in journalism, publishing, and folklore.]

Colored Blunder

There is in this city a Negroes' temperance society. One of the whites who presides over their deliberations informs us that one of the members was discoursing most furiously upon the evils arising from intemperance, and so enthusiastic did become, with eyes strained most out of their sockets, he thundered away, "If I had the arms of Caesar, I would grap the whole University (universe) and fly to the uttermost parts of the world!"

An old Negro who was near him exclaimed in an undertone, "La! Pompey! would you take the Pispical Simnary?"

[*The Rasp* (Raleigh), 12 February 1842.]

Tales from Guilford County

MAN ABOVE.—Man was jealous of his wife, an' he come in one day an' ask her who had been there. An' she said, "No one."

But he said, "Yes, there have, an' I'm goin' to beat you."

She said, "Well, you can, but there's a man above knows all things."

An' the man above said, "Yes, an' there's a man under the bed knows as much as I do."

[Bill Cruse.]

THE TURNIP.—One say there was a man in this country. An' he called to de man to stay all night. His name was John. He 'plied to him, "What's your occupation?"

Says, "Turnip-grower." Says he cultivated an acre of land. He put it knee-deep manure. He sowed de seed. Didn't but one come up. It growed so big that they put a fence aroun' it. It raised de fence. Says, "What's your occupation?"

He said, "Pottery." He was three weeks amouldin' a big pot. It wore out three-power hammer before it struck the ground.

He 'plied to him, "What you better do in that big pot?"

He said, "Jus' to cook that turnip in."

[Bill Cruse.]

AS BIG A FOOL.—Man was goin' cortin', an' he tol' de girl, an' de ol' woman an' de ol' man both, he wasn't agwine to marry her. He tol' em he'd ride three miles, an' ef he could fin' three as big a fool as they was, he'd come back an' marry her.

An' he went on 'bout a mile, an' the first man he see was tryin' to pull a cow up on de house to eat the moss off the house. He axed the man what was he doin'. He said he was haulin' the cow up to eat the moss. He axed him why didn't he get up an' throw it down. "Thank you kindly, Sir Stranger, many a cow's neck I've broke tryin' to pull it up to eat the moss off my house."

He went on, an' the nex' man he come across was tryin' to put on his pants. He had 'em hangin' on a tree, an' he was runnin' an' tryin' to jump in 'em. Man axed him what he was doin', an' why didn't he take 'em down an' put 'em on right. "Thank you kindly, Sir Stranger, many a time I've cracked my shins tryin' to put on my pants."

He went on about a mile furder, an' seed a little boy runnin' through the house with a wheel-bar' as hard as he could go. He axed him what he war doin'. He said he was haulin' sunshine to dry the house. He went back then, an' married the girl.

[George Marshall.]

THE BLACK CAT.—A man had a house an' lot. He'd give it to any man who'd go an' stay all night. An' one ol' black man said he could stay dere. An' he took his Bible an' his light, an' sot down dah an' went to readin'. An' he looked 'round, an' da sat an ol' black cat aside of him.

De ol' black cat said, "Dere's nobody here but I an' you to-night."

He said, "Dere'd be nobody here but you directly, neither."

He broke out an' run, an' got powerful tired, an' sat down on a log to rest; an' he looked around, an' dah sat de ol' black cat again. An' he [the cat] said, "Dat was a right good race we had up here."

An' he [the man] said, "We're goin' to have anoder one too."

[George Marshall.]

[Elsie Clews Parsons, *Journal of American Folklore* 30 (April-June 1917).]

Announcements

An old Negro preacher was holding a series of meetings in his church. On Sunday morning, just before he started to preach his sermon, he made the following announcements for the week:

Monday: Directly after the service, there will be baptism of one adult and two adulterers.

Tuesday: There will be a meeting at the north end of the church at three o'clock and the south end at six o'clock. Children will be baptized at both ends.

Wednesday: The Prayer Circle will meet at 8:30 when Sister Johnson will sing "Put me in my little bed," accompanied by the pastor.

Thursday: The Ladies Benevolent Society will serve supper from six to eight-thirty. All sisters giving milk will kindly come early.

Friday: At seven-thirty the Little Mothers Society will meet. All sisters desiring to become Little Mothers will kindly see the pastor before Saturday night.

Saturday: These meetings will close by the singing of "Little Drops of Water." Will some kind sister please start little drops of water. The pastor and congregation will all join in.

[Source unknown.]

A Vocabularic Duel

One of our local smart elecks was standing on the steps of the postoffice here at Moravian Falls the other day, when an old colored man came up, and, touching his hat, asked:

"Kin you tell me is dis de place where dey sells postage stamps?"

"Yes, sir, this is the place," replied the smart eleck, thinking he saw a chance to have some fun, "but what do you want with a postage stamp, uncle?"

"To mail a letter, sah, of co'se."

"Well, then, you needn't bother about stamps. You don't have to put on any this week."

"Don't I?"

"No, sir."

"Why-for not?"

"Well, you see, the conglomeration of the hypothenuse has differentiated the parallelogram so much that the consanguinity don't temulate the ordinary effervescence, and so the government has decided to send letters free."

The old man took off his hat, dubiously shook his head, and then, with a long breath, remarked:

"Well, boss, all dat may be so, an' I don't say it ain't; but s'pose dat de ecksentricty ob de aggregation transsubstanshuates de ignominiousness ob de puppindickler an' sublimites de puspicuity ob de consequences—don't you qualificate dat de guv'ment would confiscate dat dar letter? Guess I'd jes' as well put on a stamp anyhow, fer luck."

And the old man mailed his letter and passed solemnly down the road.

[James Larkin Pearson, *The Fool Killer*, January 1911. Pearson, born in Wilkes County in 1879, is poet laureate of North Carolina. *The Fool Killer* was issued 1910-29.]

Theology

Another yarn with a theological twist . . . is said to come from North Carolina.

A negro preacher, referring to the Judgment Day, cried out: "Dere shall be weepin' and gnashin' ob teeth! and dem what's got no teeth will hab to gum it!"

[Charles Johnston, "Old Funny Stories of the South and West," *Harper's Weekly*, 4 January 1913.]

Buck Newton

Buck Newton was a colorful character well known around Wadesboro forty or more years ago. He was seen frequently walking the streets, or the roads in the area between Lilesville and Wadesboro, where he made his home.

The dull-witted fellow went barefoot with pants legs rolled up to his knees. He sported a floppy hat and an ill-fitting shirt, and always carried a large club or stick, which he would often shake at a passerby, with some muttered word or epithet. In his jaw rolled a wad of tobacco, and at times he flaunted a cigar from one corner of his mouth. A large red bandanna handkerchief, nearly always dirty, swung from his belt.

Buck was a champion loafer, spending much of his time fooling around with cotton buyers, farmers, politicans, and lawyers, as they gathered in Wadesboro for business. If he ever got in a hurry to go somewhere, he would hit his legs with a switch and say, "Get up, Buck, and go along!"

Of the many humorous tales told on Buck, one of the best was about his flagging the through, limited passenger train while it was near Wadesboro on its Birmingham-Washington run. The incident probably occurred between Wadesboro and Lilesville, for Buck frequently walked this stretch of track.

Buck honed for a fresh chew of tobacco as the alcoholic thirsts for strong drink.

As he saw the fast train approaching down the gleaming rails, Buck hit upon an idea. Taking his red bandanna handkerchief from his belt and tying it to his stick, he began flagging the train and making frantic hand signals.

The engineer saw flag and signal, reduced speed, and came to a dead stop. Buck sauntered over to the train as the conductor stepped down from the platform with visions of danger ahead.

When the unkempt, odd-looking character approached the train, the conductor asked, "What's the matter, buddy?"

"Say, mister," said Buck, with a squint in his eye, "have you got a chaw of tobacker on you?"

By this time the engineer strode up. "What's going on here?" he asked.

"This dam' fool jest wants a chaw of tobacker."

"Have *you* got one?" Buck asked the engineer.

"Naw!" exploded the engineer.

"Well, what in hell did you stop the train for?"

[Mary Louise Medley, *North Carolina Folklore*, July 1957.]

Six Oral Narratives

THE PREACHER AND THE RUNAWAY LION.—One Sunday an old preacher was telling his congregation about belief and faith in prayer before the eleven-o'clock services began. He had been informed just a few minutes before that a lion had broken loose from a nearby zoo. So he was telling the members of his audience to have faith in God, and not be afraid of the lion if they should run across him on the way home after services. "If you pray hard enough," he said, "fear not, for the lion outside will not bother you." He shouted very loudly, "Fear not, for thou art with me; watch, and I will show you a way to git out; I have the faith in God that all ya'll should have."

But after the services were over, before the preacher had gone more than a few yards from the church-house steps, he was met by the lion. The preacher got down on his knees, and said, "Oh Lord! please hear my prayer. You saved Daniel from a lion, and I know you gonna save me from this here lion." His prayer was loud and sincere; but, all the same, he raised his head after a while to see what the lion was doing. To his surprise, he saw that the lion was also kneeling with his paws clasped over his eyes. So he said, "Brother lion, are you praying wid me?"

The lion looked up at him and replied, "No, brother, I's saying mah grace befo' meat."

[Joseph C. Biggers, Durham.]

THE PREACHING OF THE SINFUL BROTHER'S FUNERAL.—A man's brother died. He was so wicked that none of the preachers in the community would preach his funeral. So his brother went around into all of the neighboring communities to see if he could find somebody to preach the sinful brother's funeral. Finally, he succeeded in finding a raggedy and hungry preacher who had no church, and who told him he'd preach his brother into Hell for $2.98, into Purgatory for $3.98, and into Heaven for $5.00. So the live brother told him he'd pay him $5.00 to preach the dead brother into Heaven.

The man then took the preacher out to his house, in his horse and buggy. When they got there all the relatives and friends of the sinful brother were there. So the hired preacher began to conduct the funeral services. He preached for about thirty minutes, but just before he reached the end of the sermon he turned to the dead brother's brother who'd hired him, pointed his finger at him, and said, "Well, brother, I'se got him jes' one step out of Heaven now;

so I tells you what I'll do—for another fifty cents I'll preach him right on into Heaven."

"I ain't gonna pay you another cent," replied the live brother, looking up at him. "If he cain't step dat other one step into Heaven, he can jes' go on to Hell."

[Grady E. Moss, Sr., Rowan County.]

JESSE JAMES AND THE BURIED MONEY.—It is said that Jesse James, the famous robber, robbed a bank one time in North Carolina, right after slavery times, and wanted to hide the money, but he knew not where to hide it. His brother Frank told him to hide it in the colored graveyard, because all the ex-slaves were afraid of dead folks, and the money would be safe there.

What Jesse and Frank did not know was that a Negro runaway from justice was hiding out in the graveyard, and that when he saw Jesse and Frank coming he went and climbed up in a tree and hid.

Jesse buried the money and put a sign over it which read, "Dead and Buried." After Jesse and Frank left, the Negro dug up the money, took it, and made his escape.

When Jesse returned for the money several months later the sign read, "Risen and Gone."

[Rev. James L. Hunt, Marion.]

HOW COME "HENRY."—The new colored parson visiting one of the sisters in his church for the first time was puzzled to hear her call her children Eenie, Meenie, Minie, and Henry.

"Why you name dat last boy Henry?" inquired the parson.

"Cause," replied the sister, "us don' want no Mo."

[Robert Cuthrell, Mocksville.]

THE CHEROKEE INDIAN SOUP LINE.—In the hills of North Carolina where the Great Smoky mountains begin, there is an Indian Reservation for the Cherokee Indians controlled by the federal government.

Right after the First World War, during President Hoover's administration, when there were some really tough times and soup-lines were being formed all over the country, a soup-line was formed on this Cherokee Reservation, where all the Cherokees and passers-by were served except Negroes.

One time a hungry Negro passed through that section, got in line with the others, and waited to be served. In front of him were a Cherokee Indian, a Chinaman, and a Japanese.

There was a government man checking the nationality of all those passing through the soup-line. So when the Cherokee got to where he was, the government agent asked him what his nationality was. The Cherokee replied, "Me Cherokee." When the Chinaman reached him and was asked his nationality, he replied, "Me Chinese." When the Japanese got to where the government was, and was asked his nationality, he replied, "Me Japanese."

The Negro was next. So he walked over to where the man checking the races was standing, and when asked his nationality replied, "Me Spookanese."

[George Maye, Cherokee County.]

WHY DOOGER CHANGED HIS TEXT.—Dooger Woods was quite a character. He was pastor of the Sugar Hill Baptist Church in Caldwell County, but had been born and raised in the adjoining county, Wilkes County, which was called by people living in Caldwell County, because of its bigness, "the State of Wilkes."

One of the most talked-of characters in Caldwell County was a Negro preacher by the name of Dooger Woods. He was a good friend of my father's and grandfather's, and, I could say, of mine too, because I knew him quite well, and used to talk to him all the time when I was a boy.

It is said that Dooger was unable to read and write, but he had a good memory and a powerful voice. My grandfather said that one Sunday morning when Dooger got ready to deliver a sermon that he had prepared he looked out into the congregation and saw a Negro man from Wilkes County named Edward who knew him before he started preaching and was a sinner. So, as grandfather tells it, as soon as old Dooger saw Edward he said: "Now, brothers and sisters, you knows sometime a preacher fix hit in his mind what he gonna preach about before he gits to de church an' after he gits dere he see somebody or sump'n an' switch his mind clear around about what he gonna preach about. Dat's de dickment I find myself in dis mornin'. Hit done come to me right out of de blue to change my tex'; so I'm gonna change my tex' dis mornin' to the second chapter of de Book of Edward, which say, 'To all dem dat sees me

and knows me say nothin' and do nothin' till I sees 'em later.' ''
[Bert Roberts, Caldwell County.]

[Collected by J. Mason Brewer, *North Carolina Folklore*, July 1961.]

Conversations

"Say, ole nigger, yo' face look lak po' man's dinner wrapped up in dish rag."

"Well, you look lak mushmellon in slop bucket."

"Yo' face look lak a coffee-pot, yo' mouth look lak the spout, yo' nose look lak the fireplace wid de ashes pokin' out."

"Yo' feet look lak burnt pine poles."

"Yo's look lak tarpin on dry lan'."

"Go on, nigger, yo' feets ain't mates, you don't love yo' Jesus."

"Huh, I see yo' feet mile round corner 'fo' I see you."

"Yo' feets look lak stalled ship on dry lan'."

"Yo' eyes look lak two burnt holes in a blanket."

"Yo's look lak dime wid a hole through it."

"You too cheap to buy a mus'rat smokin' jacket."

"You's a cheap screw—don't eat nothin' but beef stew."

"Yo's head's so nappy it stop ever clock from runnin'."

"Say, ole nigger, if I was to cut off yo' hair an' put it in bottle, it rattle lak shots."

"You needn't be talkin', you ain't got 'nuf hair on yo' head to wad er musket."

"Gwa'n, nigger, you ain't got no sense. If I was to ketch hold o' one stran' o' yo' hair an' pull, I'd ravel yo' whole brains out."

"Say, ole darky, don't be tryin' to size me up; I don't weigh no ton."

"Wait till I come back an' I'll fix you."

"Huh, wait broke down a bridge once, an' if I *wait* you might break me down."

"You look lak fifteen cents in copper—a whole heap an' ain't nothin' neither."

"Say, ole man, what's the biggest ham you ever seen?"

"Well, the biggest ham I ever seed weighed 'bout twenty pounds."

"That must have been a dog ham."

"No, it was a hog ham. What's the biggest ham *you* ever seed?"

"Well, I seen a ham so dad-bob big till horses an' wagons an' trains an' all them dad-bob thing run through it."

"Well, well, what kind er ham was that?"

"Birmingham, you fool—haw-haw-haw."

"Say nigger, what's the fastes' train you ever rode on?"

"Who, me?"

"Yes, you, durn you."

"Well, I guess about a mile a minute."

"Huh, that train wasn't runnin' at all."

"Well, what's the fastes' train you ever rode on?"

"I rode on train so dad-bob fas' till conductor had to hold hair on fireman's head."

"Who hold hair on his head?"

"Two little girls."

"Well, who hold hair on they heads?"

"I got you to know, two ole men 'bout fifty years old."

"Well, who hold hair on *they* heads?"

"They was bald-headed, didn't have no hair—caught—haw-haw-haw."

"Say, ole man, I see you are bald-headed; what made it?"

"Well, old age, I guess."

"Oh, no, I know."

"Well, if you know what'n the devil you ax me for?"

"To see if you knowed. Now I tell yo: yo' brains have got water on them an' yo' hair fall in an' get drowned—haw-haw."

"Well, bygod, that is funny story."

"Talkin' 'bout buyin' God, damfool, you better buy mule an' peck o' peas an' go to farmin'. You ain't got 'nough money to buy lumber to build backhouse."

"Well, you sho' God got big talkin' mouth. If God hadn't held steady hand, yo' mouth would have been clean back to yo' years."

"Well, you needn't be talkin', you big stiff. How high is you?"

"I'se six feet two."

"Well, you would been a heap taller if you hadn't turn' down so much o' yo' legs to walk on. What size shoe you wear?"

"Seven an' half."

"Yea, seven cows' hides an' half barrel tacks."

"Well, ole strumpet, I know cows glad when they goes to make yo' shoes, 'cause don't have to cut hide at all 'cept tail, an' that goes to make shoe strings."

"Yea, when you go to shoe sto' you cain't ask fer number, jes' ask how big can they make 'em."

"Well, folks think yo' feets yo' waterwings, ole slew-footed nigger."

"Well, goodgod, wish I had yo's fer snowshoes."

"Snow, nothin', you so black you look like dam' lump o' coal."

"Well, you so dam' black you spit ink."

"Well, goddam, you so ugly you have to slip up on dipper to drink water."

"Yes, bygod, you so ugly you have to cover up yo' head so sleep come to you."

"Well, you better wish you had sense like I got."

"Huh, if yo' sense was powder, you wouldn't have 'nough to blow 'yo nose off if got set fire to it."

"Well, if yo' head was shaved down to yo' senses, peanut hull make you good-sized head."

"Well, anyway, ole nappy-haired nigger, I'm fool what knows it, an' you fool don't know it. You got rabbit hair, eve'y knot balls up an' squats."

[Howard W. Odum, *Rainbow Round My Shoulder: The Blue Trail of Black Ulysses* (Indianapolis: Bobbs-Merrill Company, 1928).]

Morphine

An insurance agent told me that he went over to the colored section of my town to collect some insurance premiums. He knocked at the front door of Aunt Dinah's house. Receiving no answer, he started around to the back of the house and heard Aunt Dinah calling: "Morphine, Morphine, you lazy, triflin', no 'count niggah, if you don't come on heah, I'se gwine beat the life outen you."

The agent inquired: "Aunt Dinah, why in the world did you name your daughter Morphine?"

Aunt Dinah replied: "Well, suh, I'se done read in a book one time dat morphine is de offspring ov de wild poppy. . . ."

[Felix E. Allen, *Random Thoughts and the Musings of a Mountaineer* (Salisbury: Rowan Printing Co., 1941).

Why the Holy Amen Church Has Two Doors

Dicksonville is the largest colored community in Salisbury, with the largest church. The Holy Amen Church is situated just outside the city limits, and now it has two doors.

Here, as in other Negro churches in the South, it was a common practice to try church members who had committed some act they regarded as sinful. Such a trial took place when Deacon Pennybacker Robinson was accused of "cussing" Holy Amen Church. Following is one account of the incident:

When the prayer was finished and the rustling and craning of necks had subsided and the fanning begun, the meeting was turned over to Deacon Wassail White, who arose and addressed the gathering.

"Brudders an' sisters, as you all knows, we is assembled here today ter try and 'reak justice on a po', miserable back-slidin' member of dish here church. We is gonna gib 'im er fair tri'l an' effen he has got ennything ter say fer hisself, we is gonna hear 'im through befo' we drives 'im frum de flock. An' I don' want no hollerin' at 'im 'twill he gits through.

"Mister Pennybacker Robinson, you has bin 'cused of a most ser'ous crime. You has bin 'cused of cussin' de church. Now nemmine who repo't you an' nemmine what evidence we got ergin you, what has you got to say fer yo'se'f? Is you guilty er not guilty? Answer me dat!"

Pennybacker arose and came forward, proud and unashamed. His head was lifted high. His lanky length seemed to grow under the hostile gaze of his erstwhile friends and neighbors. In his eyes glowed the fire of a martyr.

He was a dignified man. His skin was a dark roan color, somewhat brindled in the darker spots. His grizzled hair, heavy gold-rimmed spectacles, and jim-swinger walk gave him the walk and air of a dusty esthetic. Calmly and in a firm voice he answered his accusers, anonymous though they were.

"Deacon White, brudders an' sisters, I don't 'zackly know how ter answer dat question. I is guilty an' yet ergin I ain't guilty. De thing happen lak dis:

"You all, leastways de mos' of you, 'members 'bout er month ago when we was funeralizin' Sister Erferlia Johnson. Well, I knows you also 'members how, when dey opens de kaskit so de family cud hab de las' look, an' when de lid wuz tooken off, er big black cat jump outten de kaskit an' start spittin' an' den start runnin' eroun' er tryin' ter git outten here. Well, in de tumult an' de fight at de do', Sis Elby Crawford wuz on mah back, an' Brudder Sam Frisbee was tryin' ter git 'tween my legs, and Sis Peebles wuz er beatin' me ober de haid wid her umbrelly, 'cause I couldn't git outten her way fas' ernuf. . . .

"Well, right den and dare I turn ter Brudder Mose Benson, an' I says ter 'im, sez I, 'Mose, damn a church ennyway dat ain't got but one do'!' "

[J. Mason Brewer, *American Negro Folklore* (Chicago: Quadrangle Books, 1968).]

When I Worries

Nobody can accuse us of being slow or backward, because the state has made tremendous progress during the last twenty years. At the same time, our people realize that there's something else to life besides work and that there are other interests besides merely making money.

Perhaps we're somewhat like the old Negro mammy whom John Bragaw, of Washington, told me about one time. She stopped him on the street and asked him to lend her ten cents. John pulled out the money and said: "Aunt Emma, how old are you?"

"I'se eighty-five," was her answer.

"Eighty-five!" he repeated. "That hardly seems possible. Why, you don't look a day over sixty-five. How do you keep looking so young?"

The old woman hesitated a moment and then she said: "Well, I'll tell you, Mr. John. Hit's disaway: When I works, I works hard; when I sets, I sets loose; and when I worries, I goes to sleep."

Which, after all is said and done, is pretty good philosophy— particularly that part about "setting loose."

[Carl Goerch, *Down Home* (Raleigh: Edwards and Broughton Co., 1943).]

Rolling Tom

A colored woman, it is related, knocked at Saint Peter's gate, seeking to learn if her deceased husband had come that way.

"What name?" asked the gatekeeper.

"Name ob Jones," replied the portly investigator.

"Got lots of Joneses here," said the gatekeeper. "What was his first name?"

"Name Tom Jones," answered the widow.

"Lots of Tom Joneses here," said the representative of St. Peter. "Wasn't there some distinguishing characteristics or unusual idiosyncracies about him?"

"Dunno none," replied the old Negress, " 'cept he told me when he wuz dyin' ef I war onfaithful t'him arter he gone, he gwine t'turn ober in his grave."

"Oh," exclaimed St. Peter's gatekeeper, "you're talking about Rolling Tom Jones."

[Thomas Johnston Henderson, *Homespun Yarns* (Yanceyville: p.p., 1943).]

Tired of That Man

The whole affair reminds me of a doctor who had a Negro boy to clean up his office and do odd jobs. One day he showed up with both eyes swollen almost shut, his face scratched and a decided limp in his walk.

"Why, Sam," the doctor asked, "what in the world happened?"

"Well, Boss, me and another gentleman got to argufying about a lady and I ups and called him a liar. He then knocked me down, kicked my ribs, scratched my face and bit my ear nearly off. Honest, Boss, I was never so sick of a nigger in all my life."

[George Franks Ivey, *Humor and Humanity* (Hickory: Southern Publishing Co., 1945).]

Progress

"What you have described shows one type of progress," Roberts said. "It is a report of one item of a vast number of modern accomplishments. In many respects, ours is not the same world that your grandfather knew. What would he have done if a jet had flown over this place?"

"I've no idea what he would have thought. Maybe he would have reacted as an old Negro in the neighborhood of Linwood did. About fifty years ago, a man brought an airplane to Lexington at the time of the County Fair. He wore goggles, a helmet, and a long white coat when he flew the plane. One day the plane gave him trouble, and he had to land in a cotton field where the old man was working. When the plane landed, the old Negro dropped to his knees and said, 'Lord, I am ready to go.' "

[A. C. Reid, *Tales from Cabin Creek* (Raleigh: p.p., 1967).]

A Literal Mind

Speaking of maids: Raymond Pollock, of New Bern, was in Raleigh while the legislature was in session and told me of a little experience that he and Mrs. Pollock had with a maid whom they had hired a couple of weeks before.

She was a girl from the country and hadn't worked out before. She found it mighty hard to get the hang of things and made a lot of mistakes. However, Mrs. Pollock was very patient and did her best to teach the girl how her work should be done.

One day Mrs. Pollock had to go to some kind of a meeting down town. Before she left, she made out a list of things she wanted the maid to get from the store while she was gone. She wrote out the various items very plainly and distinctly. Like this:

1. Chicken
2. Tomatoes
3. Potatoes
4. Biscuits
5. Lemon pie

The maid was determined that this was going to be one job that should be done right. She took the list and went to the store. She bought the various items. When Mrs. Pollock got home, she found one chicken, two tomatoes, three potatoes, four biscuits and five lemon pies.

[Carl Goerch, *Characters . . . Always Characters* (Raleigh: Edwards and Broughton Co., 1945).]

Protocol

On our farm in western North Carolina, I have spent many happy hours. During the summer months, I usually work as a helper to the foreman. It was on a warm, uncomfortable day that I had to haul a load of manure and a hog into Boone.

I suppose it is about a five- or six-mile drive. I was taking my time getting to town. On the way I picked up an old colored man who was also headed into Boone.

Half way to town I was stopped by some friends and questioned about my cargo. I replied, "I am hauling a load of manure, a hog, and an old colored man."

After this brief conversation, I resumed my lazy drive into town. On the outskirts of Boone, I met the town constable, and in the course of our conversation he inquired about my load.

Again I replied, "A load of manure, a hog, and an old colored man."

I resumed the drive, and before many minutes had passed I was surprised to hear the old man speak.

"Mister Bill, mind if I axes a favor of you?"

I replied that he was perfectly free to ask a favor and that I would be glad to accommodate him if possible.

"Well, suh," he said, "the nex' time we is stopped, Mr. Bill, an' somebody axes you what you is haulin', would you please, suh, introduce me fust?"

[William R. Bibb, *North Carolina Folklore*, September 1954.]

The Devil at the Revival

For several nights two white boys were spectators at a Negro revival meeting, and they heard the preacher say over and over that there was no reason why a man should be afraid of the Devil. They decided to have some fun.

They made a devil's costume out of red flannel, packing the tail with sand, and fastening cow horns to the head. Before preaching one night they hid themselves in the church loft.

As usual, the preacher brought up the folly of fearing the Devil. To drive the point home, he put a question to them. How many of them, if they met the Devil on their way home that night, could stand up to him, look him in the eye, and say, "I'se not afeard!"

While the audience pondered that question in breathless silence, the Devil was seen to descend from the loft directly behind the preacher. The congregation had the jump on the preacher and cleared the church first, but the preacher picked up speed. As he passed them on the road, he panted, "I'se not sceared—I'se just too good to 'sociate wid him."

[A. M. Owens, *North Carolina Folklore*, June 1948.]

Devil's Loyal Servant

During one Duke University fraternity hazing a freshman was taken far into the country from Durham, put out of the car, and left to make his way back the best he could.

The lonely way offered no rides to hitch, and after trudging a long way he grew very cold. Then he came upon a church where Negroes were holding a meeting. He squeezed through the back door to warm beside the stove.

The Congregation caught sight of him, dressed in his Blue Devil suit, standing behind the preacher. The congregation fled helter skelter, and so did the preacher when he turned to see what had startled his audience.

Only one arthritic old woman remained. She sprawled at the "Devil's" feet and proclaimed: "Mr. Devil, I'se been going to this church all my life, but I'se been serving you all the time!"

[F. Roy Johnson, as told by Sam Boone, *Witches and Demons in History and Folklore* (Murfreesboro: Johnson Publishing Company, 1969).]

The Patrolman

I was walking along Fayetteville Street in Raleigh. Two colored men were standing in front of the Wachovia Bank building, waiting for a bus. As I passed, I heard this portion of their conversation:

"What happened to him then?"

"I dunno, but I think he was arrested by a highway patroleum."

[Carl Goerch, *Just for the Fun of It* (Raleigh: Printed by Edwards and Broughton, 1954).]

At Harvard

When I think of Harvard, I am reminded of what the Negro at Charlotte said when someone asked him where his brother was, and he said he's at Harvard. And then someone asked him what he was studying, and he answered and said, "He ain't studyin' nothin'; they is studyin' him."

[Chub Seawell, *News and Observer* (Raleigh), 5 May 1969.]

From a Collector's Treasury

THE TRUTH ABOUT MULES.—A northerner making his first trip south, picked up a young Negro hitchhiker on U.S. 301 in North Carolina and as the two drove along, the man from New York became aware that he was seeing quite a few mules in the fields along the road. They didn't look at all like the cantankerous, stubborn, sometimes treacherous creatures he had read about.

Finally he turned to his young passenger and asked him if he had ever done any farming.

"Yes," the young man replied. "I used to farm down home in Florida with my folks."

"Then maybe you can tell me," the northerner asked, "why mules have such a bad reputation. Are they really as mean as people say?"

"Why, no," the ex-farmer replied. "Mules aren't especially mean. It's just that they won't let themselves be imposed upon."

HELL AT THE LOCAL LEVEL.—A northern minister, attending a service up-country in North Carolina, was astonished to hear the local preacher portray Hell as a region of ice, snow, and eternal cold. Later, the visitor commented to his host:

"Your description of Hell was very impressive, but I couldn't help feeling it was quite unorthodox."

"Reverend," the up-country pastor replied, "it's like this. Things ain't too bad around here in the summertime but when the frost sets in, and the wind finds the chinks in your cabin, and you got no heavy clothes to wear outdoors, *and* you got one less blanket on your bed than you would like to have, *and* you come to church on Sunday, and it's none too warm *there*; now on top of that they hear me telling how warm Hell is—why, some of my congregation might develop a powerful yearning to get there."

THE HOTTEST DAY.—This is a lie that's been told on a lot of people in a lot of places, so let's just say this man's name was Henry Dorsey and it happened in North Carolina quite a while back. What happened to him was this:

On the hottest July 17 they'd had there in twenty-two years, Henry's boss sent him down to the cornfield to lay by some corn. So Henry hitched up a mule to the cart, went down to the field and started pulling corn. After a while it got so hot the corn began to pop. The air got so full of popped corn that it looked like it was snowing. When the mule saw that, he lay down in his tracks and froze to death.

[Philip Sterling, *Laughing on the Outside: The Intelligent White Reader's Guide to Negro Tales and Humor* (New York: Grosset & Dunlap, 1965). A New York state native who grew up in Ohio, Sterling has made a career in journalism, writing, and broadcasting.]

Here and There in North Carolina

HOW THE PARROT BROKE UP THE CHURCH MEETING.—A preacher was running a revival, and every night he would tell the people that they were going to hell by the wagonloads. Old boss had a parrot, so he told the parrot to go down to the church and ask who was going to bring the wagon back. The next night as the preacher made the statement, the parrot said, "Who'll bring the wagon back?"

Everybody ran out of the church but one old lady, so the parrot lit on her shoulder and said, "Who'll bring the wagon back?"

The old lady said, "I don't know, Mr. Jesus. I'm ain't a member here, I'm just a visitor."

SHE WASN'T THE FUSSY KIND.—One time a colored woman named Carrie was workin' for my mother. Mother worked her about three days a week, over and above the laundry work she did for mother.

One day when Carrie got to work she looked at Mama and said, "Missy, I's got to be off tomorrow; I can't come to work."

Mama was surprised, because Carrie had never asked to be off from work before. So she said, "Carrie, what you got to be off for?"

And Carrie replied, "It ain't me, Missy. I's got to take my li'l boy to de doctor."

"Yo' little boy to de doctor," replied mother. "I thought you told me you was an old maid."

"Yassum, dat's what I is," said Carrie. "But I ain't the fussy kind."

THE TOBACCO STACKER'S MISTAKE.—One year, during tobacco-stacking time, a tobacco grower near Winston-Salem brought some Negroes up from Georgia to stack his tobacco for him. The reason he did this was that he could hire the Georgia Negroes cheaper.

The Georgia Negroes had heard about how bad Winston-Salem Negroes were, so every Saturday when they got their week's pay they would slip off, two or three at a time, and go into town and buy guns, knives, and wine. The reason they could not stay in town long at a time was that they worked all day Saturday—they just got paid off at ten o'clock in the morning and had two hours off for the day—from ten to twelve.

There was one in the bunch who never went into town but who'd always send by some of the others for a quart of "Eleven Star" wine every Saturday. He kept up this practice for about four weeks, but finally, on the fifth Saturday after they had started to work on the tobacco farm, he decided that he'd go into town himself and get his "Eleven Star" wine. When he got there he went into the first store he saw, which was a hardware store, and told the owner that he wanted a bottle of "Eleven Star" wine. The owner said, "We don't have nothin' but hardware here."

So the Negro said, "Well, gimme a bottle of that."

THE SPELLING BEE AND THE COUNTY SUPERINTEN-
DENT.—My gran'ma say when she was a little bitty girl jes' startin'
to school out to Tobaccoville, dat dey jes' hab a one-room school
wid one teacher, dat mos' o' de little school scholars was boys. Some
o' de little boys' names was Tom Miller, Jimmy Brown, Bob
Thomas, Chuck Connor, Raymond Moore, and Bill Johnson, but
dey was one little fellow dat was named Damn-it Jones.

Gran'ma say dat little Damn-it was a top scholar in rifmetic—
dat he could work wid figgers real good, but dat he was a de bottom o' de class when it come to spellin' day. Gran'ma say dey'd
have a spellin' bee ever' Friday jes' 'fo' school turned out, and dat
little Damn-it was always at de botton o' de row.

One Friday, howbeever, gran'ma say, de county sup'inten't
comed by de school an' tuck him a seat whilst dey was havin' de
spellin' match. Gran'ma say dat her an' de other li'l girls an' all de
boys spelled all de words de teacher give out till finally de teacher
ask 'em to spell de word Nebuchadnezzar an' dey all missed out,
cep'n she ain't got to Damn-it Jones yet, so li'l Damn-it riz up his
han' real high in de air an' say, "Teacher, let me spell it."

"Damn-it Jones, you can't spell it," say de teacher, an' when
she say dis, de sup'inten't stan' up real quick and say, "Hell,
teacher, let him try!"

THE BOY WHO PLAYED JESUS.—One time a ol' boy what
lived out to Pleasant Plains, in Winton Township, what belong to
dat "almos'-white" bunch o' folks dey calls "Free Issues," come to
learn how to play de organ an' de piana real good, so no sooner'n he
done finish up in de high school he tells his mama an' papa dat he
wanna go up de road an' come to know mo' 'bout how to play de
organ an' de piana. But his mama an' his papa say "No"—dey
ain't gonna have him lightin' out from home at no sixteen years ol'.

After dis de boy sit 'roun' de house an' won't open his mouf to
his mama an' papa, but dey hol's fas' to what dey says 'bout him
not goin' up de road to come to know how to play de organ an'
piana better'n he do now.

Howbeevuh, one Saddy when his mama an' papa done drive
into Ahoskie to git some tools for de farm, dis ol' boy packs his

clothes into a bag an' goes out to de highway to catch him a ride. He gets him a ride as far as Norfolk, an' from dere he catches de train an' goes on to New York.

When he gets to New York he goes down to Harlem, an' rents him a li'l room in a basement. He got a little money dat he kin call his own, so it las' him a li'l while, but putty soon hit 'gin to give out, an' he starts lookin' for a job. But since his folks was land-ownin' farmers an' hire dey help, dis ol' boy don't know nothin' 'bout no work an' he can't fin' nothin' to do.

Dis worry him a lots, 'cause his money 'bout all gone, so one day whilst he was stannin' on de corner thinkin' 'bout he might have to go back home, a man passed him an' say, "Man, you looks like Jesus"—de ol' boy done really growed a beet-nick beard, so when de man tell him dis he hurry down to his li'l room an look in de lookin'-glass at hisse'f, an' sho nuff, he do look like Jesus.

No sooner'n he done peeked at hisse'f in de lookin-glass he goes down to a Jew store on de corner an' buys him a long white robe. Dat nex' comin' Sunday he puts de robe on an' goes down to a big Baptist Church in Harlem, an' starts walkin' comin' down de aisle towards de pulpit, when de preacher see him an' say, "Hol' de singin' a minnit. Here comes Jesus. Let's take up a collection for him." So dey takes up $200 an' gives it to de ol' boy.

Dat nex' comin' Sunday he goes down to a big Catholic Church an' goes in an' starts walkin' down de aisle wid his han's stretched out, so de priest sees him an' say, "Here comes Jesus. Let's take up a collection for him." So dey takes up $200 an' gives it to him.

De ol' boy say to hisse'f, "I sho' got sumpin good workin' for me now." So nex' comin' Sunday de ol' boy puts on his long white robe again, an' goes down to a Jew synagogue an' starts walkin' down de aisle wid his han's stretched out. Dere was two rabbis 'ductin de services, so when dey seed de ol boy walkin' down de aisle, one of 'em yells to de other one, "Go an' git de hammer an' nails quick; de fool's off de cross again."

THE CABARRUS COUNTY BOY WHO TOLD THE CHURCH WHAT TO DO.—One time dere was a boy what left home in Cabarrus County, went up to New York, an' comed to be in good shape. When he done come to be in good shape, an' have him a little money on de side, he makes his way back to see his mama

an' papa what done been his standbys 'fo' he lef' home. Dey is real proud of de boy, 'cause he got a lots of fancy clothes, a bran' new car, an' some money in his pocket. So dat next comin' Sunday dey all gets ready an' goes on down to de church.

Dey gets dere a little 'fo' de services starts, so de boy shuck an' reshuck de hands of most de members what know him from a little chap, and den goes on into de churchhouse wid his mammy and pappy.

After de sermon am over de preacher gets up an' say, "Now brothers an' sisters, I has sumpin' dat got to be 'cided on right here dis mornin'. It's 'bout de money we done raised; an' de question am, what must us get wid de money, a piano or a chandelier?"

Den one of de members what been knowin' de boy from time he was knee-high to a duck riz up an' say, "Brother pastor, we has a visitor 'mongst us dis mornin' what done been up de country an' done come to be a knowledge man. Sposin' we asks him what we ought to buy wid de money?" De pastor say dat's awright wid him; just whatsomever de membership want to do wid de money, an' whosomever dey wants to pass judgment, cause dey raised it.

So de boy gets up, pokes his chest way out, rams his han's way down in his pockets an' say, "Well now, I tells you. If'n I was ya'll I believe I'd buy a piano wid de money, 'cause as far back as ya'll is in de woods I don't believe you gonna find nobody out here can play no chandelier."

[J. Mason Brewer, *Worser Days and Better Times: The Folklore of the North Carolina Negro* (Chicago: Quadrangle Books, 1965).]

Carl Goerch

Although he has maintained that "there is no such thing as an entirely new joke [and] that every one that comes out masquerading as a new one is in reality an old one dressed up," Carl Goerch is an avid collector of the "old" and the "new," the unusual and the strange—whatever is amusing and laughable. Scattered among the pages of The State *magazine and his half dozen books are anecdotes and stories he has heard, acted out (he is not adverse to playing practical jokes), or reconditioned to suit his readers. Like his famous "Zipper Story," most of his yarns turn on mishaps and misunderstandings. Born in New York state in 1891, he came to North Carolina in 1913 as a newspaper editor. In 1933 he founded* The State *and has been writing for it ever since.*

The Zipper Story

It may sound funny to you and to me, but it was almost tragic to the people who were involved in the incident.

It happened in the State Theatre in Raleigh.

There's a certain gentleman in Raleigh (we'll call him Mr. Brown for the sake of convenience) who weighs well over 200 pounds. One night last week he went home to supper and found that his wife had prepared backbone and dumplings—a dish of which he is particularly fond.

So he sat down at the table and gorged himself until he could hold no more.

Then he suggested that they go to the State Theatre and see a picture. Mrs. Brown was agreeable, so down town they went.

They found seats at about the center of the theatre, and after

217

they had settled themselves comfortably, proceeded to enjoy the picture. Mr. Brown began to feel that his belt was too tight. Inasmuch as the theatre was dark, he didn't hesitate to unloosen it. But even then he didn't feel exactly right: there was still too much pressure around his middle.

He had on a pair of trousers with zippers down the front, so he reached down and ran the zipper-jigger down a few inches.

After that he felt fine and gave a huge sigh of relief as he prepared to enjoy the picture.

Everything went along fine for ten or fifteen minutes, and then a lady, sitting on the same aisle, about three or four seats away, decided that she had seen all she wanted of the show and got ready to leave. The people sitting next to her obligingly rose in order to make way for her. When she approached Mr. Brown, he too rose to his feet. And then he suddenly remembered that his zipper was unfastened, so he reached down hurriedly to pull up the jigger.

When he did, he caught the lady's dress in the zipper and couldn't work the thing up or down to save his life.

She felt a tug at her dress and turned around to give him a hard look. She felt another tug, whereupon she leaned forward and hissed: "What are you trying to do?"

That attracted Mrs. Brown's attention. She turned to her husband and whispered hoarsely: "John, what are you trying to do to the lady?"

"Not a thing," whispered back John.

"He is, too," said the lady. "He's tugging at my dress."

Mrs. Brown half-way rose from her seat. "Turn her loose this instant!" she commanded. "Whatever in the world has come over you?"

"I can't turn her loose!" protested Mr. Brown.

"Why not?"

"Her dress is caught in my pants."

Mrs. Brown gasped, and so did the other lady. People sitting behind them were beginning to get impatient and there were cries of "Sit down!" and "Down in front!"

Mr. Brown began to perspire freely. He tugged at the zipper for all he was worth, but the more he tugged, the more firmly the lady's dress became entangled in its meshes.

"What are you-all trying to do?" asked a gentleman sitting directly behind Mr. Brown.

"Her dress is caught in my pants!" hissed Brown.

"Good Lord!" said the man behind, and after that he didn't say another word.

"Do something!" insisted the lady.

"I'm doing all I can," growled Mr. Brown, "but it's getting worse and worse all the time."

By that time everybody in the neighborhood was taking a keen and unholy interest in the proceedings.

"We'll have to go out in the lobby, " finally said Mr. Brown.

"Together?" she asked.

"You're darned right—together," he told her. "Think I'm going to take off my pants and let you walk off with them?"

She agreed that there was nothing else to do but act upon his suggestion. Moving slowly toward the end of the aisle, she led Mr. Brown along with her.

Then they started toward the lobby. It was the side of her dress that had been caught in the zipper and so, while she was able to walk along all right by taking rather short steps, Mr. Brown had to go sideways somewhat like a crab on the beach.

Folks sitting on the aisle almost fell out of their seats as they saw what was taking place. Their eyes followed Mr. Brown and the lady as they waltzed in the direction of the lobby.

By the time they got there, both of them were so mad that they couldn't see straight. One of the ushers—after the situation had been explained to him—took them into a little sideroom, where Mr. Brown took out his knife and proceeded to do some effective work with it.

At last the lady was free. She shook down her dress, shook herself all over, gave Mr. Brown a final dirty look and sailed majestically out of the theatre.

Mr. Brown returned to his seat, where he had to listen to Mrs. Brown's whisperings and also to the chuckles emanating from all the seats in his immediate neighborhood.

He sat through the rest of the show with his belt tightly fastened and with the zipper pulled all the way up, but the damage had already been done and he really didn't get much pleasure or enjoyment out of the picture.

If anybody wants a pair of pants with zipper attachments, I

can tell him where he can get them at a very reasonable price.

He'll have to be a rather fat man, however.

[Carl Goerch, *Down Home* (Raleigh: Edwards and Broughton Co., 1943).]

One Way of Paying for a Meal

For a number of years it has been my pleasure to enjoy the friendship of two very fine North Carolinians: Mr. and Mrs. Henry Ingram, of Asheboro. Henry—as splendid a gentleman as I've ever known—died not long ago. He was Department Commander of the American Legion at the time of his death. Mrs. Ingram still lives in Asheboro.

During the early part of June, several years ago, I attended the commencement exercises of High Point College. On the way back home, I passed through Asheboro.

It was just about lunch time when I got there, so I went around to the hotel and ordered lunch.

The hotel, by the way, is run by Mrs. Ingram's mother.

When I had finished my meal, I walked up to the desk in the office and asked the young lady there how much I owed her.

"Fifty cents," she told me.

I paid her. And then I said to her: "Do you happen to know if Henry and DeEtte are in town?"

"I believe they are," she replied. "Would you like for me to get them on the phone for you?"

I told her I would.

So she called their number, and in a moment DeEtte was on the line.

"Just thought I'd say hello," I told her.

"Where are you?"

"Down at the hotel. I've just finished lunch and am heading back to Raleigh."

"You stay right there for a minute or two. Henry and I will be right down."

After an interlude of about five minutes, Mr. and Mrs. Ingram appeared upon the scene. They were very cordial in their greeting and had a lot of questions to ask about Raleigh and their friends in the capital city. They also said they were planning to go to Mexico shortly to attend the International Rotary convention down there.

They planned to go as far as Brownsville, Texas, and then take the train from there.

We had a very nice little visit. Finally, however, I announced that I had to leave, inasmuch as I had an engagement in Raleigh at four o'clock and just naturally had to be there by then. Henry, too, said that he had to get back to his oil plant. He was distributor for Standard Oil in that section.

I shook hands with them, got into my car and started to get underway.

Suddenly I heard my name called. Looking around I beheld Mrs. Ingram running toward the car.

"Wait a minute!" she hollered. So I waited.

"Did you pay for your lunch here?" she demanded, as she stood beside the car.

I told her that I did.

"What in the world made you do that?" she inquired. "You ought to have had better sense."

"Now just wait a minute," I broke in. "I don't mind sponging off you when you invite me to take a meal at your house, but this time I insist upon paying. I went into the hotel of my own free will and accord, and if you don't let me pay this time, darned if I'm ever going to stop here again."

"We'll never let you stop here again if you do pay," she retorted. "You give me back that fifty cents."

"I'm not going to do it," I told her. "I'm going to pay for my lunch."

"You are not!" she insisted. "Give me back that fifty cents, I tell you; and don't argue with me any longer."

Well, you know how it is. When a woman gets that insistent there's no use arguing with her. So with a deprecatory shrug of the shoulders, I reached down into my pockets and handed over the fifty cents.

"It really isn't fair, though," I informed her. "You ought to have let me pay."

"No such thing," she said. "We want you to consider yourself our guest whenever you pass through here. We'll be glad to see you at any time, and you're always welcome to a meal. So don't you try to pay any more."

Whereupon we said good-bye again, and I drove off.

And do you know, I'd almost driven as far as Franklinville when—all of a sudden—I straightened up with a sudden start.

I tried to figure out exactly what had happened and how it had happened, but I actually had to stop the car by the side of the road and do a little mathematical work with pencil and paper before I realized what had taken place.

And then, with a sigh, I resumed my way in the direction of Raleigh. Next time I pass through Asheboro, however, and stop for lunch, I'm going to insist that I be permitted to pay. I believe it'll be a whole lot cheaper.

[Carl Goerch, *Carolina Chats* (Raleigh: Edwards and Broughton Co., 1944).]

Belongs to Us

U.S. Marshal Charlie Price drove me around Asheville one day last summer. As we cut across Pack Square, he called my attention to the Vance monument which stands in the center of the square.

"Not long ago," said Charlie, "a tourist was wandering around town and he saw the monument. He was standing where he couldn't see Vance's name on it.

"A native of Buncombe County, from out in the rural sections, happened to come along. 'I say,' said the tourist, 'can you tell me whose monument this is?'

"The native looked at the monument, then looked at the tourist and said: 'Hit's our'n.'

"And with that he calmly proceeded on his way."

[Carl Goerch, *Characters . . . Always Characters* (Raleigh: Edwards and Broughton Co. 1945).]

Taming of the Wife

It may be old but I'd never heard it until Henry Hulick told it at Warlick's Soda Shop in Raleigh while several of us were having our mid-morning coffee together.

Reporter visited a couple who had been married fifty years. "I understand," he said, "that you two good people never have had an argument or a fuss in all your fifty years of married life."

"That's right," said the old man.

"How did you manage to do it?"

"Well, I'll tell you. When we were first married, I took my wife horse-back riding over a rough trail. Her horse stumbled, and I said: 'That's once.' A little while later the horse stumbled again, and I said: 'That's twice.' Going over some rocks, the horse stumbled again, and I said: 'That's three times.' Then I told my wife to get off the horse and I shot the animal. After that I lifted her up on the horse with me and we headed for home. She started bawling me out for shooting the horse: said I was a brute and a lot of other things along that line. I listened until she ran down, and then I said: 'That's once!' "

[Carl Goerch, *Just for the Fun of It* (Raleigh: Printed by Edwards and Broughton Co., 1954).]

Taking up the Collection

This little tale was told me by my good friend Tom Henderson of Yanceyville some time ago. He got it from Benton Stacey, former state legislator and well know throughout North Carolina.

It has to do with a doctor by the name of Jordan—a good, kind, generous, tender-hearted physician and a staunch member of the Methodist Church. He had one weakness, however: he would cuss on certain occasions. Most of this profanity was of an involuntary nature: not deliberately planned, and it would burst forth in the most unexpected places.

On one occasion Dr. Jordan was taking up the collection in church. In the third pew from the front sat a good friend of his, Jim Powers. Doc held the plate in front of Jim. The latter had a dollar bill in his hand and apparently desired to get change from the plate. Unmindful of the reverence of the occasion and the sanctity of the place, Dr. Jordan blurted out in a voice that carried through the silence of the church: "Aw, dammit, Jim: put the whole thing in!"

[Carl Goerch, *Just for the Fun of It* (Raleigh: Printed by Edwards and Broughton Co., 1954).]

Mixed-up Sentences

One of the colored boys at the S & W Cafeteria in Raleigh got slightly mixed up the other day. He hollered into the speaking tube: "Send up one span of paghetti!" He hesitated a moment and then said rather cautiously: "I mean one span——" Pausing briefly once more he finally shouted: "We need some spaghetti up here!"

Which brings to mind something that happened many years ago while we were living down in Washington, North Carolina. My wife went to the post office, greeted the clerk cordially and said: "Give me a dam's worth of stimps, please." The clerk laughed and said: "You mean a stam's worth of dimps, don't you?"

"No, a dim's worth——"

That's as far as they got before reaching a state of almost complete collapse. Then, after a short interval, they regained their composure and the clerk gave Mrs. Goerch her dime's worth of stamps.

[Carl Goerch, *Just for the Fun of It* (Raleigh: Printed by Edwards and Broughton, 1954).]

An Ineffective Prayer

I always enjoy having Mr. R. S. Eckles of Black Mountain drop in to see me because he always has a good story to pass on.

During the course of his last visit he told us about Uncle Pres Watkins who was quite a hunter and guide up in the mountain country many years ago.

There was a meeting of Presbyterian preachers in Montreat and they wanted to take a trip to the top of Mount Mitchell. The services of Uncle Pres were engaged with the understanding that he would act as guide on the journey.

At the present time there's a paved road up to the top of the mountain, but when this little incident took place there was only a narrow dirt road. Inasmuch as there were a number of branch roads emanating from it, a person could get lost very easily. That's why a guide was essential.

The party made the top of the mountain in safety. While there, a terrific electrical storm broke out, and the preachers were scared to death. They offered up individual prayers for their safety. One of them turned to Uncle Pres and said: "Brother Watkins, wouldn't you like to join us in prayer?"

Uncle Pres shifted his cud of tobacco around a little bit, hesitated slightly; finally spoke up and said: "Well, to tell the truth, preacher, I only know one little prayer and I don't think that would be worth a damn in a storm like this."

[Carl Goerch, *Just for the Fun of It* (Raleigh: Printed by Edwards and Broughton Co., 1954).]

Governor Scott and Ungah

The clipping was placed on my desk recently and came from one of the newspapers we receive at the office from all parts of North Carolina. I'm not positive but I believe it was Bill Horner's paper in Sanford.

It featured a story that was being told by Bill Fitts and starts off by saying that Mr. Fitts had been entertaining his friends with an account of what happened when Governor [W. Kerr] Scott made a speech at Cherokee following a performance of the pageant, *Unto These Hills*.

The story goes like this:

The Indians sat in stolid silence as the Governor started his speech. He paid his compliments to the pageant, said he had thoroughly enjoyed seeing it and hoped it would be continued for many years to come. Then he began talking of other things. He told them: "Your ancestors received a raw deal and were treated very unjustly, but I believe that our nation and our state have made amends for this. You have many good roads already, but I intend to pave all the roads in the Indian reservation before the end of my administration."

The Cherokee chief, sitting on the front row, considered this statement a moment. Then he nodded his head and said: "Ungah!" Other members of the tribe took it up, and Cherokees all over the hillside could be heard saying: "Ungah! Ungah!"

The Governor smiled brightly at this appreciation of his remarks and continued, "You have not had the best schools but I intend to see to it that you get as fine schools as there are in the United States, and staff them with the best teachers available."

The chief also gave this due consideration, nodded his head and said: "Ungah!" Other Indians also nodded approvingly and came forth with the same expression.

Well, to make a long story short, the Governor promised them more telephones, better medical service and a number of other things, and in each case he received the same response. There was a general and enthusiastic outburst of Ungahs as he continued his speech and he was deeply appreciative of the reaction which his audience had displayed.

When the meeting broke up, the Governor walked through the group of Indians and shook hands with a number of them.

"Ungah, eh?" he said smilingly.

They nodded solemnly and said: "Ungah!"

Turning to the chief, the Governor remarked: "I don't know when I've spoken to a finer audience. I believe my little talk went right to their hearts."

The chief nodded.

It was getting late, so the Governor and his party went to the Boundary Tree Lodge close by, where they spent the night.

The next morning the chief came around and said: "Governor, we would like to show you around the reservation so that you may obtain a better idea of what we have here."

"I'd be delighted," said Governor Scott.

So they got into a car. Our chief executive was shown the school, the museum and a number of other places of interest.

"Do you folks do much farming around here?" he inquired.

"Yes, indeed," said the chief. "Would you like to see some of the farms?"

"I certainly would," said the Governor.

So the chief drove him around for several miles and showed him a number of fine farms, together with the homes in which the people resided. Everything was neat and attractive and the Governor was greatly impressed.

"By the way, Governor," said the chief, "you're interested in the dairying business, aren't you?"

"Yes. We've got some mighty fine dairies in our part of the state and I'm glad to see that you people here in western North Carolina are getting interested in dairying."

Said the chief: "We have several fine cows here, and we also have a prize bull of which we are very proud. He's a registered animal and one of the finest that can be found anywhere in this part of the state. Would you like to see him?"

"Yes, I would. Where is he?"

"Just about a mile from here. We'll drive over there right now."

So they proceeded to drive down a dirt road until they came to a little valley in the middle of which was a fine pasture with several barns at one side of it.

"This is our dairy farm," explained the chief.

"Where's the bull you were talking about?"

"In that barn on the other side of the pasture. If you don't mind, we'll get out here and walk."

So they got out of the car and started to walk across the pasture. They hadn't gone far when the Governor slipped and almost fell to the ground. The chief grabbed him by the arm and said: "Careful, Governor!" And then, pointing toward the ground, he added: "Look—Ungah!"

And then, all of a sudden, a great light dawned upon Governor Scott.

[Carl Goerch, *Just for the Fun of It* (Raleigh: Printed by Edwards and Broughton Co., 1954).]

Did It Hurt You, John?

One of the legendary figures of Caswell County was Sheriff Jesse Griffith, a giant of a man with huge hands. With all his strength and heartiness, the sheriff was a kindly man. One time it was his duty to hang a prisoner.

But when the trap was sprung, the rope broke and the condemned man plunged to the ground.

The sheriff rushed down to the victim, and cried out in distress and anxiety: "Did it hurt you, John?"

John assured him it had not.

"Thank goodness!" said Griffith in a greatly relieved tone of voice. "Well, get up, John, and we'll try again."

[Carl Goerch, *The State*, 15 January 1968.]

Friendly

We still like this friendly comment by a Tar Heel upon meeting an acquaintance:

"If I'd a-knowed it was you when I driv by, I would have flang out my arm and wove at you."

[Carl Goerch, *The State*, 15 September 1968.]

New Locution

One of our lawyer-friends in Raleigh was telling us about a conversation he had with an elderly woman about some business dealings in which her husband had participated.

"Mr. Jack," she said, "You know Jim had no business signin' them papers, because he was gone-minded and really didn't know what he was doin'. 'Twas about three weeks later they had to take him to the 'sylum."

Gone-minded! There's one for you!

[Carl Goerch, *The State*, 1 October 1968.]

Bridge Game

This lady in Raleigh was having a bad time at the bridge club. She trumped her partner's ace, reneged twice, and passed an informatory double. She seemed confused and uncomfortable. Finally she excused herself and went to the powder room.

When she returned, her playing picked up and she and her partner made the rubber. "What happened to you?" asked the partner. "You're really back in the game."

"Took off my girdle," replied the lady calmly.

[Carl Goerch, *The State*, 1 March 1969.]

Santa Claus

A couple of weeks before Christmas, teachers and other members of the Parent-Teachers Association decided to put on a rip-snortin' Christmas observance in the local school. The children got tremendously interested and one of the first things they wanted to know was whether Santa Claus would be there. They were told that every effort would be made to bring the old gentleman to the schoolhouse.

Arrangements were made with Mr. Jim Walker to dress up and take the part of St. Nicholas. Mr. Walker said he would get his wife to make him an appropriate suit and they could depend upon his being present.

Another group, not knowing about all this, called on Mr. Tom Hadley and made him the same proposition, and Mr. Hadley said he'd be glad to cooperate.

The celebration took place on the night of December 21. When the program started at eight o'clock, the school auditorium was packed and jammed with children and grown-ups. Several carols were sung, the preacher made an appropriate Christmas talk and then—and then—in walked Santa Claus—in other words, Mr. Walker. The children applauded joyously.

Santa had come all the way from the North Pole to pay them a visit and they were delighted.

And now, momentarily, we turn to Mr. Hadley.

It was close to Christmas. Mr. Hadley felt that the advent of the Yuletide season justified him in taking a drink. So he drank a toast to himself, followed by one to Santa Claus, Mrs. Santa Claus and the nine reindeer, including Rudolph.

Then he started for the schoolhouse. He entered the back door of the auditorium and walked out on the platform. The children gasped in amazement. They hadn't been sure whether one Santa Claus would show up and here—all of a sudden—were two of them.

They yelled, stamped their feet and clapped their hands.

Mr. Hadley bowed in appreciation of such a wonderful reception. Then he happened to look over toward the side of the stage and saw Mr. Walker.

Ha-ha! An interloper. An imposter.

He walked somewhat unsteadily over toward Mr. Walker and asked, "What are you doing here?"

Said Mr. Walker, "I'm Santa Claus!"

"You're not—I'm Santa Claus, and besides—you're drunk."

Mr. Hadley looked around him. Members of the school orchestra had left their instruments on the stage. A guitar was within easy reach. He grabbed it, held it firmly in his right hand, took a long swing, and crowned Mr. Walker with it.

Mr. Walker staggered back from the blow. The children went wild. Mr. Walker reached on a table, picked up a book and slung it at Mr. Hadley. He socked him squarely in the face with it.

Then the two of them went at it with their fists, and the children really went wild. "Hit 'im, Santa Claus! In the jaw—sock him in the jaw. Hit 'im in the belly." The entire auditorium by this time was in an uproar. Four or five men sprang forward and succeeded in separating them. They were ushered unceremoniously out of the building and were told to stay out.

Then the school principal said that in view of unforeseen circumstances, he, himself, would enact the part of Santa Claus. The kids didn't give a rap about the rest of the program. They had seen enough to last them a lifetime, and to this day they haven't quit talking about the dandy fight that Santa Claus and his brother put on for them.

Mr. Walker and Mr. Hadley still don't speak to each other.

[Carl Goerch, *The State*, 1 March 1969.]

Disagreement

Superior Court Judge Chester Morris once tried a new wrinkle in jurisprudence. In Wayne court, after the testimony was related on a larceny charge, the judge turned to the colored defendant and asked a question:

"What do you think this sentence ought to be? You've been thinking about this for some six weeks, haven't you?"

"Yes, sir."

"Well, I'd appreciate any suggestions you have to make. I've been thinking about it for ten minutes. Surely you can give me a good idea."

Silence.

"Which sounds best—six, twelve, fifteen years?"

"Don't neither one of them sound so good to me," the man said.

[Carl Goerch, *The State*, 15 May 1969.]

No Blame

The other night a group of married couples were sitting around the fire enjoying a nice quiet evening. The subject got around to circumstances under which the couples met. Finally one of the group turned to a husband who evidently wasn't enjoying the conversation too much and asked, "Who introduced you to your wife?" The man

promptly came back, "We just met. I don't blame anybody."
[Carl Goerch, *The State*, 15 May 1969.]

Humor in Fiction

Novels and books of short stories without a touch of humor can be glum experiences indeed, and most writers manage to season the basic content of their works with at least a few sprightly moments. Although solemn enough on most occasions, a few writers can, and often do, publish fiction whose principal intent is humorous. Joseph Mitchell's Miss Copey, in his short story, "I Blame It All on Mama," is a woman to brighten our lives, and Dave Morrah's Wilbur Hare in "Algebra for Football Players" makes us wonder if all is right with our educational system. Guy Owen's con men in "Lightning Rods" and Burke Davis's tobacco farmers in "Goings-On in John M. Virden County" are contemporary evidence that the rural humor of the Old South survives vigorously in the New.

I Blame It All on Mama

Mrs. Copenhagen Calhoun, who lives on a riverbank watermelon farm in Black Ankle County, about a mile from the town of Stonewall, is the only termagant I have ever admired. She has no fondness for authority and is opposed to all public officials, elected or appointed. Once a distinguished senator came to Stonewall and spoke in the high-school auditorium; just after he finished telling how he made it a practice to walk in the footsteps of Thomas Jefferson, she stood up and said, "Senator, you sure are getting too big for your britches." A mayor of Stonewall once tried to get her fired from her job as cook in the restaurant of the Charleston, Pee Dee & Northern Railroad. A woman who got drunk in public, he said, was a disgrace to the town. She kept her mouth shut until he came up for reelection; then she went up and down Main Street making speeches which helped defeat him. "Why, the stuck-up old hypocrite!" she said in one of her speeches. "He goes to the country club on Saturday night and gets as drunk as a goose on ice, and Sunday morning he stands up in the Methodist choir and sings so loud the whole church echoes for a week." She believes that public officials are inclined to overlook the fact that Americans are free, and when she is brought into court for disturbing the peace she invariably begins her address to the judge by stating, "This is a free country, by God, and I got my rights." She has a long tongue, and Judge Elisha Mullet once said she could argue the legs off an iron pot. She has many bad qualities, in fact, and her husband often complains that she has made his life a hell on earth, but when I go back to Stonewall for a visit and find that she is still insisting on her rights, I always feel better about the vigor of democracy.

I was in the tenth grade when I became one of her admirers. At that time, in 1924, she was unmarried and had just come up from Charleston to cook in the station restaurant. It was the biggest restaurant in Stonewall; railroad men ate there, and so did hands from the sawmill, the cotton gin, and the chewing-tobacco factory. After school I used to hang around the station. I would sit on a bench beside the track and watch the Negro freight hands load boxcars with bales of cotton. Some afternoons she would come out of the kitchen and sit on the bench beside me. She was a handsome, big-hipped woman with coal-black hair and a nice grin, and the station agent must have liked her, because he let her behave pretty much as she pleased. She cooked in her bare feet and did not bother to put shoes on when she came out for a breath of fresh air. "I had an aunt," she told me, "who got the dropsy from wearing shoes in a hot kitchen." Once I asked her how she came to be named Copenhagen. "Mamma named all her babies after big towns," she said. "It was one of her fancy habits. Her first was a boy and she named him New Orleans. Then my sister came along and she named her Chattanooga. Mamma was real fond of snuff, and every payday Pa would buy her a big brown bladder of Copenhagen snuff. That's where she got my name."

One Friday night, after Miss Copey had been working at the restaurant a couple of months, the station agent wrote her a pass and she went down to Charleston to see her family. When she returned Monday on the 3:30, she was so drunk the conductor had to grab her elbows and help her down the train steps. She paid no attention to him but sang "Work, for the Night Is Coming." She bustled into the kitchen, kicked off her shoes, and began throwing things. She would pick up a pot and beat time with it while she sang a verse of the hymn, and then she would throw it. "Work till the last beam fad-eth, fad-eth to shine no more," she would sing, and then a stewpot would go sailing across the room. I stood at a window and stared. She was the first drunken woman I had ever seen and the spectacle did not disappoint me; I thought she was wonderful. Finally the chief of police, who was called Old Blunderbuss by the kids in town, came and put her under arrest. Next day she was back at work. In the afternoon she came out to sit in the sun for a few minutes, and I asked her how it felt to get drunk. She gave me a slap that almost knocked me off the bench. "Why, you little shirt-tail boy," she said, "what do you mean asking me such a question?" I rubbed my jaw and said, "I'm sorry, Miss Copey. I didn't mean any harm."

She leaned forward and held her head in her hands like a mourner and sat that way for a few minutes. Then she straightened up and said, "I'm sorry I slapped you, son, but that was a hell of a question to ask a lady. Drinking is a sad, sad thing, and I hate to talk about it. I was a liquor-head sot before I got past the third grade, and I blame it all on Mamma. I had the colic real often when I was a little girl, and to ease the pain Mamma would take Pa's jug and measure out half a cup of liquor and sweeten it with molasses and dose me with it, and I got an everlasting taste for the awful stuff. If I knew then what I know now, I would've got up from my sickbed and knocked that liquor outa my mamma's hand." She sighed and stood up. "Still and all," she said, and a broad smile came on her face, "I got to admit that it sure cured my colic."

Miss Copey had not worked at the restaurant long before she got acquainted with Mr. Thunderbolt Calhoun. He has a watermelon farm on the bank of Shad Roe River in a section of the county called Egypt. He is so sleepy and slow he has been known as Thunderbolt ever since he was a boy; his true name is Rutherford Calhoun. He is shiftless and most of his farm work is done by a Negro hired boy named Mister. (When this boy was born his mother said, "White people claim they won't mister a Negro. Well, by God, son, they'll mister you!") Mr. Thunderbolt's fifteen-acre farm is fertile and it grows the finest Cuban Queen, Black Gipsy, and Irish Gray watermelons I have ever seen. The farm is just a sideline, however; his principal interest in life is a copper still hidden on the bank of a bayou in the river swamp. In this still he produces a vehement kind of whiskey known as tanglefoot. "I depend on watermelons to pay the taxes and feed me and my mule," he says. "The whiskey is pure profit." Experts say that his tanglefoot is as good as good Kentucky bourbon, and he claims that laziness makes it so. "You have to be patient to make good whiskey," he says, yawning, "and I'm an uncommonly patient man."

After Miss Copey began buying her whiskey from him, she went on sprees more often; his whiskey did not give her hangovers or what she called "the dismals." At least once a month, usually on a Saturday afternoon, she would leave her kitchen and walk barefooted down Main Street, singing a hymn at the top of her voice, and she seldom got below Main and Jefferson before she was under arrest. Most of the town drunks meekly paid the usual fine of seven dollars and costs or went to jail, but Miss Copey always took advantage of the question "What have you got to say for yourself?" First she would claim that the right to get drunk is guaranteed by the Constitution, and then she would accuse the judge of being a hypocrite.

"I got a right to let loose a hymn when I feel like it," she would say. "That don't harm nobody. Suppose I do make a little noise? Do they put 'em in jail for blowing the whistle at the sawmill? And anyhow, I don't drink in secret. There's nothing so low-down sorry as a man that drinks in secret. You're a secret sot, Judge Mullet, and don't try to deny it."

"I like a drop now and then, to be sure," the judge would reply, "but that don't give me the right to run up and down the highways and byways in my bare feet."

"Now you're trying to tell me there's one law for a judge and another for a railroad cook," Miss Copey would say triumphantly. "That's a hell of a way for a judge to talk."

Miss Copey had been cooking in the station restaurant about two years when a stovepipe crumpled up and fell down on her head, stunning her. It made her so angry she quit her job and threatened to sue the railroad for a thousand dollars. She settled out of court, however, when a claim agent offered her a check for seventy-five. "I haven't got the patience to fight a railroad," she said. She cashed the check, insisting on having the sum in one-dollar bills, and hurried out to Mr. Thunderbolt's to buy a Mason jar of tanglefoot. When he saw her roll of bills he said he felt they ought to celebrate. He drew some whiskey out of a charred-oak keg that had been buried in the swamp for five years, and they sat in rocking chairs on the front porch and began to drink to each other. After an hour or so, Mr. Thunderbolt told her he was a lonesome man and that he had grown mighty damned tired of Mister's cooking. He wound up by asking her to be his wife. Miss Copey broke down and sobbed. Then she said, "I'll make you a good wife, Thunderbolt. We better hurry to town before the courthouse closes. If we wait until you're sober, I'm afraid you'll change your mind." Mister drove them to Stonewall in Mr. Thunderbolt's old Ford truck. They stopped at Miss Copey's rooming house and picked up her trunk; then they went over to the courthouse and were married. Judge Mullet was surprised by the marriage but said he guessed Mr. Thunderbolt's star customer wanted to get closer to the source of supply. For a week the bride and groom went fishing in Shad Roe River in the morning, got drunk in the afternoon, and rode about the country in the Ford truck at night. Then, Saturday morning, Mrs. Copey woke up, looked out a window, and saw that the figs were ripe on the door-yard bushes; she shook her husband awake and said, "The honeymoon's over, Thunderbolt. I got to get busy and can them figs before they drop on the ground."

For a couple of months, Mrs. Copey was a model wife. That autumn I hunted squirrels practically every afternoon in the swamp that runs along Mr. Thunderbolt's farm, and I used to stop by and see her. She showed me scores of jars of watermelon-rind pickles and fig preserves she had canned and arranged on the cellar shelves. She had spaded a pit in the back yard for barbecues, and in the corncrib she had a big barrel of scuppernong grapes in ferment. She had bought four Rhode Island Red hens and four settings of eggs, and she had a yardful of biddies. She proudly told me that every night when Mr. Thunderbolt came home from the swamp, worn out after a day of squatting beside his still, he found a plate of fried chicken and a sweet-potato pie on the kitchen table waiting for him.

After a while, however, she began to get bored. "It's too damned still around here," she told me one evening. "I need some human company. Sometimes a whole day goes past and I don't get a single word out of Thunderbolt. He lived by himself so long he almost lost the use of his tongue." There is a Baptist church a half mile up the river, and one lonesome Sunday she attended a service there. She picked an unfortunate time, because there was a fight in progress in the congregation. In fact, at that period, which was the autumn of 1926, there was dissension in many rural Baptist churches in the South over the ceremony of immersion. One group believed a convert should be immersed three times face forward in the still water of a pond, and the other favored a single immersion in the running water of a river. The opposing groups were called the Trine Forwardites and the Running Riverites. Mrs. Copey became a churchgoer merely because she wanted to sing some hymns, but she soon got mixed up in this theological wrangle. The second Sunday she attended services she was sitting in a back pew when a man got up and advocated changing the name of the church from Egypt Baptist to Still Water Trine Forward Baptist. He said any sensible person knew that a calm pond was more spiritual than the troubled waters of a river. This did not seem right to Mrs. Copey; she arose and interrupted him. "Jordan wa'n't no pond," she said. "It was a running river. On that rock I stand." "That's right, sister!" exclaimed a man up front. "You hit the nail on the head." He went back and asked Mrs. Copey to come forward and sit with the Running River faction. "Why, I'll gladly do so," Mrs. Copey said. "What's this all about, anyhow?"

Presently the argument between the factions grew bitter, and Mrs. Copey arose again and suggested singing "On Jordan's Stormy Banks," a revival hymn. The leader of her faction said, "Let's march out of this church as we sing that hymn." Thereupon seven men and women marched up the aisle. Mrs. Copey got up and followed them. In the yard outside, they held a meeting and decided to organize a new church and call it the Running River One Immersion Baptist. "You can meet at my house until you locate a more suitable place," Mrs. Copey suggested. "Let's go there now and sit on the porch and do some singing. I feel like letting loose a few hymns." The Running Riverites were pleased by this suggestion. With Mrs. Copey leading, they marched down the road singing

"There Is a Green Hill Far Away." When Mr. Thunderbolt saw them heading up the lane, he was sitting on the porch, playing his harmonica. He leaped off the porch and fled to the swamp. Mrs. Copey arranged chairs on the porch and announced that her favorite hymns were "There Is a Fountain Filled with Blood," and "The Old Time Religion Is Good Enough for Me." All afternoon they sang these hymns over and over. At sundown Mrs. Copey said, "If you're a mind to, we'll meet here again next Sunday. We'll show those Trine Forwardite heathens!" Then the meeting ended. Late that night Mr. Thunderbolt came in, raging drunk. "Listen, you old hoot owl!" he shouted. "If you bring them hymn-singers to this house again, I'll leave you and never come back!" "Don't threaten me, you drunk old sinner," Mrs. Copey said. "You start threatening me, I'll pull a slat out of the bed and fracture your skull."

Next Sunday afternoon the hymn-singers held another meeting on Mrs. Copey's porch, and that night Mr. Thunderbolt did not come home at all. Monday night he was still missing. Early Tuesday morning, Mrs. Copey went down to Mister's cabin and found that he was missing too. She looked in the barn and found that the Ford truck was gone. On my way home from the swamp that afternoon I stopped by to see her, and she was sitting on the front steps, moaning. There was a carving knife in her lap. "I'll cut his black heart out," she said. "I'll put my trademark on him. The wife-deserter!" I sat down and tried to comfort her. Presently two of the hymn-singers came up the lane. "How are you this fine fall day, sister?" one called out. Mrs. Copey ran out to meet them. "You come another step closer, you old hymn-singers," she said, "and I'll throw you in the river! You've turned a man against his wife! You've broke up a happy home!" After a while we went in the house and she made some coffee. We were sitting on the back porch drinking it when Mister drove up in the Ford truck. "Hey there, Mrs. Copey!" he yelled. "They got Mr. Thunderbolt in jail down in Charleston." "Why, bless his heart," said Mrs. Copey. She ran in the house and got her hat and her purse. "Get back in that truck," she said to Mister, "and take me to him." The three of us climbed in the seat.

In Charleston, the jailer let us go in and see Mr. Thunderbolt. He was lying in his cell playing his harmonica. He was in fine spirits. He told us the hymn-singing had made him so angry he had ordered Mister to drive him to Charleston. There was a moving-picture theatre near the place they parked the truck, and Monday night he decided to go in and see a show; he had never seen a moving picture. Mary Pickford was in it, he said, and he became so absorbed in her troubles that he crouched way forward in his seat and got a cramp in his left leg. At first he tried not to notice it, but when he could bear it no longer he decided to try the old-fashioned remedy of kicking the cramp out. He got out in the aisle, held on to an end seat, and began kicking backward, like a mule that is being shod. All the time he kept his eyes on the picture. "I didn't want to miss a thing," he said. People began to yell for him to sit down, he said, and an usher hurried up and told him to stop kicking. "Please go away and don't bother me," he told the usher. The usher got the manager and together they grabbed him. "I couldn't properly defend myself," Mr. Thunderbolt told us. "I couldn't fight them two busy-bodies and keep up with what was happening to Miss Mary Pickford and kick the cramp out of my foot all at the same time. It was more than any one human could do." The usher and the manager hustled him to the lobby, and when he realized he wouldn't be able to see the rest of the picture, he put all his attention on self-defense and knocked the two men flat. Then a policeman came and arrested him for disorderly conduct.

"Why, it's a damned outrage, honey," Mrs. Copey said. "I'm going right down and bail you out."

"Just a minute," Mr. Thunderbolt said. "You're not going to bail me out until I get your solemn promise to leave them hymn-singers alone. It's real quiet in this jail."

"Oh, hell, Thunderbolt!" said Mrs. Copey. "I threw them hymn-singers in the river before I left home."

[Joseph Mitchell, *McSorley's Wonderful Saloon* (New York: Duell, Sloan and Pearce, 1943). Reprinted by permission of Harold Ober Associates Incorporated. First published in *The New Yorker*. Copyright © 1940 by Joseph Mitchell. Copyright renewed. Mitchell, born in 1908 in Robeson County, graduated from The University of North Carolina at Chapel Hill. Since 1938, he has been a writer on the staff of the *New Yorker*.]

Algebra for Football Players

[*Wilbur Hare, gentle and willing to please if somewhat thick-headed, arrived at King City College because his girl wished to*

marry only a college man. Months passed before he learned that,
instead of a scholarship student, he has been employed as a
groundskeeper.]

Come next morning, I seen whole bunches of boys and girls
going into this one big building, and I figured them that had come
to the college before, and knowed where to go, was leading the
others. I got in with a bunch, which it happened they was a lot of
the football boys. We kind of shuffled into this big room and, first
thing, I seen Professor Litman. I grinned and flang my hand up at
him, and he come over to where I was setting.

"Good morning, Wilbur," he said. Then he told me he was
glad to see me, but he didn't think I was on his rooster.

Well, I knowed that, and I told him I hadn't never been, best I
could remember. Professor, he turnt his back towards me a minute,
and then he kind of looked around and said I could audit if I
wanted to. Whatever that was, I didn't feel no need to do it right
then; so I just set there in back of the room and listened.

It taken up right smart of a time for Professor Litman to call
out everbody's names and shift them around to where he had a notion they ought to set. He never called out my name, I reckon because of we was old friends and had spoke; and I was already set,
anyhow.

All the football boys, and me, too, was getting kind of restless,
when Professor Litman took and written something across the
blackboard. It didn't make no sense at all, on account he had got
his letters and numbers all mixed up. I guessed how come he done
that was, he was maybe flustered the first day; but no, it come about
he meant to. "Gentlemen," he commenced, "our subject is algebra.
I realize this is a special class for football men, so just to review
what you should have learned years ago, I have written a simple,
elementary algebraic equation on the blackboard." What he had
wrote was $X - 3 = 22$. "Now," he said, "who can tell me the value of
X?"

Nobody said nothing at all, and I seen Professor Litman was
upset and wanted to know real bad what was the value of that X,
which it didn't seem to be worth much to me. He asked again, and
nobody said nothing again.

The professor taken a new start. "Gentlemen," he said, "let's
suppose X is something hidden in a bag." He drawed what looked

like a bag around it. "Now, X is unknown. In the bag we have a certain unknown number of things, represented by X. We don't know how many there are, but if we take away 3, we have 22. How many were in the bag before we removed three? In other words, what is the value of X?"

Right then a bell rung, and everbody jumped up and run like they was going to a fire! I come out kind of at the tail end. . . .

There weren't nothing else to do but go, which I went; but all day long it worried me about how much Professor Litman was fretted over the value of that X. By the time it come night, I knowed what I was going to do, and I done it.

All them football boys was staying at the same building, so I run over there and got together ever one which was in Professor Litman's class, even them as had went to bed.

"Boys," I told them, "I have knowed Professor Litman for some while, and there ain't hardly nobody nicer. You all seen he was plumb worried, because of he don't know how much is the value of that X, or maybe had forgot. Now, if we don't want him frazzling hisself to death, we best do all we can to find out for him."

There weren't no doubt they all wanted a go at it. First thing we done was send one boy over to the College Shoppe for some big paper bags. He brang back near onto thirty, and we given them out, one bag each. Two was left over, and I taken them back next day.

We mighty near never decided on what to put inside them bags. One boy said the professor had told us eggs was in the one he drawed; but everbody else, they said no, what was in it was that X. Then it come out X had to be unknowed, being the professor had said it was. Well, that weren't easy to figure out, on account of anybody would know what it was he put in a bag, unless he didn't have no sense at all. What we done in the end was, each boy taken a bag out and filled it up, secret like, with whatever he had a notion to. Then, when we was all back, everbody swapped them full bags around, till nobody had no idea what was in which one.

Next it come up, how was we going to count out three from each bag, without everybody finding out what was being took away? Well, that weren't too hard, being there was a lot of us thinking on it. We voted, and what won was to turn off the light; and then we all taken out three from his bag, whatever was in it.

Now, there weren't no way at all to find out nothing more, till we turnt the light back on, which I done it, being I was kind of the leader. Well, we opened up all them bags and begun to hunt for what there was just 22 of left in a bag. It weren't apples, and it weren't rocks, and it weren't nothing at all, till we come to next to the very last bag in the bunch. Dog it, that was it, and it was raw hot dogs! 22 raw hot dogs, smack dab on the nose!

Some boys was of a mind there weren't nothing else at all to it, but I said no, the professor wanted us to find out how much the value of it was.

"Dollar and sixty-five cents," one boy said, which he was the one that had put in the hot dogs, and knowed for sure.

"Professor Litman, he'll be plumb glad to learn that," I said, wondering who would ever of thought X would turn out it was hot dogs?

Most everbody was all for going out and making a fire to cook the X, but it had got late; and just then the coach come in, which he run us all off to bed.

Next morning . . . I didn't have me no time to fool around with going to a class, but I taken that bag of hot dogs by to Professor Litman. "Well, we found what it was," I told him, and I given him the bag.

"What's this?" Professor Litman asked me.

"This here's a bag full of hot dogs, which it come out they was that X you was worried so about in the bag you drawed."

Professor Litman, he looked in the bag, and then he given a look towards the blackboard, where that $X - 3 = 22$ was still wrote on it. All of a sudden, he kind of grinned. "How many hot dogs are there in the bag?" he asked me, and I seen he was fishing for something.

"After we taken out 3, there was 22," I told him. "But that ain't the point. What you wanted me and them football boys to find out was, what was the value of the X, which it happened it was hot dogs."

"And what was the value?" Professor Litman asked me.

"It was a dollar and sixty-five cent," I told him.

Professor Litman, he set down. "Wilbur, my boy, how in the world did you figure this out?"

I told him everything we had did, and what he said next made me feel real good. "Wilbur," he said, "mathematical history was made last night!"

And I reckon it was, if it learnt something to anybody as smart as Professor Litman. I told him I sure wished I could stay for his class, in case he got stumped again. . . .

[Dave Morrah, *Me and the Liberal Arts* (New York: Doubleday & Company, 1962). A native of Greensboro, Morrah graduated from North Carolina State University at Raleigh in 1935, and is currently public relations officer for Guilford College. He made his mark in comic mock-German. A second humorous novel is *Our Honor the Mayor* (1964).]

Lightning Rods

[*This is one episode in the Cape Fear County odyssey of narrator Curley Treadaway, banjo-picking deserter from Fort Bragg, and Mr. Mordecai Jones, the Flim-Flam Man. The sole purpose throughout their wanderings is to outwit those so gullible and greedy that they are entitled to a fleecing.*]

Mr. Jones put on his Stetson hat, straightened his shoestring tie and brushed the rumples out of his black suit. A jay flew over him and fussed on the limb above his head. He just whistled back at it, a few bars of some symphony or other, his oyster eyes taking in the situation good. It was what he called one of the vissisitudes of life. Of course, it had me stumped a good deal more than I let on at the time.

What he did next was a surprise in this world. Without so much as a go-to-hell, he took the battery out of the truck, grunting as he unloosed the connections. Then he gathered up a coil of tangled wires he'd picked up back there at Lovick's store and threw it under the tarp with the forty-rod. I watched him fasten the wires to the battery, leaving two ends loose and dangling. It made the most ungodly infernal-looking contraption I ever did see, the complicated way he twisted them old electric wires.

When he finished he took out the beat-up gas can from the cab and says, "We're in business, lad. Keep in touch. I may have something for you." Winking, you know.

He might of been in business, but I sure God wasn't. Of course I kept still and waited. I didn't want to show my ignorance.

The Flim-Flam Man commenced walking toward the road,

humping his long legs, me lugging the wired-up battery at his heels and sweating like a mule, staying close to his shadow.

"Where we heading now?"

"That big white house on the hill there," he says, casual-like. "We'll see if they can advance us a little gas money or some gas, one. I wouldn't be surprised if they can."

Thinks I, fooling ignorant rednecks and greedy snuff-pushers is one thing, but that white house on the hill is a horse of a different complexion. People that live in big places like that, with indoor plumbing and all—why, they don't turn up their backsides every time somebody says pick up the soap. They ain't that easy fleeced. High muckety-mucks has more gumption.

"You watch now, Curley," my pardner says. "I'm going to show you how nobody can resist a real bargain these days. You can call it Mordecai Jones's Second Law." . . .

I had to admire Mr. R. J.'s house. It set back from the road a good piece, with a green lawn in between. It had two white columns and a little balcony that looked pretty and useless—except for maybe standing on to admire the scattering of magnolia trees. They was still blooming enough to scent the air, along with the Confederate jasmine. Around back I saw a walnut tree and two or three big papershell pecans, with a fenced-in garden behind them and a white-painted pumphouse beside it.

First news I knew, here come a brindle bulldog tearing out from under the piazza steps. I almost broke and run, would of if my foot hadn't got hung up in them all-fired octopus wires.

But not Mr. Jones. He just stood his ground talking to the son-of-a-bitching dog as polite as you please, calling it by name. He had a nice manner with mean dogs. Gentle.

Directly, this woman calls out, "You, Tut," and come out on the veranda. She was a little old lady, and her white hair was done up in a bun that was scraggling loose. She put me in mind of poor Aunt Doshie, flapping her apron at that mean-looking Tut, only my aunt never had her high-class air nor lived in such a high-toned house.

"That dog bite, ma'am?"

"Only strangers sometimes," she says.

I tried to look awful familiar, I tell you. Mr. Jones patted Tut's head, but I'd as soon pat a diamondback rattler, sooner.

"A fine animal," he goes on. "I use to own one like him myself, not purebred though like Tut here, although his sire was Solomon the Second. I named him Daniel Webster."

Then he asked if Mr. R. J. was home, which he knew already he wasn't. She said she wasn't expecting him in till noon.

"Could I see R. J., Jr., then?" he asks.

Mrs. MacDougald said she was the only one home. She asked if there was something she could do for us.

"I'm right sorry none of the menfolks are in," Mr. Jones says. "It's rather urgent that I see Mr. McDougald this morning." He took out one of his little white cards and handed it to her, standing by the bottom step. I saw that it said he was Mr. Oppenheimer, electrical engineer.

Mrs. McDougald held the card up close to her glasses, then looked down at us, puzzled.

Mr. Jones nodded at me. "Mr. Wigglesworth," he says, "my assistant."

By now the battery was feeling like a hunk of lead.

Mr. Jones went on then, telling how he worked for the Acme Lightning Rod Company that sold the rods for her house. "I'm making a survey of this district, ma'am, to see if any of our rods need recharging."

I looked up at the rods, and they was a pretty special collection. You could see a whole mess of them spear-looking things sticking up above the roof line. The housetop fairly bristled with spears with funny knobs and doodads on them.

"How long you all owned this system of rods, ma'am?"

"Six—no, seven years, come next Fourth of July."

Mr. Jones, he took out his little black book, licking his thumb and flipping the pages. "Just as I thought," he says. "Even an expensive system like yours needs to be recharged every five years, Mrs. MacDougald. After that, those rods aren't good for anything but ornaments. They wouldn't repel a speck of lightning, let alone a good-sized bolt."

He motioned to me to set the wired battery down by a green boxwood, where one of the rods was grounded.

"Just one wire, Wigglesworth, please."

I set the contraption down, glad to get shut of it. Then I hitched the end of a wire to the rod. Mind you, I had to turn my head, I was so near to busting a gut laughing. The very idea of having a set of lightning rods *recharged!*

"That man sold those rods to R. J. never mentioned anything about recharging. He didn't say they would ever run down."

Mr. Jones looked kind of sheepish and hangdog. He went on to explain how he knew it, and the company had found it out too. Said they had to let that salesman go when they found out he was dishonest and misrepresented their product, even though he was a crackerjack salesman. They didn't want a blot on the company's good reputation. And he went on apologizing for the salesman's dishonesty.

"I don't know now, my son—"

But Mr. Jones never let up. He never allowed the old lady to get a word in edgewise. He went on holding forth on how it stood to reason those rods would get stale after five years and lose their full potency. He used some words that would of choked a billy goat, going on about neutrons and proteins and such like. Said the electrical juices in lightning rods need to be swapped about ever so often for maximum protection, and so on and so forth. It was enough to convince me, almost. He was that eloquent when he got to cutting loose with what he called his polysyllables.

"Look here, Mrs. McDougald," he says. "I've not seen this battery since my assistant hooked it up, but I'd be willing to bet the water in the battery is not acting at all. Not one bit. It ought to be sending up bubbles now—if your rods are sufficiently charged, that is."

I unscrewed the cap, and sure enough there wasn't any bubbles. Not even one teentsy bubble.

Mrs. McDougald, she walked down the steps slow and peered into the little round hole, squinting her eyes. She was so close I could smell the snuff on her breath. Old Tut, he come over and sniffed some too, looking at me suspicious-like, not wagging his tail a fraction.

"I'd wager there's not a sign of photosynthetic activity," Mr. Jones says.

I'd wager the same, thinks I.

Mrs. McDougald shook her head, and I swear it was right pathetic. "I declare, Mr. Oppenheimer, I didn't see a sign of any bubble."

Talk about being downright *gullible,* as Mr. Jones calls it. People ought not to be so ignorant. They purely *deserve* to be flim-flammed.

Mr. Jones, he give a little snort and slapped the rod. "I'm not surprised at all. What'd I tell you just now? Ma'am, these rods are deader than a coffin nail."

"I declare to goodness. I don't know—"

"Dangerous. It's right dangerous to depend on them any longer." He went on to tell how just last week lightning struck a house in Brownsville with a set of rods like hers, only newer by a couple of years. "It burned out two radios, the TV set and stove, and a pair of skates in the garage. It even burst a set of false teeth in a tumbler setting on top of the commode."

"My stars above!"

"I tell you what, ma'am. Our usual fee for recharging an expensive and complicated set like yours is ten dollars. But since our agent misrepresented our product to Mr. R. J. in the first place, I'm authorized by the president of Acme Incorporated to give you good folk a reactivating job for five dollars."

Then he says to me, "Mike, boy, hook up that other wire."

I did and when I looked up he caught my eye and winked. I screwed the cap back on the battery.

The Flim-Flam Man looked at his gold watch, which was bigger than a biscuit, and checked the time. "That'll be five minutes to each ground unit."

"I don't know if I've got five dollars in the house," Mrs. McDougald says, going back up the steps.

"You're getting a real bargain here, ma'am. And I can see a delicate lady like you has a mortal fear of lightning."

I moved the contraption to the next rod and fastened the wires. I was having to hold myself in to keep from hooting out loud.

Mrs. McDougald, she stayed in the house the longest kind of time. So long I was in a sweat that she might of got wise and was phoning the Law. When she came out I was hooking to the last rod, at the back of the house, and Mr. Jones was testing the recharged rods with a gadget he'd took out of his pocket. It was an air pressure gauge, for God's sake, and it broke to boot.

All the sweating and worrying I did was misspent. Because the upshot was she'd made us a pitcher of ice-cold lemonade and I saw she'd even took the time to powder her face and take off her apron. She'd even cleaned the specks off her gold-rimmed glasses and spit out her snuff.

Mr. Jones pocketed the five dollars and we both fell over ourselves thanking her kindly for the lemonade. It sure tasted good after lugging the battery around in the hot sun. But to tell the truth, it didn't go down right somehow, that lemonade. It just didn't set right at all.

Then she had to go and give us two gallons of gas out of the tank beside the garage and tell us how she'd appreciated all we'd done. I never looked her in the eyes, and I never hope to, because we didn't naturally *need* the five dollars nohow, only the gas. I reckon the Flim-Flam Man did it just to see if it could be done, or maybe just to keep from getting bored. . . .

I hoped she learned a lesson from being stung thataway. Maybe she did. You can never tell.

[Guy Owen, *The Ballad of the Flim-Flam Man* (New York: Macmillan Company, 1965). Copyright © Guy Owen. Reprinted by permission of Macmillan Publishing Co., Inc. Born in 1925 near Clarkton in Bladen County (the Cape Fear County of his novels), Owen received three degrees from The University of North Carolina at Chapel Hill. Now professor of English at North Carolina State University at Raleigh, he has written several books of poetry and four novels, the last being *The Flim-Flam Man and the Apprentice Grifter* (1972).]

Goings-On in John M. Virden County

[*In the tobacco-growing country of the northern Piedmont just south of the Virginia state line, Henderson Starling's large family, including sons Jimroe and Fairfax (the narrator), harvested a bumper crop in the summer of 1916. Among those participating in the comic events of that long-ago summer were Grandpa and*

*Grandma, Cousin Tree Poindexter, and the villainous Indian half-
breed Jess Sixkiller.*]

Papa claimed he had gone to school just one day in his life.
"The first time I went was on a Friday," he would say. "Then I went
back on Saturday and nobody was in the schoolhouse, so I came
home and told Pap that school was out—and I never went back
again."

It gave Mama the whiffets to hear him tell me things like that.

Tree and Papa had worked together on the railroad over on the
Virginia side of the river when they were young, and Papa had
funny tales that were still good to us even after years of telling. This
time Papa thought of one we hadn't heard before.

"Well, sir, one night T. finally got a bellyful of that railroad.
You know that high trestle over Gravitt's Creek? In the middle, it's
a drop of about fifty feet to the bottom."

Tree began to shake, laughing, as soon as Papa said that,
keeping his eyes on Papa like he wanted to make sure he told it
straight and was half afraid that he would.

"Old Tree was just prancing, so full of corn juice that his back
teeth were afloat, when 'The Creeper' came chugging up behind
him. He could see her headlight in the gorge and hear the engine
bell, and he went up on his tippytoes, flying over the crossties as fast
as he could go.

" 'The Creeper' got so close that old Tree had to give up, she
was gaining so fast. He dropped down between two crossties and
hung on for dear life."

Tree beat himself on the thighs like he couldn't stand to hear
another word, and tears rolled down his cheeks. We couldn't see
that it was all that funny but we laughed at Tree's antics, except for
Jimroe, who looked from Tree to Papa as if he saw something
nobody else could see. It was one of his ways. He understood funny
things, all right, but he was anxious to look behind the laughing
and see what else was there.

"Poor old Tree hung there till his fingers like to have popped
off," Papa said. "When that freight train got past he tried to pull
up, but he couldn't make it. He was stuck between ties and had to
hang there or give up the ghost. His arms most came out of his

sockets, but he hung and he hung and managed to last till daylight.

"And then, when it was light enough to see"—Papa grinned at us—"why, then old Tree looked down, and after all his suffering saw his toes hanging just about eight inches off the ground. He'd come that close to making the bank."

We laughed over that, and when he got a little pause Papa said, "*Ah-whoo!* And that ain't all. It made Tree so mad that he hung there till dinnertime that day, just out of spite."

A one-lung gasoline engine chugged behind the store and we knew that Biscoe was out grinding corn for somebody. Tree took his jug on the porch, where a line of men sat propped against the wall with their heels hooked in chair rungs. One of them yelled, "Evening, Pinedexter. Whatcha know good?"

"Well, we just saw Wash Strawn have a mighty close call."

The men turned their heads all at once, grinning, to see what lie Tree had thought up.

"Why, how's that, T.?"

"You know he's always said he'd hang himself if he had just one more youngun, and this new baby at his house had mighty near drove him crazy."

"Yeah."

"Well, we passed his place just now and Wash was poling up from the barn with a rope, shaking his head and saying he couldn't bear to take his own life. When Fax asked him how come him to change his mind, you know what that scannel said?"

"No telling."

"Why, he said, 'Boys, it come over me in a flash. I got to thinking, hi God—what if I was about to hang the wrong man?' "

One of my cousins broke in, "Grandpa, how come you to shoot them Yankee spies at sunrise?"

"Why, to keep from giving the sons of bitches their breakfast, that's why!" He looked at the boy like he must have been wrong in the head. The old man told a new story:

"Didn't you boys know Ginral Lee hisownself come up to me at the battle of Sharpsburg in Maryland, where Yank bodies were piled hip-deep around me? He rode up on that dapple-gray horse of his and said, 'Hold on there, Sergeant Starling, they ain't nothin but Yankees. After all's said and done they're human beings. Think of the widders and orphans you've made this day. Stop it, I say. You've spilled blood enough.' "

I tried to get Grandpa talking about the war again, but he wouldn't say much, 'Ah, Buddy, dammitall, I've lied so much about the War that I've clean forgot what really happened."

He finally cleared his throat and rumbled a little and said, "I can tell you one thing I ain't lied about—when I was in that Army, way back yonder, they put some kind of stuff in our eats to keep us from hankering so after women. Saltpeter, I think it was. Oh, Lordy. That's been fifty years ago and more. Long time. You know, Buddy—I think that damn stuff is beginning to take effect on me." He cackled.

After a while he said, "Ah, me. Youth. By God, if I had teeth I'd run out and bite me a damn woman this evening."

The next thing we knew he [Papa] was on the church steps, talking to a knot of men. Papa said he was going to preach a little sermon. He spouted a lot of Bible talk, and lit in on Jess Sixkiller for being a bully and a moral coward, and once pointed his finger at Jess and told him the Lord would have his way with him. Jess glowered and worked his hands together at his sides. People cheered, but not those near Jess. Others came from around the grove. Mama froze when she saw what was going on. I thought she might yank him down by the shirttail, but she didn't dare. Papa harangued the hide off Jess, then came down. Jess stopped him. The Indian was as red in the face as a turkey gobbler. "I heard you out, Hence. Now git ready. I'm agoing to whale you."

"I just gave you the gospel, Jess, and I'm not half your size. How come you want to fight?"

"It's too late for begging, Hence. You're going to get it."

My brothers moved in close. "Step back," Papa said to them. "I'm twisting this monkey's tail." Then he turned to Jess. "Well, then, Mister Sixkiller, could I have time to say a prayer before I take my thrashing?"

Jess began to look uncertain. "Yeah, pray if you want, but it's got to be short and sweet."

Papa took off his hat and some of the other men did, too, even

Judge Bucktarrel. Papa bowed his head and began to call in a voice I had never heard him use before. There was something laughable about it, but nobody smiled.

"Oh, Lord God Almighty, Thou knowest that when I killed Shep Rouse and Cecil Houck I fought in self-defense. And when I cut out the black heart of Will Pyne and strewed the ground with his blood, that I did the deed with agony of soul—but Lord, Thou knowest that he drove me to it."

Men looked at each other and Jess gaped at Papa. Nobody looked like they even guessed Papa was lying about his killings.

"And Lord, lay Thy hand upon the sons of my loins and bid them stand aside and commit no lynching, for Thou knowest that Thee and Thy servant, Henderson Starling, will punish this wayward youth.

"Now, Lord, I call upon Thee to care for the soul of this poor wretch who has assailed me on Thy holy ground, hard by Thy tabernacle—and who is about to compel me to lay him in his coffin. Lord, care for the widow and orphan children and his poor old ma when he is gone. In the name of our Redeemer, Amen."

Jess was studying the ground. Somebody went tipping away in the sandy path behind. It was Pembroke [Sixkiller], getting along from there.

Papa unfolded the long blade of his knife and whetted it on the sole of his shoe, and as he straightened, broke out singing in a high voice:

"Ye living man come view the ground
Where ye must shortly lie."

There was a scuffle in the crowd, and when Papa turned to find Jess, the big Indian was dusting along the road, trying to gain on Pembroke. He shouldered among the hitched horses and mules, hopped into his saddle and left. Mama looked at Papa and began crying, like relief was flowing in her. The crowd broke up in a laugh, and people beat Papa's back and said he was a good man and a brave one, but there was some nervousness because there was no telling what Jess would do next.

The big boys were so proud of Papa that I thought they would stay all night, taking it in. But I was scared and wanted to leave. I knew that Jess wouldn't rest until he got even with Papa, and with Jimroe too. I wanted to tell Tree about it.

The crowd parted a little and Tree spoke to Papa. "I was ready to help you out. My old rifle's there in the carpet. He was as good as covered all the time."

"I wish you'd let me know, now, Tree. Me and the Lord felt mighty lonesome before that big hooligan."

They tagged off with the other little girls but were soon back, deviling Grandpa to tell them tales. Grandpa loved children so that he couldn't keep his hands off them, and they all got in his lap and he told them outlandish yarns. Grandma, who was his second wife, got watery eyes watching him entertain the children. "He always loved the least ones so. He'll not be with us much longer, but it'll be the children he'll hate most to leave behind. You know, he was away over fifty when I married him, and we had five quick babies in a row—just blip, blip, blip. And he always took a baby to bed with him every night for years and years. When we finally ran out of babies he had trouble. He couldn't sleep of a night until I poured a pitcher of warm water over him." We laughed with Aunt Lumbie and went back to work. Grandpa didn't even look up from his story-telling.

"I'm talking about back there when men were men and women were glad of it," Grandpa said. "I remember when Sug Kinnamon was eighty-three years old and her old man was eighty-six, and she went down to Doc Kiger and told him the old man was losing interest in her and wouldn't play sex no more, and said she needed medicine to cure him. Doc asked her when she first noticed it and she said, 'Why, the first time was last night—but it happened again this morning.' "

"Goddlemighty," Jess said. "Here it is Saturday evening and I've got to go to town and get drunk, and I sure do dread it."

"Pshaw, if it was me I'd go to Tootsy's instead," Grandpa said. "You don't see many of them tasty quarter-ton women these days."

Tree guyed Jess about the time he had gone on a spree to Richmond, Virginia, and spent two or three weeks in cat houses up there. "It's a wonder to me a ragged-tailed Indian tobacco farmer could afford that."

"Hell," Jess said. "It never cost me a dime. We was all kinfolks."

"Don't mention home to me," Tree said. "If you ask me, the three most overrated things in this world are home cooking, home loving, and the State of Virginia."

"Well, Roller's our best hound. Last night something got into the hen house and raised a fuss and Papa went out with his shotgun to see about it. He had on his nightshirt, and was stooped down on hands and knees by the hen house when old Roller came up behind him and touched him just right with his cold nose. Papa had his finger on the trigger, so I've been picking chickens all morning."

"Fax, where on earth have you been? Do your folks know you played hooky?"
"Yes'm. I had to take the cow. . . ."
She [the teacher] understood me, but wouldn't stop. "Couldn't your papa have done it?"
Jimroe laughed. "Hell, Miss Cassie. Papa ain't even registered."
Miss Cassie didn't laugh with us, and Jimroe had to stay in school until dark, and she never said a word to him.

Tree told his worn-out story about bullbat time—about how gentlemen never drank until dusk, when the nighthawks were flying. Tree claimed he had known a man who'd been such a hard drinker that he had caught a bullbat and tamed him, and carried him in his shirt so that he could turn him loose any time of the day or night, and then take a drink and still be a gentleman. Grandpa popped Tree on the back and asked for another sip.

Tree still felt like joking. "It puts me in mind of the fellow who was running for President of Hell," he said. "He run on the platform of cutting down the heat and establishing water. Who in Hell wouldn't be for that?"
Papa and the Judge laughed enough to be polite, almost enough so that Tree wouldn't know they'd heard it so many times—but Grandpa carried on like he'd never heard it at all, and they had a time stopping him laughing.
"I take it to heart," Grandpa said, "seeing's I'm damn soon going to be down there, trying it out."
[Burke Davis, *The Summer Land* (New York: Random House, 1965). From

college Burke Davis, born in Durham in 1913, drifted into journalism. His many books include biographies, Revolutionary and Civil War histories, and four novels. Since 1960 he has been on the staff of Colonial Williamsburg, Inc.]

Harry Golden

The middle years of the twentieth century brought a roly-poly, cigar-smoking, controversial humorist who made us laugh at our racial troubles. In addition to his Golden Vertical Negro Plan, Harry Golden proposed other outlandish schemes to lighten the pressures. Beneath the chuckling was a serious campaign against pomposity and pretense, against the denial of civil rights, against prejudices of any sort. In his autobiography The Right Time *(1969), he wrote: "I will always believe that if Galileo had used humor, the Inquisition and the Popes would have let him alone." Golden was born in 1902 on the lower East Side of New York, son of an Austrian immigrant. In 1941 he settled in Charlotte, founded his own monthly newspaper* The Carolina Israelite, *and later hit the best-seller lists with his first book,* Only in America.

The Golden Vertical Negro Plan

It is only when the Negro "sets" that the fur begins to fly.

Now, since we are not even thinking about restoring *VERTICAL SEGREGATION*, I think my plan would not only comply with the Supreme Court decisions, but would maintain "sitting-down" segregation. Now here is the *GOLDEN VERTICAL NEGRO PLAN*. Instead of all those complicated proposals, all the next session [of the North Carolina Legislature] needs to do is pass one small amendment which would provide *only* desks in all the public schools of our state—*no seats.*

The desks should be those standing-up jobs, like the old-fashioned bookkeeping desk. Since no one in the South pays the slightest attention to a *VERTICAL NEGRO*, this will completely solve our problem. And it is not such a terrible inconvenience for young people to stand up during their classroom studies. In fact, this may be a blessing in disguise. They are not learning to read sitting down, anyway; maybe standing up will help. This will save more millions of dollars in the cost of our remedial English course when the kids enter college. In whatever direction you look with the *GOLDEN VERTICAL NEGRO PLAN*, you save millions of dollars, to say nothing of eliminating forever any danger to our public education system upon which rests the destiny, hopes, and happiness of this society.

[Harry Golden, *Only in America* (New York: World Publishing Company, 1958).]

It's the Spirit That Counts

I do not want to lose any speaking assignments and so I promise that this will never happen again, but I have to tell you of a terrible tragedy on one of my speaking engagements last year in a South Carolina city.

It was a small literary group, and I had been asked to review a book. I was introduced, and they provided me with a table and a chair. I carry a zipper brief case for my papers, etc. Since I was reviewing a book, I wanted to take out a copy of the volume, and keep it in front of me as I spoke. Everything was quiet. I sat there, and took my brief case and zipped open the zipper, when lo and behold a pint bottle of whiskey pops out. I had forgotten all about it.

Earlier in the week I had developed a very dry throat and someone suggested that I try whiskey, and I had forgotten all about it. The bottle actually bounced on that mahogany table, and you have no idea the noise it made in the schoolroom. I made a dive for it just as it was ready to fall on the concrete floor and luckily I caught it.

The audience meanwhile was in hysterics. Men and women were rolling in the aisles laughing and some of the women were running out toward the ladies' room. Meanwhile I had sort of collected myself, put the book out, and the bottle back in the zipper case, and I sat there, trying to be as nonchalant as possible. I went on with my lecture telling the folks about Professor Harry Overstreet and *The Mature Mind*, but it was no go. Every few minutes someone would burst out laughing; then everybody would laugh; and I had to laugh, too.

As I was getting into my car to leave, I heard folks laughing down the street, and through the night. Oddly enough, this meeting has resulted in more lasting friendships than any other in which I have participated. The folks write to me from time to time and they are nearly all regular subscribers [to Golden's newspaper *The Carolina Israelite*].

From the angle of "interfaith," the meeting was a tremendous success.

[Harry Golden, *Only in America* (New York: World Publishing Company, 1958).]

Ginger Rogers and Napoleon

One of the great series of newspaper stories of all time is the manner in which the Paris press handled the escape of Napoleon Bonaparte from Elba. I have capsuled the time into a few days, but the headlines are substantially true.

First day: The monster has escaped.

Second day: The criminal is laying waste to the countryside.

Third day: The dictator is on his way to Paris.

Fourth day: Bonaparte is at the gates of the city.

Fifth day: All France rejoices as our glorious Emperor Napoleon makes a triumphant entry into Paris.

Now we come to Ginger Rogers.

The merchants of Charlotte spent a lot of money and effort on the annual Thanksgiving Day parade. It was a worthy event, a sort of R. H. Macy parade in miniature, and great fun for the children. Each year a famous personality is engaged to attract the thousands of people in the surrounding rural and textile mill communities. One year it was Hopalong Cassidy, another year it was Fulton Lewis, Jr., and this year it was Ginger Rogers.

But at the last moment, Miss Rogers canceled the date and left the managers of the parade without the name attraction (it was a success anyway).

Here is how the Charlotte press handled the Ginger Rogers project (I have again capsuled the time into a few days, but, as in the case of Emperor Napoleon, the Ginger Rogers headlines are substantially accurate).

First day: Ginger Rogers, gorgeous star of stage and screen, will be our guest this year.

Second day: The delightful Ginger Rogers, dancing partner of Fred Astaire, tells the secrets of her beauty.

Third day: Ginger Rogers, Oscar-winning screen star, will also lead the parade.

Fourth day: Ginger Rogers, stage, screen, and TV star, has agreed to sign all autographs.

Fifth day: Ginger Rogers, 54-year-old former motion-picture actress, has canceled her appearance in Charlotte.

[Harry Golden, *For 2¢ Plain* (New York: World Publishing Company, 1959).]

One Hundred Years of the American Novel

1856:—"She has canceled all her social engagements."
1880:—"She is in an interesting condition."
1895:—"She is in a delicate condition."
1910:—"She is knitting little booties."
1920:—"She is in a family way."
1935:—"She is expecting."
1956:—"She's pregnant."

[Harry Golden, *For 2¢ Plain* (New York: World Publishing Company, 1959).]

The Secret of Interfaith Work

In 1943 the national office of the National Conference of Christians and Jews asked me to help in the formation of a chapter in Charlotte.

I immediately enlisted the services of two very charming ladies—a Presbyterian, let's call her Mrs. G., who had also been president of a local Woman's Club, and Mrs. Minnie R., a Jewish woman of dedication and wisdom. I gave them the printed material and further briefed them on the work and the value of the organization and I furnished each with a list of fifty prospects, twenty-five Christians and twenty-five Jews.

At the end of the first week, Mrs. G. had nine applications and five-dollar checks, and Minnie had two. At the end of the second week Mrs. G. brought me fourteen and Mrs. R. three. I knew that Minnie was a very hard worker and I figured that it must be in the method of approach. So I asked Mrs. G. to tell us how she achieved this success.

Mrs. G. told us, "I go to see my prospect. I say to him that we are trying to organize a local chapter of a famous national organization which had been founded by Chief Justice Charles Evans Hughes and that this National Conference of Christians would be a good thing for Charlotte and—"

At this point I interrupted my co-chairlady: "Mrs. G., the name of this organization is the National Conference of Christians *and Jews.*"

Mrs. G. looked at me very innocently and said, "I know that, Mr. Golden, but I can get more applications the way I do it."

[Harry Golden, *Enjoy, Enjoy!* (New York: World Publishing Company, 1960).]

Summing It Up

One of the best political speeches I've ever heard came from a Southerner running for a county office. He said, "Remember the symbol of the Republican Party. It is the elephant, the giant that stomps through the jungle clumping little animals underfoot and swinging its weight around. But the symbol of the Democrats is the little mule, the same blessed animal our Saviour rode in Jerusalem two thousand years ago."

[Harry Golden, *Enjoy, Enjoy!* (New York: World Publishing Company, 1960).]

The Trouble with Women

Aside from the fact that they are not philosophers, what is the trouble with women?

Number one: women are possessed of this terrible compulsion to move furniture about. There is no end to the myriad number of mathematical arrangements of the furniture. You can leave the house one morning, off to the shop, to bring home the goodies for the wife and kids, and when you return that night you wouldn't recognize the place. You are reduced to a form of blindness, groping your way around what should be your own familiar home. But this is getting off easy.

Number Two: no man has yet found the wife or secretary who is able to make the adjustment to either air conditioning or central heating. On the hottest day of the summer, you can return to the office after lunch to find the staff sitting there clothed in babushkas, shawls, and sweaters, teeth chattering and knees blue. It seems the air conditioner produces a draft. And in the winter they will burn you out of the place. They seem never able to understand that moving the thermostat up one degree will ignite the oil burner. Ah, no! They move it up twenty degrees and, to boot, will insist it does not work properly, that it's likely to explode.

Number three: no man does right by a woman at a party. If it is not asking for that extra drink which enrages and disgraces them, then it is putting salt on your salad before tasting it. Coming home from a party with a woman is worse than having the boss put you on the carpet for sheer negligence.

I remember an old *Saturday Evening Post* cartoon where the husband about to depart the party looks at his wife and remarks, "From your expression I can tell I had a wonderful time."

[Harry Golden, *You're Entitle'* (New York: World Publishing Company, 1962).]

The Car Salesman

Car salesmen are the last true believers in the powers of hocus-pocus.

They are men loaded with secrets and they keep these secrets under their blotters on their desks. There is no mystery about how much a brand-new car costs since such statistics are prominently displayed. It's what the agency will offer you for your old car that's the great secret. It's the trade-in value that sets the gears of secret signs and signals grinding.

The salesman and the agency appraiser look over your old car with a more careful scrutiny than you give the new one. You think they are trying to evaluate the old wreck. But you are wrong. They are indulging in mental telepathy. They are trying to communicate with each other on how much they think you intend to spend.

You walk back into the office with the salesman, who adds the cost of white-wall tires, radio, and sun visors, and then he takes a deep breath, lifts up that blotter, and says, "We can give you eighty dollars on the old car." He watches your face. If your expression doesn't change, he lifts the blotter up higher, looks around to see that no one is listening, and whispers, "Make it one hundred dollars." If you say something to the effect that the dealer on the other side of town offered more, he peeps once again under the blotter, this time with a flashlight, expels his breath like a high diver, and says, "One hundred and thirty dollars!"

If you peek under the blotter while his back is turned, all you'll find is a picture of his wife and kids and a two-year-old shopping list.

[Harry Golden, *You're Entitle'* (New York: World Publishing Company, 1962).]

Hi Ya, Tar Heel

 Some time ago I lent my car for a couple of days to a fund-raiser from Brooklyn. He represents (while studying for the Orthodox rabbinate) a famous Jewish orphan asylum, and he had to make a few stops between Charlotte and Chattanooga. I have known the fellow for some years—a charming, cultured man. He speaks English haltingly, and I enjoy his annual visits because it is an opportunity for me to speak Yiddish for hours and hours. When he returned my car he told me that on the highways of Tennessee he had three or four experiences which puzzled him. Every once in a while a passing motorist would lean out of the window of his car and yell, "Hi ya, Tar Heel!" The third time it happened, the young rabbinical student pulled over to one side to see if anything was wrong with the car. He asked me in Yiddish, "Mr. Golden, what's this *Tar Heel* business, is it good or bad?"

[Harry Golden, *You're Entitle'* (New York: World Publishing Company, 1962).]

Gradual Intergration

In the emergency room of the Alachua General Hospital at Gainesville, Florida, there are three thermometers. They stand in a row on a small shelf with nothing else. The first is in an open container labeled: *"WHITE-ORAL,"* the third is in an identical container labeled, *"COLORED-ORAL,"* and the middle one, which protrudes through a cork, in its otherwise sameness, is labeled, *"RECTAL."*

This is what I call *gradual* intergration.

[Harry Golden, *You're Entitle'* (New York: World Publishing Co., 1962).]

Repartee

In Charlotte not too long ago, a civic group convened to try to discuss the problem of juvenile delinquency. One of the speakers was particularly concerned about perversion and during the course of his remarks, he leaned over the table and asked a colleague, "What do you call a man who loves another man?"

One of the ladies on the committee immediately spoke up. "A Christian," she said.

[Harry Golden, *So What Else Is New?* (New York: G. P. Putnam's Sons, 1964).]

Interracial Unity

In the men's room of the Hoke County (North Carolina) Courthouse there are three stalls, marked, *WHITE, COLORED, INDIAN*. However, there is only one urinal.

[Harry Golden, *So What Else Is New?* (New York: G. P. Putnam's Sons, 1964).]

Dixie Dictionary

You may have seen some of this before, so I thought I'd pick my own favorites—everyday words and how us Sothron boys pronounce them:

Abode—Wooden Plank
Balks—Containers
Beckon—Meat from a pig
Coat—Place of justice
Faints—Barricade
Frustrate—Tops, The Best
Lack—To enjoy, as "I lack fried chicken"
Tarred—Weary
Tin sin stow—Ten-cent store

[Harry Golden, *So What Else Is New?* (New York: G. P. Putnam's Sons, 1964).]

Where Are the Names of Yesteryear?

There was a time when everyone had a nickname. People don't have them nowadays. Perhaps it is because we are all too busy to familiarize ourselves with the personal idiosyncracies of others. Where are the names of yesteryear? Where are Fatso, Stinky, Butch? Where are Mouth, Schnozz, and Lard?

They are now Melvin, Lester, Everett, or Ellsworth. In fact, I was in a supermarket the other day trailing a woman with two kids, one of them a little boy in the cart. As she waited to check out her purchases, the little kid started to fuss and the lady said to the older, "Randolph, shuckle Williston."

[Harry Golden, *So What Else Is New?* (New York: G. P. Putnam's Sons, 1964).]

The New South

Down here, things have changed since the Civil Rights Act of 1964 was signed. Restaurants integrated so quietly that it seemed segregation had been forgotten. One of the girls in the office returned from lunch with the following account:

A timid, elderly Negro lady approached the downtown drugstore lunch counter, leaned over and whispered confidentially, "Do you serve colored here?"

The teen-aged white waitress looked blank. "Colored what?"

[Harry Golden, *Ess, Ess, Mein Kindt* (New York: G. P. Putnam's Sons, 1966).]

Let Jews Forgive Christians, Too

I have a suggestion to offer the Jewish leaders of the world. It is in the form of an invitation addressed to the Chief Rabbis of Israel, United Kingdom, France, Denmark, Argentina, as well as to the Rabbinical Councils of America, the B'nai B'rith, American Jewish Committee, and American Jewish Congress.

My plan is to call a Jewish Ecumenical Council in Jerusalem some time in 1967, for the purpose of issuing a Jewish Schema on the Christians.

The Catholics and many of the Protestant brotherhoods have recently issued the Christian Schema on the Jews. We have been absolved from personal responsibility in the crucifixion of Jesus.

Now it is our turn. I propose that we forgive the Christians for the Inquisition, the Crusades, the ghettoes, and the expulsions. I think we can also include forgiveness for the usurpation of property which continued unabated for one thousand six hundred years, the worldwide discrimination; and we may also waive our annoyances at the barriers that guard country, city, and fraternal clubs.

The Christians have been nice. Now we can be nice. There is no reason for us to hold bitterness in our hearts because Crusader Godfrey of Bouillon drove the Jews of Jerusalem into the synagogue and set it on fire.

There is no reason in the world why our Christian neighbors

today should be held responsible for the wholesale slaughter of the Jews in the cities on the Rhine by the Christians of the Second Crusade. Nor should they be held responsible for the murders perpetrated by Peter the Hermit and Peter of Cluny.

And why should we let the memory of the Inquisition haunt us? England's crime of expulsion and expropriation in the year 1290?

And there is every political reason these days to forgive the Germans, Ukrainians, Hungarians, Croats, Poles, and Roumanians, the traditional anti-Semites. The Germans are even on our side in the Cold War against Communism.

As for the quotas in the medical school and the colleges which had been used to control the influx of Jews, why there is no doubt they will disappear now that we are no longer guilty of the death of Jesus, and when the Christians read our own Schema of forgiveness.

For all this terrifying history, let us clear those Christians living today. The Jewish Schema on the Christians would not only express appreciation for the recent events at the Catholic Ecumenical Council, but would clear the air for brotherhood and remove our own memories of bitterness. I strongly urge the Jewish leaders to call this conference. It is time for—love.

[Harry Golden, *Ess, Ess, Mein Kindt* (New York: G. P. Putnam's Sons, 1966).]

What the Americans Worry About Most

1. Calories
2. Communism
3. Body odor

[Harry Golden, *So Long As You're Healthy* (New York: G. P. Putnam's Sons, 1970).]

The Message

A socially prominent matron invited her doctor to dinner. She asked RSVP. The doctor was prompt in his reply, but the matron couldn't make out his scrawl. Was he or was he not coming? Her dear hubby came to the rescue. He said he would take the doctor's reply to the local druggist, who had years of experience deciphering the longhand of many doctors.

The druggist read the scrawl, bent down, and put a big black bottle of medicine on the counter: "That will be three eighty, please."

[Harry Golden, *So Long As You're Healthy* (New York: G. P. Putnam's Sons, 1970).]

My Grandson's Car

In order to popularize its new two-thousand-dollar sports car, the Ford Motor Company offered a plastic scale model of the Maverick. My daughter-in-law, the proud mother of an eighteen-month old son, immediately sent off for it. The little boy goes into ecstasies over anything on wheels. Promptly the model arrived. The first time my grandson wheeled his new car across the floor, the little plastic bumper fell off. My daughter-in-law wrote a letter to Ralph Nader.

[Harry Golden, *So Long As You're Healthy* (New York: G. P. Putnam's Sons, 1970).]

Cemetery Segregation

City Councilman Fred Alexander's proposal to remove the fence between the Negro and white sections of the municipally owned cemetery was defeated by the Charlotte City Council.

Opponents of Alexander's proposal argued that there had always been a fence. One part of the cemetery was for whites and one part was for Negroes, they pointed out. Why not let folks alone?

Mr. Alexander cautioned the council that it is precisely this meaningless intransigence which results in what mayors and police chiefs euphemistically call a "long hot summer." There is neither integration nor segregation in a grave, just the dead. Most of the souls have departed for points north and south, some whites sharing heaven with blacks, some hell.

In Georgia I saw an animal cemetery. The color of the *owner* of the dog was the determining factor in which section of the cemetery the dog would find its final resting place. A black dog owned by a white man was somewhat curiously buried in the white-dog section;

a white dog owned by a Negro was even more curiously buried in the colored-dog section.

[Harry Golden, *So Long As You're Healthy* (New York: G. P. Putnam's Sons, 1970).]

Comic Wind-Up

Children's sayings, epitaphs, essays, character sketches, epigrams and episodes are grouped together here. The writers, among others, are O. Henry, James Larkin Pearson, (Private) Marion Hargrove, Robert Ruark, Weimar Jones, William T. Polk, Willie Snow Ethridge, and Thad Stem, Jr. Each of them is fortunate in having developed a comic point of view about himself, about the people around him, and about life in general.

Out of the Mouth of Babes

OVERHEARD.—"She's getting married next month and she's awfully busy collecting things for her torso."

HALLOWEEN.—Mrs. Ed Rowland got the butcher knife out and prepared to carve the jack-o-lantern from the fat pumpkin.

"Mama!" wailed her two-year-old son Drew. "You gonna kill it?"

BIRD FUNERAL—A young Chapel Hill foursome . . . were burying a pet bird that a cat had killed.

One little girl was telling her mother about it all.

"We put it in a box and we dug a hole under the crabapple tree," the youngster said wistfully. "And Tommy prayed about the bird and we covered it up then. And then we sang a song. . . ."

"What did you sing?" asked the child's mother.

269

"We sang 'Don't Give a Damn for Duke University' 'cause that was the only song that all four of us knowed," she replied.

NEW SHOES.—A Raleigh father was taking his young son to have corrective shoes fitted. The lad, who loved his tennis shoes, protested vigorously.

"My leg's gonna hurt a whole lot," he promised.

"Yeah, I know," said his Dad.

"And I won't be able to play ball."

"Maybe you can."

"Well, I'm probably gonna flunk arithmetic!" he threatened.

TRAGIC INCIDENT.—Probably the most tragic incident involving truth and children occurred when some Asheville friends called the home of a couple they play bridge with.

"Let me speak to your mommy," the lady asked the little boy who answered.

"She's in the bathtub," he said.

"Let me speak to your daddy."

"He's in the bathtub with mommy," the little fellow explained.

[A. C. Snow, *Raleigh Times,* 1 November 1967; 30 October 1968; 31 May 1969; 4 October 1969; 4 December 1971.]

Epitaphs

Reported originally in the *Wasp* (Raleigh), cemetery not cited:
> Beneath this stone, a heap of clay,
> Lies Arabella Young,
> Who, on the twenty-fourth of May,
> Began to hold her tongue.

[Kemp P. Battle, *The Early History of Raleigh* (Raleigh: Edwards and Broughton Co., 1893).]

From the *Newton Enterprise* in the winter of 1880:
> A boy once took it in his head
> That he would exercise his sled.

He took that sled into the road
And, lord a massa, how he slod.
And as he slid he laughing cried,
"What fun upon my sled to slide."
And as he laughed, before he knewed,
He from that sliding sled was slude.
Upon the slab where he was laid,
They carved this line: "This boy was slade."

[Billy Arthur, *Durham Morning Herald*, 7 November 1954.]

Elon College Cemetery:
"Our little darling has gone home to be an Angle."

Snow Camp:
"Here lies a virgin with her babe resting in her arms."

Providence Cemetery, Graham:
Lydia J. Moon
"She was the sunshine of our home."

Monument to his second wife, Salisbury:
"The Lord giveth and the Lord taketh away;
Blessed be the name of the Lord."

Cedar Grove Cemetery, New Bern:
Miss Mary E. Oliver
daughter of John & Eliz
Pearson Oliver. Died Mar. 6, 1836
Aged 82 yrs.
"Him that cometh to me I will in no wise cast out."

In the Beaufort Cemetery:
Michael Arundell
1819-1884
"I was sick and ye visited me"

[Collected by Alonzo C. Hall, *North Carolina Folklore*, December 1957. Hall, born in Burlington in 1886, was professor of English at The University of North Carolina at Greensboro until his retirement in 1956.]

From the repertoire of Edmund Harding:
"Here lies the body of Maggie McGinnity,
A native daughter of Chocowinity.
She lived 80 years in a state of virginity,
And that's damn good for Chocowinity."

[A. M. Patterson, *News and Observer* (Raleigh), 8 February 1972, reports the epitaph is "apocryphal, no doubt."]

Snoring

There are various kinds of snoring and as many kinds of snorers. I need not take the reader's time to describe all the different kinds of snores, as I take it for granted other people are as well posted as I am; but I do want to mention a few of them—if, for no other reason, to let the reader understand that I have been an appreciative hearer of that midnight music which some sensitive people pretend they do not admire.

In the first place, there's what may be termed the "smoking snore." That's the simplest form of snoring, and the easiest executed, as a man has simply to lie on his back and puff, as if he were smoking a pipe. It doesn't require any exertion whatever and, consequently, it doesn't tire the snorer. He can keep up his "pooh" from the moment he begins to puff until the sun rises the next morning. And what makes it so aggravating, if you punch the fellow and make him promise to stop, he'll begin again right where he left off. And should you shake him again and beg him to stop his puffing, he will say, "All right—p-o-o-o-h!" and go right ahead as if there had been no interruption. I have a very dear friend in Smithfield who graduated with distinction as a "smoking snorer" and, as far as I have been able to inquire into the matter, he stands at, or about, the head of that class. It is worth the loss of a night's sleep to be permitted to room with him and satisfy one's self as to his proficiency in the art of p-o-oh-ing.

The "goose hissing snore" is somewhat like the smoking snore; but it differs from it in two particulars. In the first place the mouth is partly open and the snorer "s-s-s-h-e-s" instead of "p-o-o-h-s"; and, in the second place, the hissing gets louder and louder until it becomes a sort of whistle, which generally scares the snorer and wakes him up, when he will be pretty apt to remark: "I believe I was snoring." And then he will most likely turn over and sleep quietly the remainder of the night.

The next snore, in order, is the "frog snore," or rather a cross between the noise made by filing a handsaw and the croaking of a meadow frog. Such a snore is enough to make the flesh crawl on a person who is nothing but skin and bones, and make him forget all the other troubles and disagreeable things in this world. Beware of a person who snores that kind of a snore.

The next snore is what might be called "the snort." The noise is made through the nose, and sounds as savage and quite as discordant as the roar of a young lion mixed with the braying of an ass. That snore is known as "the baby-waker," and is therefore a terror to the household; but the one good feature about it is, it soon exhausts itself, or it would exhaust the snorer.

Lastly, though there are other kinds, I mention the "gourd-sawing snorers." There are two distinct kinds of these: the hand-sawyers and the crosscut sawyers. The handsaw fellows are those who blow out, simply—the crosscut fellows are those who snore "a-gwine and a'comin'." Of all snorers this last mentioned class, by all odds, stands highest, and is entitled to a premium as a sleep disturber; for no man with a bad conscience can sleep while the crosscut snorer runs his machine.

[Richard Harper Whitaker, *Whitaker's Reminiscences, Incidents and Anecdotes* (Raleigh: Edwards and Broughton Co., 1905). In his later years, Whitaker (*ca.* 1830-1907) was a Methodist preacher in eastern North Carolina.]

The Confession of a Murderer

He is dead and I killed him.

I gaze upon him, lying cold and still, with the crimson blood welling from his wound, and I laugh with joy. On my hand his life blood leaped and I hold it proudly aloft bearing its accusing stain and in my heart there is no pity, no remorse, no softness. Seeing him lie there crushed and pulseless is to me more than the pleasure of paradise. For months he escaped me. With all the intense hate I bore him at times, I felt admiration for his marvelous courage, his brazen effrontery, his absolute ignorance of fear. Why did I kill him? Because he had with a fixed purpose and a diabolical, persistent effrontery, conspired to rob me of that which is as dear to me as my life. Brave as I have said he was, he scarcely ever dared to cross my path openly, but with insidious cunning had ever sought to strike me a blow in the dark.

I did not fear him, but I knew his power, and I dared not give him his opportunity.

Many a sleepless night I have spent, planning some means to rid myself of his devilish machinations. He even attempted to torture me by seeking to harm her whom I love. He approached her with the utmost care and cunning, wearing the guise of a friend, but striving to instill his poison into her innocent heart.

But, thank heaven, she was faithful and true and his honeyed songs and wiles had no effect. When she would tell me of his approaches, how I would grind my teeth and clench my hands in fury, and long for the time when I would wreak a just vengeance upon him. The time has come. I found him worn and helpless from cold and hunger, but there was no pity in my heart. I struck him down and reveled with heartfelt joy when I saw him sink down, bathed in blood, and die by my hands. I do not fear the consequences. When I tell my tale I will be upheld by all.

He is dead and I am satisfied.

I think he is the largest and fattest mosquito I ever saw.

[O. Henry, *Postscripts* (New York: Harper & Brothers, 1923). William Sidney Porter (1862-1910), native of Guilford County, used the pseudonym of O. Henry. His mature years were spent in Texas and New York.]

Idiotorials from The Fool Killer

A citizen of this county died last week, leaving all he had to his wife's folks. All he had was his wife.

A subscriber in Alabama writes me as follows: "Dear Mr. Editor: What is your opinion about the hen? Does she sit, or does she set?" Aw, shut up! I don't bother about such things as that. What concerns me when she cackles is, Has she laid, or has she lied?

A little girl aged three had been left in the nursery by herself, and her brother arrived to find the door closed.

"I wants to tum in, Sissie," said Tom.

"But you tan't tum in, Tom."

"But I wants to."

"Well, I's in my nightie-gown, an' nurse says little boys mustn't see little girls in their nightie-gowns."

After astonished and reflective silence on Tom's side of the door, the minature Eve announced triumphantly: "You tan tum in now. I's tooked it off."

Whoever gets the Nobel Peace Prize this year will have to fight for it.

The slowest way to become a millionaire is to work for the money.

The less religion people have, the harder they can fight and fuss over it.

[James Larkin Pearson, *The Fool Killer*, June 1910, April 1912, June 1912, September 1914, October 1920, April 1925.]

Guard Duty at Fort Bragg

"One of the most solemn and responsible trusts of a soldier," Sergeant "Curly" Taylor said today, "is his guard duty." Sergeant Taylor, who has been in the Army for nineteen years and probably knows more about guard duty than any man in Fort Bragg, is teaching us about guard duty now.

The soldier is called to this duty about once a month. For a twenty-four-hour period, he is on two hours, and off four hours, and he "walks his post in a military manner," guarding the peace and possessions and safety of a part of the post. He is responsible only to a corporal of the guard, a sergeant of the guard, an officer of the day, and his commanding officer.

The guard, or sentry, is known chiefly to the reading and movie-going public by two expressions, "Halt, who goes there?"

and "Corporal of the guard! Post number three!" The former, Sergeant Taylor said with his best poker face, has given the Army considerable worry at times.

According to the sergeant, the guard is instructed to give the "halt" order three times and then shoot Overenthusiastic rookies from the back counties, he said, had been known to go like this: "Halt halt halt! Ka-POW!" (You can believe it or leave it; I never question what the sergeant says.)

There was one rookie guard, he said, who halted him, questioned him and allowed him to pass. After he had gone several steps, the sentry again shouted, "Halt!" Sergeant Taylor came back and wanted to know—politely, of course—how come. "My orders," said the guard, "say to holler 'Halt' three times and then shoot. You're just on your second halt now!"

The other popular expression is the come-a-running call that goes up the line to the guardhouse when a guard takes a prisoner or "meets any case not covered by instruction" (General Order No. 9). If the guard is on the seventh post, he sings out, "Corporal of the guard! Post number seven!" The guard on the sixth post picks up the cry and it goes down the line like that.

There's the story about the officer of the day who questioned a new sentry, as officers of the day frequently do in order to test the sentries. "Suppose," the O. D. asked, "that you shouted 'Halt' three times and I kept going. What would you do?"

The guard was apparently stumped by the question. Finally he answered, "Sir, I'd call the corporal of the guard."

The officer of the day gloated. "Aha!" he said. "So you'd call the corporal of the guard, would you? And just why would you call the corporal of the guard?"

This time the answer was prompt and decisive—and correct. "To haul away your dead body, sir!"

Another promising young guard, Sergeant Taylor says, was **questioned by a sergeant of the guard. "Suppose you saw a battleship coming across that drill field over there. What would you do?"**

The guard thought furiously. The answer—General Order No. 9—didn't come.

"What would you do?" the sergeant insisted.

A light came into the sentry's eyes. "I'd torpedo the thing and sink it."

The sergeant gasped. "Where would you get a torpedo?" he demanded.

The guard smiled brightly. "The same place you got that damned battleship," he said.

Heroes are born, not made.

[Marion Hargrove, *See Here, Private Hargrove* (New York: Henry Holt and Co., 1942). Born in Mt. Olive in 1919, Hargrove attended high school in Charlotte. His later writing career carried him to Hollywood and New York.]

Coining a Word

Mr. Waters' son had been knocked off his bicycle as he rode along the highway, knocked off by a fast-driving motorist, and Mr. Waters was agitated as he told me about it.

"I'm goin' to sue him if the Lord lets me live! I shore am, Mr. Begaw, for he hadn't no need to hurt my boy like he done! He was drivin' reckless and speedless, I tell *you!*"

I wanted to be sure I had heard him correctly, so, equally indignant, I exclaimed: "You don't mean *speedless* and reckless *both,* do you?"

"Yes, sir, I do! He was drivin' reckless *and* speedless!" insisted Mr. Waters, and even Daniel Webster, let alone Noah, could not have done better than that on coining a word.

[John G. Bragaw, *Random Shots* (Raleigh: Edwards and Broughton Co., 1945.]

Gray's Elegy at Duke University

This is the way the boys at Duke University think Gray might have written his "Elegy," had he lived today:

> The curfew tolls the knell of parting day;
> The line of cars winds slowly o'er the lea.
> Our friend jay-walked his absent-minded way—
> And left the world most unexpectedly.

[Bennett Cerf, *The Laugh's on Me* (New York: Doubleday & Company, 1959).]

A Man I Remember

Old Dr. Brack Lloyd died last year, which might be the reason the University of North Carolina is putting in a four-year medical school and its own four-hundred-bed hospital. They got to do something to take up the slack Dr. Lloyd left.

Dr. Lloyd was one of the last country doctors. He wore a pinched-up black hat, slept in his clothes, and had dirty fingernails. If he had an office, it was on the sidewalk of Franklin Street or in Eubanks' drugstore in Chapel Hill. But he was a mighty good doctor. The big boys often called him in on the tough cases. He was using sulfa drugs on pneumonia long before its use was sanctioned by the State Medical Association. His obstetrical record was probably the best in the state.

Dr. Lloyd was picturesquely profane, vastly irreverent, and he never sent out a bill in his life. He would just as leave take a pint of whisky as a fee for delivering a baby, and often did. He always wore his black hat when he was operating. Said he couldn't see to cut without it. He loved animals, and his hogs were always fatter than anybody else's.

When one of the university's most revered, venerable sages died, to the accompaniment of much written and spoken elegy, Dr. Lloyd spat and said:

"He's a-sittin' in a front pew in hell right now. Any man who'll let his livestock perish to death out of pure stinginess is duty-bound to go to hell." The departed professor had been notorious for his bony horses and emaciated dogs.

A friend of mine once had a huge ulcer on the back of his neck. Dr. Lloyd looked at it and said: "That thing needs cuttin'. Wait'll I get my hat."

He went outside to his car and came back with a crusted mustard jar full of surgical instruments. His greasy old black hat was perched on his head. He straddled the patient, wiped off a scalpel on his sleeve, and commenced to hack. The patient's wife was horrified.

"Don't worry," the doctor said, chopping away. "I was born sterilized. I eat germs." The patient got well in a hurry.

Dr. Lloyd loved to play poker, and he always carried a straight flush of cards in his pocket. It was signed by the cronies who were present when he hit the flush, and was grimy and tattered from handling. But his fondness for poker deprived him of sleep.

On a maternity case one time he decided it would be at least an hour before baby came, and he was yawning. It was pretty late at night.

"You got another bed in this house, sister?" he asked the expectant mother, a colored woman. He called all women, from professors' ladies to servants, "sister."

"Naw suh, Dr. Brack," she said. "This is the only one."

"Then move over a mite, sister," said Dr. Lloyd. "I aim to ketch me a little snooze." He flopped down beside the pregnant patient and caught a two-hour nap before the baby announced its desire to be born.

Although Dr. Lloyd had topped off his medical instruction at a famous Eastern university—and had, I believe, headed a big hospital up north before he came home—he was not an admirer of fine-haired education. Especially when it concerned women. He once remarked to a lady who was acquiring knowledge somewhat late in life: "Cut it out, sister. It'll make you no money and get you no friends."

Dr. Brack thought that education was too heady a draught for most folks and they'd be happier if they stayed stupid. And his opinion of women was something less than exalted. To Brack, a lady was a kind of automat which produced babies instead of coffee cups, with the added nuisance value of taking him away from his poker games. He never was very much impressed with the super-sanctity of motherhood as an institution.

I mentioned that Brack never sent a bill, and he never dunned a patient. One time he went on a country call to see a farmer's wife about the rheumatism, and as he started to climb in his rackety old car the farmer approached him sheepishly.

"Don't want you to think I'm forgettin' my rightful debts, Doc," the farmer said. "Seems to me I never did pay you for birthing that boy of mine."

Brack couldn't remember, but he argued on the side of logic.

"Don't reckon you did," he said.

"You got ary farm?" the farmer inquired.

"Got a little farm," Brack said.

"Could you use ary heifer?" the farmer asked.

"Might," Brack said.

The farmer turned and cupped his hands around his mouth. "You, boy!" he yelled. "Come here."

Out from behind the barn came a shock-haired, husky youth of some nineteen years.

"Yes, Paw," he said.

"You, boy, go down and ketch that heifer for the doc," the farmer said. "It's little enough fer ye to do to pay for your birthin'."

He turned to Dr. Lloyd.

"That's the boy you birthed, Doc," he said. "I'm trying to teach him respect for his rightful obligations."

They say an early, unfortunate love affair turned Dr. Brack sour, made him into a character, and led him away from a distinguished medical career to a small-town routine of baby-snatching and throat-painting. He was also a practicing agnostic and never went near a church.

But it is interesting to recall that there were three preachers of different faiths at his funeral. They all made sermons about Dr. Lloyd. They tumbled all over themselves to excuse him for his lack of surface godliness.

At least, one good dominie turned and reprimanded the surprised congregation. This sky pilot said that maybe Brack would have joined the church if the people in the church had been better people.

[Robert Ruark, *I Didn't Know It Was Loaded* (New York: Doubleday & Company, 1948). Ruark (1915-1965), native of Wilmington, attended The University of North Carolina at Chapel Hill. After apprenticeship as a reporter, he became a columnist whose writing was syndicated nationwide. He was also the author of twelve books.]

A House, Swimming, Insults, and Sweet Music

THE EXTERIOR IS THE FUNCTION OF THE INTE-RIOR.—Let me tell you about the house I live in. We wanted to enjoy the building of it, for we were not likely to build another. We went to friends who were the best architects around—they were modernists and we wanted a house in the Colonial tradition—and put this question to them: "Will you help us build the house we

want, and not the one you think we ought to have?" "Yes," they answered. "Well, go ahead and draw us a picture of it," I said, "we
want to see what is is going to look like." Right solemnly they replied, "You are putting the cart before the horse. You don't live on
the outside." And just as solemnly I replied that I had never
thought about that profound and penetrating observation which
was worthy of the brain of an architect, and told them to go ahead
and draw the inside plans.

They did, and brought the plans to us and asked how we liked
them. "All right for the time being," I said, "but I am not going to
move a step till I see the outside." "There is nothing you can do
about the outside," they said. "What do you mean there is nothing
I can do about the outside?" "The exterior is the function of the interior," they answered. "What does that mean?" "It means that
once the floor plans are drawn, the walls and roof lines fall into
place—the exterior is controlled by the interior." "Well," I said, "I
have heard about predestination in religion; maybe it will work in
architecture. Go ahead and let's see how it comes out."

Two weeks later they brought us the outside plans, with a tree
already rooted and growing in the yard. I've noticed that architects
never put in the tree until they think they've got you in the bag. I
did not need a split second of thought before exclaiming: "I won't
live in it! My father might have paid five hundred dollars for a tenant house in that general form, size, and dimension, but he
wouldn't have put thousands of dollars in it, and I am not going
to!"

"But you don't live on the outside," they said. "You miss my
point," I replied. "If I had to walk home at the end of the day for
the rest of my life and see that thing at the end of the road, I would
not need a television screen to see limned in midair that exterior following me into that perfect interior and spoiling it like a fly in a
bowl of soup. I won't live in it!"

At that point one of the architects went haywire and started re-
peating: "The exterior is the function of the interior, the exterior is
the function of the interior"—over and over again, like a stuck pho-
nograph record. "Hold on a minute," I finally said, "I have heard
that one time too many. There is not a word of truth in it. I can
show you two girls with the same interior floor plan, functions,
mechanisms, and objectives—-one as pretty as she can be and the

other one as ugly as hell. Don't tell me the exterior is the function of the interior!"

[Albert Coates. *In Appreciation* . . . (n.p., 1962.)]

SWIMMING.—I was in Yellowstone National Park a few years ago and spent a night at the great Canyon Hotel where college boys are summer bellhops and some of the prettiest college girls in the country are summer waitresses. My wife and I were sitting around the table after dinner with two of the boys who were from Chapel Hill and a collection of the girls from everywhere.

The girls told us they had found a pool at the foot of the canyon where they would go in swimming after they had washed the luncheon dishes—not in the nude, which has a sorry connotation from nudist camps, but without clothes, which is an entirely different matter. While they were in the pool on that particular afternoon, one of the many rambling bears in the park came up and sat down on their clothes, and for an hour or more they were imprisoned in the water. Then someone came along and threw part of a lunch down the ravine; the bear went after it and the girls came out of the pool.

I looked at that collection of youth and beauty around me and took a long breath and said: "Ladies and gentlemen, in all humility, reverence and love of beauty let me say—I hope to God I never get that hungry."

[Albert Coates, Bar Association Address, n.d.]

SWEET MUSIC.—Some of you will recall the opening day of the first Patrol School in the wooden barracks after World War II. It was a cold, rainy Sunday afternoon in February. The barracks had been brought from abandoned army camps and were partially heated by antiquated coal stoves. Between the barracks was a latrine with commodes and lavatories—all ready to go. Men had been working in three shifts round the clock laying the pipes to bring hot and cold water, but they had come only halfway to the building. I knew that if the prospective patrolmen had to go to the bushes instead of the commodes, and if they had no hot water to wash and shave with next morning, they wouldn't be there another day. I was tired, sweaty, dirty and worried as I went home to clean up and dress up, and I was worried as I returned for the formal opening of the school after the evening meal.

Here was my greeting to the expectant rookies:

Gentlemen, I have heard Serge Koussevitzky lead the Boston Symphony Orchestra. I have heard Walter Damrosch lead the New York Philharmonic. I have heard Eugene Ormandy lead the Philadelphia Orchestra. But no one of these orchestras alone, nor all of their instruments together, ever made music as sweet to me as the sound of forty flushing commodes on a trial run as I came by the latrine building on my way to this opening ceremony.

[Albert Coates, from manuscript of talk to law-enforcement officers.]

INSULTS.—I was coming out of the woods across the road from the newly erected Knapp Building housing the Institute of Government, and saw a patrolman stop a woman driver for a traffic violation. She was irritated and began hurling at him a succession of abusive epithets that I didn't know women knew. The patrolman kept his head and made his point, and the woman drove on. On seeing me standing at the edge of the woods, the patrolman came over and said, "Professor, do you remember your last lecture to the Patrol School?" Yes, I responded, and he touched his hat and went on. Here was the substance of that last lecture:

No man has a right to be in the public service in general, law enforcement in particular, and even more particularly in the traffic law-enforcement service, unless he has got sense enough to know how to take an insult—sense enough to know that nine out of ten insults are not really intended, and that most of the one out of ten are regretted by the people giving them when they look back on the incident.

Let me give you an illustration. This morning a boy came to my office and in no uncertain terms asked me if I had seen So-and-So. "No," I replied. "You look like you are mad. What is wrong?"

"I have just heard that he called me an S.O.B. in front of the post office, and I am going to find him and beat the living hell out of him."

I didn't want to see that happen, and I thought a minute and said, "Son, what sort of an S.O.B. did he call you?"

He was taken a little by surprise and finally stammered out, "Why, he just called me an S.O.B."

I replied: "That is nothing to fight about. I have been called that so many times that it runs off of me like water off a duck's back. What bothers me is that there have been two or three times when they nearly proved it on me. And there was at least one time when if they had been in possession of all the facts, they could have done it. I no longer fight over the facts, I fight over the modifying adjective. You call me a certain sort of an S.O.B. and I'll fight you."

The boy got to laughing and went out of the office in a better humor, and an hour later I ran into him in front of the post office telling that story to the fellow he was going to beat the hell out of an hour before, and both of them were laughing over it.

[Albert Coates, from manuscript of a talk made to the State Highway Patrol.]

About Snakes

About as many stories are told about snakes as about fish. The only difference is that the snakes are longer.

Biggest snake ever killed in North Carolina? Doubt if it's on record. As the years pass, the snakes get longer and thicker.

Take the rattlesnake killed by the late Captain Jim Rhoades of Durant Island around the turn of the century. The tremendous rattlesnake now is said to have measured twenty-two feet and it is claimed that it took a long-armed man to reach around the middle. Shucks, a snake that big could swallow you.

There have been tales for years about milk snakes that were supposed to milk cows dry, and hoop snakes that put their tails in their mouths and rolled after their prey. These stories are untrue but they have survived from one generation to another.

We thought we had heard about the different kinds of snakes until we heard about the sewing-machine snake.

A tenant of the M. C. Braswell Company farms near Battleboro was telling Tom Pearsall about a large snake he had seen. The tenant said he had never seen one like it before. Mr. Pearsall had never heard of such a snake and wanted to see it.

The tenant said he could take him to it without much trouble. It was a hot day. The men walked down a narrow road through the pines to a big brush pile. The tenant poked a stick into the brush pile and a big rattlesnake coiled up, started buzzing his rattlers— all fourteen of them.

"Don't he sound like a sewing machine, Mr. Pearsall?" the tenant asked. But Mr. Pearsall wasn't in answering distance by then.

[Bugs Barringer, *News and Observer* (Raleigh), 18 June 1967. Osmond Long Barringer, born in Charlotte, is a Rocky Mount photographer and columnist.]

Aren't People Funny?

Aren't people funny? No matter how naturally a man acts, they seem to think what he does is strange.

I am reminded of that almost every time I am on Main Street. Having finished my errands uptown, I am ready to drive back to *The [Franklin] Press* office. I start walking up one side of the street, looking; then I go down the other side, looking.

Friends seem puzzled; so I explain:

"I've lost my automobile."

Now what, I ask you, could be more natural than that? But they don't seem to understand.

"Do you mean," they ask in alarm, "that it's been stolen? . . . or just what *do* you mean?"

"Just what I said: I've lost my automobile."

They don't literally shake their heads; they're too polite for that. But I can see from their faces they're doing a job of mental head-shaking.

Then I'm the one who's puzzled . . . and a little irritated.

"I can't remember where I parked the darn thing."

Surely that ought to clear the matter up; surely they ought to say, "Oh, I see"; surely their tone ought to suggest that nothing could be more natural, that everybody does that every day. But you should see their smiles!

So I continue to look. Let's see, did I park it here in front of the Post Office? No, it isn't here. Maybe in front of the Drug Store. . . .

I walk from Post Office to Drug Store. Still no automobile.

Maybe on the other side of the street; no, that was yesterday. . . . But it must be on the other side, because it's not on this one. So I walk from the Five and Ten to the Chevrolet place. Still no automobile.

Maybe the Main Street parking places were all full, and I left it down by the Jail. Sometimes I find it there; sometimes I don't.

It's an awful nuisance, this business of never remembering where you've parked.

It's not a new nuisance. I've done it all my life. Years ago, when I lived in Asheville, I often walked the three-quarters of a mile from the office to my home, was surprised to find the car wasn't there—and then remembered I'd left it parked within a block of the office.

Then there was the time I sold our car; planned to walk for a while and save money. But the very next day I saw a car that looked just like the one I had sold, and got home with it before I remembered I didn't own a car.

As I say, that sort of thing is an awful nuisance. But if, as I suspect, everybody does it, why are folks so all-fired amused when I do?

As I said before:

Aren't people funny? No matter how naturally a man acts, they seem to think what he does is strange.

[Weimar Jones, *My Affair with a Weekly* (Winston-Salem: John F. Blair, Publisher, 1960). Jesse Weimar Jones (1895-1968) was a Franklin newspaper editor.]

We Get Going

One July I accepted the invitation of my daughter, Shug, and her husband, Bud, to spend two weeks with them and their three children: Mark, aged seven; Sefton, five; Georgia, three; and a son of Bud's by a former marriage, Jim, fifteen, on Long Beach, North Carolina, approximately 150 miles from their home in Sanford.

Naturally my husband Mark was invited too: but he announced without a moment's hesitation that he couldn't possibly get away from his newspapers. He explained with a straight face that July was his busiest month.

A few days ahead I went to Sanford to help Shug and Bud get ready and it was well I did. I never before saw such preparations for two weeks at the beach. Cape Kennedy on the eve of John Glenn's shot around the world didn't equal them.

We packed sheets, pillowcases, pillows, blankets, spreads, washrags, face towels, bath towels, dish towels, baby cribs, cots, deck chairs, old tire tubes, rubber floats, life-saving jackets, an electric rotisserie, an electric blender, an electric toaster, a vacuum cleaner, a mop, a dustpan, two ice coolers for extra ice and soft drinks, a twenty-foot shelf of books for grownups and children, puzzles, games, sand buckets, shovels. . . . The list exhausts me even now.

Yet none of the above included clothes or food. Though there are two or three perfectly adequate grocery stores on Long Beach, we packed as if we were headed for the moon. We packed a gallon of spaghetti sauce and another gallon of homemade vegetable soup; two or three meat loaves—I stepped on a meat loaf every time I moved; an old Kentucky ham; a pot roast; loaves of pumpernickel bread; jars of homemade cookies, and heaven only knows what else. Every hour Shug sent Jim and Mark to the A & P or the Progressive to beg more cartons.

On the morning of departure—a Sunday morning—everybody was up early, excitedly hollering instructions to everybody else and hauling his own luggage from the bedrooms and the cartons from the kitchen and side porch to the front terrace and steps where Bud could reach them quickly when he got around to packing the station wagon. Bud, who is a leisurely, easygoing, even-tempered mortal—except when headed for the beach, which he is simply mad about—was ready to pack at the crack of dawn. But in spite of the days of preparation, Shug's suitcase and a box of last-minute toilet articles weren't on the terrace and, naturally, Bud couldn't start loading until everything was at hand and he could estimate the proper space for the entire cargo.

At two-minute intervals he would stride with his long legs back into the house and shout up the stairs, "Mary Snow [Shug's real name], aren't those suitcases ready yet? I can't do a thing until I have them."

"They'll be ready in just a few minutes, Bud," she'd call back. "I've just three or four things to put in."

"Well, please hurry. We're going to lose a whole day at the beach if you don't hurry."

Then he'd stride back; study the hillocks of baggage sprawled about the terrace and steps; walk over to the station wagon and order the impatient children to get out and stay out until it was time to go; give a tug at the tarpaulin, which was spread over the lawn but would eventually cover up the luggage on the roof of the station wagon, and then stride back into the house and yell once more at Shug.

Finally Shug called down that the bags were ready to be closed and up the stairs raced Bud, Jim, Mark, and Sefton to fetch them. Now Bud could begin to load. For at least an hour he lifted into the back of the station wagon and onto the roof suitcases, cartons, ice coolers . . .; then lifted them off and shifted them around. He grew fearfully hot in the fast-rising sun; sweat rolled from his forehead, nose, and cheeks and his sport shirt stuck like wet wallpaper to his back. But he wouldn't let anybody help him. "Just stay out of my way and keep quiet," he barked when anybody approached to offer a hand.

For a while it looked touch and go. There seemed at least twice too much for the available space. Still he persisted, and at long last everything was in except two cartons—one of sheets and towels and one of pillows. Maybe Shug and I could repack, he suggested, one of the large cartons of bedclothes and squeeze in the sheets and towels. As for the pillows, he'd just take them out of the carton and stuff them in cracks.

Where he was to find these cracks I couldn't imagine, for all of them, so it seemed to me, were already stuffed with bathrobes and pajamas and rubber sheets that couldn't be packed in the children's suitcases the day before.

After a heroic struggle Bud dislodged the large carton of linen from the station wagon and Shug and I did succeed in jamming most of the other linen into it—I offered to hold the left-over pieces in my lap—and Bud did locate holes that could be chinked with the pillows.

Then, with the carton back in the wagon, Bud, permitting Jim for the first time to assist him, spread the tarpaulin over the pyramid of luggage on top and tied it down with long lengths of rope. From one side of the top to the other he crisscrossed it, pulled it tight and knotted it fast. "I don't intend to have this tarpaulin come undone," he boasted, mopping his face with the sleeve of his shirt, "and let everything get wet if it rains."

Now we were ready to ride—at least, that is what we told ourselves—and loudly and joyfully we piled into the station wagon. Bud, Shug, and I sat on the front seat; Jim, Mark, and Sefton on the second seat (a nurse was still to be picked up); and Georgia, behind the seat on the floor in a little cubby hole among the luggage.

Bud turned on the ignition key, put his foot on the gas, and down the driveway we started. Then, right at that beautiful moment, Mark cried out in wild alarm, "Where's Maryburger?"

Eyes shut, I crumpled over. Oh, don't tell me, I groaned inwardly, that that stupid, fat, lazy, seemingly about-to-die, adored dog of Mark, Sefton, and Georgia is to go too? Somehow in the wild confusion of the last days I had completely forgotten to ask about her; but now I pulled myself up and did.

"Certainly, she's going," said Shug. "We wouldn't consider for a moment leaving her at home."

"But where is she?" demanded Bud.

"I don't know," answered Mark. "I haven't seen her since we started getting ready to go."

"Have you seen her, Sefton?"

"No, sir."

"How about you, Jim?"

"No, sir."

"Georgia, have you seen Maryburger?" Bud raised his voice to carry it to the hideaway.

"No, sir."

"Then she must be in the house somewhere." Bud put on the brakes, got out of the car, and went back into the house. On his heels, before Shug could stop them, streamed Jim, Mark, Sefton, and Georgia, all calling, "Maryburger, Maryburger. Where are you, Maryburger?"

In a few minutes they were back, but with no Maryburger. It was very peculiar, for she usually lay in the sun on the lawn, from all appearances half dead, from sunrise to sunset. The only stimulus that ever moved her was the station wagon going places. She then struggled to her feet, waddled over, and climbed in.

"Bud, did you look in the basement?" asked Shug.

"Yes, in the basement, upstairs, under the beds, in the bathrooms, under chairs, everywhere," said Bud. "She isn't in the house."

"Well, one thing sure, we can't leave her," Shug declared.

"No, Daddy, no, Daddy, we can't leave Maryburger," the children all wailed piteously.

"Stop that screaming," ordered Bud. "Nobody is going to leave Maryburger."

"But where can she be?" I put in.

Bud shrugged. "We'll just have to drive around the neighborhood and see if we can see her somewhere."

"Daddy, while you're driving, would you mind driving by the Wilkinsons?" suggested Jim. "I left my bathing trunks there last night."

"Oh, damn, Jim!" said the usually patient Bud. "What in God's name possessed you to do that? Didn't you know we were leaving for the beach this morning?"

"Yes, sir; but I just forgot them."

"The Wilkinsons aren't in the neighborhood," Bud went on irritably. "You know very well Maryburger would never go that far."

"I know, sir."

"Don't you have another pair of bathing trunks?"

"No, sir."

"Well, here's where we lose another twenty minutes."

The trunks recovered and stuffed between the luggage beneath the tarpaulin on the roof, we returned to the neighborhood and drove slowly up and down the streets that run parallel and horizontally to Shug's and Bud's Sunset Drive, looking, looking, looking. . . . Twice we stopped and the children scrambled out to reconnoiter: first at the little red schoolhouse where Sefton and Georgia attended nursery school (Maryburger had been known to follow them there and lie outside the door all morning, waiting for them to be dismissed); and second, at the home of close friends at the end of Sunset Drive. But still no Maryburger.

When we had circled the area for the second time, Bud said, "We can't spend all day looking for Maryburger."

"Don't leave Maryburger, Daddy," everybody wailed again, but this time with more anguish. "Daddy, don't leave Maryburger. Daddy, Daddy. . . ."

"But we'll never get to the beach today if we hang around much longer looking for her," argued Bud.

"But, Daddy, we can't leave her!" A high note of hysteria was now in their voices. "We can't, Daddy. We can't!"

Bud heaved a comber of a sigh and continued on slowly up Sunset Drive. Soon his and Shug's house came into view. Every eye anxiously raked the front lawn. It was still empty.

Then Sefton shouted joyfully, "There she is! There's Maryburger!"

And so she was, half buried in the heavy ivy that covers the foundation and the pillars of the house. Wherever she'd roamed, over land or sea or foam, it had completely exhausted her. She had hidden herself as well as possible for a long, uninterrupted summer's nap.

With Maryburger sharing Georgia's nest, Bud put the car into drive and speeded up as if now we were really off; but at the second corner he rolled into a filling station. "I suspect I'd better get filled up before we start out," he said casually.

Why hadn't he got filled up while waiting for Shug's bags, I wondered like a mother-in-law; but for once I kept my mouth shut. It was hard, though, and even harder when, a minute or two later, as he was getting his charge-a-plate for the gas out of his pocket, he exclaimed, "Oh, damn, I've forgotten the list of tobacco dealers I plan to see." (It was Bud's custom to use one day of his holiday to drive to nearby towns in South Carolina to solicit advertising from, I believe, the managers of tobacco warehouses for the radio station he owns.)

"Do you have to have the list?" asked Shug.

"Yes, I have to have it."

Back to the house we went and in went Bud to look for the list. He was gone much longer than any of us expected so we all decided to go in too, and go to the bathroom. After all, we'd been on the way for some little time.

"Did anybody move the list?" asked Bud in urgent tones when a survey of the house hadn't revealed it. "I would have sworn I left it right here on the dining room table."

"What did it look like?" Sefton asked.

"It was on a piece of orange paper."

"Was it a big piece of paper?"

"It was the size of a regular sheet of paper," Bud's voice sounded hopeful. "Did you see it, Sefton?"

"No, sir."

"Why did you want to know whether it was a big piece of paper?"

"I just did."

"Why, Sefton? Why?"

Sefton ducked his head down and squirmed his shoulders. "I just did."

As it was my turn at the bathroom, I didn't hear the end of this colloquy; but when I came out all was well. The list had been found on the buffet, weighted down with a brass samovar.

"Everybody in the car fast now!" Bud shouted. "We're going now! Hurry up, everybody! We've wasted enough time!"

Now, except for one stop at a house in the Negro section for the nurse with the lovely name of Barbara Bagely, we were on our way. This stop, however, proved unexpectedly lengthy too, for Shug felt she must go inside and assure Barbara's mother that she would take good care of her at the beach and never take her eyes off her when she was in the ocean.

But in due course she and Barbara and oops! another suitcase appeared and we were really off. At least, that's what we thought.

Almost immediately, though, while we were still in Sanford proper, an end of the rope that was supposed to be holding the tarpaulin came loose and beat a rat-a-tat like a machine gun firing against a window of the station wagon. Of course, Bud had to stop and get out and retie it. But it refused to stay tied. We hadn't gone a mile when the noise started again and Jim said, "Daddy, the rope's hanging down again."

When Bud slid back behind the wheel this time, Jim moaned, "Great Caesar's ghost. We haven't even got to Jonesboro."

"No," agreed Bud, looking down the highway to see if this suburb of Sanford was coming into view. "But maybe now. . . ." Bud put his foot on the gas and we shot ahead . . . all of an eighth of a mile. Then a series of screams rent the air. Bud slammed on the brakes and Shug and I whirled about. Georgia was in a paroxysm of shock and grief.

"What's the matter, Georgia?" Shug and I asked together. "What's the matter?"

Her continuous screams prevented speech; but she rose to her knees and pointed down the narrow aisle between the cartons and suitcases to the strip of highway we had just traversed.

"What is it?" I asked sternly, deciding it was time for me to take a hand. "Stop that yelling this minute and tell me what's happened."

A few more quick, hard screams like a woman giving birth and then, between strangled, snuffling, blubbery sobs came the news that her bathrobe had flown out the back window. (It was one of those last-minute items that had been stuffed in a crack.)

Jim hopped out, ran back, and retrieved it, but Georgia was not solaced. She buried her face in the bathrobe and wept as if her heart were broken. I lost all patience with her; but not Shug. "It's enough to give anyone a trauma," said she sympathetically, "to see one's bathrobe in the middle of the road."

The station wagon by this time was moving along at a fairly good rate; but alas, to the accompaniment of bursts of noise as if balloons were popping overhead. Bud didn't say anything about it for a while and neither did Shug or I. Maybe, if we didn't mention it, the noise would go away. It didn't, though. It went on and on. Indeed, it grew louder and steadier.

"I expect I had better stop," Bud said finally. "I'm afraid whatever it is will take the paint off the top."

He and Jim alighted. A part of the tarpaulin had torn away and was flapping against the roof. "I think I'll just take this piece of the tarpaulin off," announced Bud to us through the window. "It doesn't look as if it's going to rain."

"No, not today," I agreed, seat-sore. "Maybe tomorrow. . . ."

"Now, if we can only get to Jonesboro," said Bud, once more easing himself beneath the wheel.

For a few blessed moments no ropes dangles, no tarpaulin flapped, no garments flew out. . . . Then Mark broke the enchanted spell. "Daddy, I can see somebody's suitcase hanging down," he said.

"What are you talking about, Mark?" Bud asked impatiently. "Don't talk foolishly."

"But, Daddy, somebody's suitcase is hanging down."

And so somebody's was. Mine. It was dangling by the rope, run through the handle, halfway down the side of the station wagon.

While Bud and Jim struggled to get it back in place, Sefton inquired in a bored, weary, gruff voice, "How many times do we have to stop?"

Nobody bothered to answer him for nobody but God knew.

Very quietly, even resignedly, Bud himself announced the next misadventure. With his eyes peering into the rear-view mirror, he said, "There go Jim's bathing trunks off the top into the woods."

This time, when Jim was back in the car, Bud, grinning ruefully, remarked, "I've heared of a lot of absurd trips; but this is ridiculous."

And that it was and that it continued to be until we reached Long Beach. But I can bear to recall just so much.

[Willie Snow Ethridge, *You Can't Hardly Get There from Here* (New York: Vanguard Press, Inc., 1965). Mrs. Ethridge, born in Georgia, spent most of her life in Kentucky before "retiring" to Chatham County with her husband Mark Ethridge, formerly a newspaper editor. She has written more than a dozen books.]

Long Ago in Oxford

MR. ED SETTLE.—When I was a boy, Mr. Ed Settle preached the gospel of trees. This was at the time when conservation was a drunken truant, when many local farmers burned over stands of pines to make new grounds in which to plant tobacco.

I never saw Mr. Settle without a gunny sack of pine seedlings in his buggy. This was far into the automobile era, and Mr. Ed kept cars for members of his family. But he always rode around in a buggy. He wasn't six feet tall and he weighed about 475, and he had to go to the railroad freight depot everytime he wanted to see what he weighed.

His buggy was a two-seated carriage with the front seat removed. Even so, his improvised buggy was a tight squeeze. For a petrified fact, his sons and I used to make tents of his old shirts. I swear a small boy could play Hiding in one of his old shirt sleeves.

His belly and his knees weren't even on speaking terms. His stout young assistant, a boy named Aleck, always went with him, to help Mr. Ed in and out the buggy, and to help Mr. Ed make water. Mr. Ed not only couldn't see that far down below his bail of cotton of a belly. He couldn't unbutton his fly or find his hammer. When nature called, and she never seemed to have laryngitis, Aleck reached under the seat for a pail. Then Aleck placed the pail between Mr. Ed's legs and he unbuttoned the fly and found the hammer.

One day on College Street, in front of the music store, Mr. Ed had a terrible call from nature. But Aleck couldn't seem to find Mr. Ed's hammer.

"Hurry up, hurry up, I'm dying," the old man screamed.

"I'm sorry. I'm sorry as hell, Mr. Ed, but I can't find it nowhere."

Sweat was flooding the old man's agonized face. "Well, Aye God, boy, you better find it. You're the last man to have his hand on it."

SHE WROTE FOR THE NEWSPAPER.—Apparently, Captain Wade never read Miss Daisy's copy, and she did get carried away, now and then, by what she called the Muse. I have, at hand, three seer clippings I got from Papa's special file when he died.

One is a write-up of a wedding: "There was an allurious and lascivious wedding-cake, of five layers. After partaking of the cake and homemade blackberry wine, all the wedding guests departed in a merry and a licentious mood."

Another time the Greensboro College's "Madrigal Singers," all girls, were to give a concert at the Woman's Club. Miss Daisy learned that the group would sing some fugues. Her headline went: "Lovely Girls To Do Fugging Music."

The best one I will write down verbatim: "Last night the young ladies at Miss Jennie's school put on a performance of *Peter Pan.* Next week this charming group of lesbians will entertain the ladies of the Geneva Presbyteria."

TELEGRAPH OFFICE.—The bulletins that Mr. Thurston, the operator, pasted on the windows of the local Western Union, or "The Western and The Union" as most of us called it, belonged to the whole nation, whether they had told us about the Johnstown Flood, Christy Mathewson's pitching three shut-outs in five days, or about the sinking of the great ship, the *Titanic.*

People in town used it to get specific information or to say something explicitly. They asked the price of something, or they told someone when they would arrive in Washington City. I mean, of course, one couldn't lollygag, or socialize, or pass the compliments of the morning in ten words. (Some folks said the President of the local bank was so stingy he wouldn't use up his ten words. One time the President wanted to know the age of an out-of-town man who had applied for a line of credit. The President wired the man's firm: "How old George Hollingsworth stop." The reply came: "Old George fine stop. How you stop.")

[Thad Stem, Jr. *Entries from Oxford* (Durham: Moore Publishing Company, 1971). Stem was born in Oxford in 1916. After graduation from Duke University and a tour of military duty, he returned to Oxford to write. Among his dozen titles are many books of poetry and essays.]

The Hill Country Sayin's of Sam Ervin

"I found that an apt story is worth an hour of argument," says North Carolina's Sam Ervin. "A story that fits a point that you're trying to make sort of tends to arouse your audience, to get their attention if you're about to lose it. And a good story is a good way to relieve tension." Thus Ervin sums up his liberal use of hill-country anecdotes and other witticisms to make points in congressional debate or simply to amuse his friends. A sampling of the Senator's folksy stories on a variety of subjects:

ON DRINKING.—A constituent of mine bought some moonshine liquor and gave a portion to a friend. Sometime thereafter my constituent asked his friend what he thought of the liquor. "Well, it was just right," said his friend.

"What do you mean, 'just right'?" my constituent retorted.

"I mean that if it had been any better, you wouldn't have given it to me," the friend replied. "And if it had been any worse, I couldn't have drunk it."

ON IGNORANCE.—There is this man who is known as the most ignorant man in Burke County, North Carolina. Somebody once asked him if he knew what county he lived in, and he answered flat out, "Nope." They asked him if he knew the name of the state, and he again answered, "Nope." Well, they then asked if he had ever heard of Jesus Christ. "No," he answered. Finally they asked if he had ever heard of God. "I believe I have," he said. "Is his last name Damn?"

ON BIG WORDS.—I once knew this preacher back home who liked to use words that he sometimes didn't quite understand. One time he brought in a visiting preacher, and after introducing him to the congregation he told him to preach loud, "because the agnostics in this church are not very good."

ON LAWYERS.—There was a good young lawyer who showed up at a revival meeting and was asked to deliver a prayer. Unprepared, he gave a prayer straight from his lawyer's heart: "Stir up much strife amongst the people, Lord," he prayed, "lest thy servant perish."

ON JURIES.—One time when I was presiding over a murder trial in Burke County, they had special veniremen summoned in from another county to make sure that the accused got a fair hearing. I asked one of these jurors if he could be fair, and he answered: "I think he is guilty of murder in the first degree, and he ought to be sent to the gas chamber. But I can give him a fair trial."

ON POLITICS.—People in public life are sometimes subject to the same embarassment as that of a young man who was persuaded to become a candidate for the state legistlature. His father tried to talk him out of it. "Son, don't go into politics. Before it's over, they'll accuse you of stealing a horse." Sure enough, the young man lost and went back home where his father recalled his horse-stealing prediction. "Pa, it was much worse than that," the young man lamented. "They dern near proved it on me."

ON SENATORS.—Once a question was put to a Senate chaplain, Edward Everett Hale. "Doctor, when you pray, do you look at the tragic condition of the country and then pray that the Almighty will give the Senators the wisdom to find solutions?" The chaplain replied, "No, I do not. I look at the Senators and pray for the country."

ON NEWSMEN AND THE PRESS.—I am one of the few men in public life who doesn't complain much about his treatment at the hands of the press. The press takes me to task every once in a while, but they have always been very kind, not attributing my hypocrisy to bad motives. They have always attributed it to a lack of mental capacity.

[*Time*, 16 April 1973. Reprinted by permission from *Time*, The Weekly Newsmagazine; Copyright Time Inc.]

Souse Meat

As a tenth-generation Yankee recently transplanted to the South, I often encounter things entirely new and strange to me. I think, however, that my introduction to souse meat was the strangest of all.

While visiting some friends in Warrenton, I accompanied them to a small country store to pick up some steaks for dinner. In the course of admiring the wide range of meats on display in the butcher's case, I noticed a loaf of something that seemed to resemble an anemic, chunkily cut bologna, and was duly informed that it was souse meat. When I asked about the ingredients for this unwholesome-looking stuff, the butcher was called in to explain. To my amazement he told me that the loaf was made primarily from the remains of the meat, fat, and gristle from the heads of hogs, along with other, to me, unsavory portions of the pig. When I registered my firm disbelief that anyone would eat such a concoction, the butcher laid me low.

"I'll tell you what, son," he said. "You take a slice of that souse meat about a quarter of an inch thick. You soak it in vinegar about fifteen minutes, then you take it out and shake it off. Then you lay that slice of souse meat on the top of your head, and your tongue'll just flap your brains out trying to get to it."

[J. K. Dane, *North Carolina Folklore*, November 1969.]

The Characters of Hastings

Miss Laura Hastings once wrote A History of Hastings" in which she referred to certain of the inhabitants as "good, substantial citizens." Nothing could have insulted them more. That phrase took away their individuality and demoted them from "characters" to people. It put them outside the class of old Judge Alfred Crabtree, who hated so many people that he couldn't keep them straight and so he used to sit on his porch and ask his wife, "What am I mad at that damned scoundrel for, Marina?" as his foes passed by, or Charlie Taliaferro, who was so conceited that it got to be a common saying that "God Almighty's overcoat wouldn't make Charlie a vest."

[William T. Polk, *Southern Accent* (New York: William Morrow & Co., 1953). Polk (1896-1955) practiced law in his native Warrenton (which he often called Hastings) until he became associate editor of the *Greensboro Daily News* in 1941.]

A Final Word from O. Henry

I never beat a rotten egg,
   I never hope to beat one;
But this you'll understand, I beg—
   I'd rather beat than eat one.

[Quoted in John G. Bragaw, *Random Shots* (Raleigh: Edwards and Broughton Co., 1945).]

Bibliography

Newspapers and Periodicals

Asheville Citizen-Times.
Atkinson's Saturday Evening Post
(Philadelphia).
Carolina Journal of Pharmacy.
Carolina Watchman (Salisbury).
Chapel Hill Weekly.
Charlotte Observer.
Durham Morning Herald.
Edenton State Gazette.
Elizabeth City Star and North Carolin
Intelligencer.
Fool Killer (Moravian Falls).
Greensboro Patriot.
Harper's Weekly (New York).
Journal of American Folklore.
Live Giraffe (Raleigh).
Milton Chronicle.
Mooresville Tribune.
New York Times.
New York World.
News and Observer (Raleigh).

Newton Enterprise.
North Carolina Folklore.
North-Carolina Journal (Halifax).
North Carolina Minerva (Raleigh).
Publications of the Texas Folklore
Society.
Raleigh Register.
Raleigh Times.
Rasp (Raleigh).
Reader's Digest.
Rocky Mount Telegram.
Southern Literary Messenger
(Richmond)
Spirit of the Times (New York).
State (Raleigh).
State Port Pilot (Southport).
Tarborough Southerner.
Time (New York).
University Report (Chapel Hill).
Williamston Mercury.

Books and Pamphlets

Adler, Bill, ed. *The Wit and Wisdom of Billy Graham.* New York: Random House, 1967.

Alley, Felix E. *Random Thoughts and the Musing of a Mountaineer.* Salisbury: Rowan Printing Co., 1941.

Avery, Isaac Erwin. *Idle Comments.* Charlotte: Avery Publishing Co., 1905.

Battle, Kemp P. *The Early History of Raleigh.* Raleigh: Edwards and Broughton, 1893.

―――. Scrapbook of North Carolina History. University of North Carolina Library, Chapel Hill, n.d.

Botkin, Benjamin Albert, ed. *A Treasury of Southern Folklore.* New York: Crown Publishers, 1949.

Bragaw, John G. *Random Shots.* Raleigh: Edwards and Broughton, 1945.

Brewer, J. Mason. *American Negro Folklore.* Chicago: Quadrangle Books, 1968.

―――. *Worser Days and Better Times: The Folklore of the North Carolina Negro.* Chicago: Quadrangle Books, 1965.

Bunting, John N. *Mose's Letters: Life As It Is, or, The Writings of "Our Mose," Written by "Tall Mose," Correspondent of "The Life Giraffe."* Raleigh: Whitaker & Bunting, 1858.

Burman, Ben Lucien. *It's a Big Country.* New York: Reynal & Company, 1956.

Byrd, William. *William Byrd's Histories of the Dividing Line Betwixt Virginia & North Carolina.* Edited by William K. Boyd. Raleigh: North Carolina Historical Commission, 1929.

Cerf, Bennett. *The Laugh's on Me.* New York: Doubleday & Company, 1959.

Coates, Albert. *In Appreciation. . . .* N.p., 1962.

————. *What the University of North Carolina Meant to Me.* Richmond: p.p., 1969.

Craven, Charles. *Charles Craven's Kind of People.* Chapel Hill: Colonial Press, 1956.

Davis, Burke. *The Summer Land.* New York: Random House, 1965.

Dowd, Clement. *Life of Zebulon B. Vance.* Charlotte: Observer Printing and Publishing House, 1897.

Dugger, Shepherd M. *The Balsam Groves of the Grandfather Mountain.* Banner Elk: Printed by J. B. Lippincott Co., 1892.

————. *The War Trails of the Blue Ridge.* Banner Elk: p.p., 1932.

Ethridge, Willie Snow. *You Can't Hardly Get There from Here.* New York: Vangard Press, Inc., 1965.

Fun Fare: A Treasury of Reader's Digest Wit and Humor. Pleasantville, N.Y.: Reader's Digest Association, 1949.

Goerch, Carl. *Carolina Chats.* Raleigh: Edwards and Broughton, 1944.

————. *Characters . . . Always Characters.* Raleigh: Edwards and Broughton, 1945.

————. *Down Home.* Raleigh: Edwards and Broughton, 1943.

————. *Just for the Fun of It.* Raleigh: Edwards and Broughton, 1954.

Golden, Harry. *Enjoy, Enjoy!* New York: World Publishing Company, 1960.

————. *Ess, Ess, Mein Kindt.* New York: G. P. Putnam's Sons, 1966.

————. *For 2¢ Plain.* New York: World Publishing Company, 1959.

————. *Only in America.* New York: World Publishing Company, 1958.

————. *So Long As You're Healthy.* New York: G. P. Putnam's Sons, 1970.

————. *So What Else Is New?* New York: G. P. Putnam's Sons, 1964.

————. *You're Entitle'.* New York: World Publishing Company, 1962.

Green, Paul. *Words and Ways: Stories and Incidents from My Cape Fear Valley Folklore Collection.* Raleigh: North Carolina Folklore, 1968.

Hargrove, Marion. *See Here, Private Hargrove.* New York: Henry Holt and Co., 1942.

Henderson, Thomas Johnston. *Homespun Yarns.* Yanceyville: p.p., 1943.

————. *Honeysuckles and Bramblebriars.* Yanceyville: p.p., 1943.

————. *Plain Tales from the Country.* Yanceyville: p.p., 1943.

Hewlett, Crockette W. *Between the Creeks.* Wilmington: p.p., 1971.

Ivey, George Franks. *Humor and Humanity.* Hickory: Southern Publishing Co., 1945.

Johnson, F. Roy. *Witches and Demons in History and Folklore.* Murfreesboro: Johnson Publishing Company, 1969.

Jones, Weimar. *My Affair with a Weekly.* Winston-Salem: John F. Blair, Publisher, 1960.

Lawson, John. *A New Voyage to Carolina.* Edited by Hugh Talmage Lefler. Chapel Hill: University of North Carolina Press, 1967.

Lefler, Hugh Talmage, ed. *North Carolina History Told by Contemporaries.* Chapel Hill: University of North Carolina Press, 1956.

London, Melville D. *Wit and Humor of the Age.* Chicago: Star Publishing Company, 1890.

Mitchell, Joseph. *McSorley's Wonderful Saloon.* New York: Duell, Sloan and Pearce, 1943.

Morrah, Dave. *Me and the Liberal Arts.* New York: Doubleday & Company, 1962.

Nye, Edgar Wilson, and James Whitcomb Riley. *Nye and Riley's Wit and Humor.* Chicago: Thompson & Thomas, [c. 1900].

Oates, John A. *The Story of Fayetteville and the Upper Cape Fear.* Fayetteville: p.p., 1950.

Odum, Howard W. *Cold Blue Moon: Black Ulysses Afar Off.* Indianapolis: Bobbs-Merrill Company, 1931.

————. *Rainbow Round My Shoulder: The Blue Trail of Black Ulysses.* Indianapolis: Bobbs-Merrill Company, 1928.

O. Henry. *Postscripts.* New York: Harper & Brothers, 1923.

Owen, Guy. *The Ballad of the Flim-Flam Man.* New York: Macmillan Company, 1965.

Pearce, Thilbert H. *How to Sell a Dead Mule.* Freeman, S.D.: Pine Hill Press, 1971.

Polk, William T. *Southern Accent.* New York: William Morrow & Co., 1953.

Porter, William T., ed. *The Big Bear of Arkansas and Other Tales.* Philadelphia: Carey & Hart, 1845.

Reap, Charles A. *A Story Is Told.* Albemarle: p.p., 1968.

Reid, A. C. *Tales from Cabin Creek.* Raleigh: p.p., 1967.

Robertson, Judge Braxton, ed. *Gems of Truth in Stories of Life.* Burlington: p.p., 1932.

Ruark, Robert. *I Didn't Know It Was Loaded.* New York: Doubleday & Company, 1948.

Seawell, Joseph Lacy. *Law Tales for Laymen.* Raleigh: Alfred Williams and Company, 1925.

Southern Historical Society Papers. Vol. 14. Richmond, Va., 1886.

Stem, Thad, Jr. *Entries from Oxford.* Durham: Moore Publishing Company, 1971.

Sterling, Philip. *Laughing on the Outside: The Intelligent White Reader's Guide to Negro Tales and Humor.* New York: Grosset & Dunlap, 1965.

Taliaferro, Harden E. *Carolina Humor: Sketches by Harden E. Taliaferro.* Edited by David K. Jackson. Richmond, Va.: Dietz Press, 1938.

————. *Fisher's River (North Carolina) Scenes and Characters, by "Skitt," "Who Was Raised Thar."* New York: Harper & Brothers, 1859.

Tucker, Glenn. *Zeb Vance: Champion of Personal Freedom.* Indianapolis: Bobbs-Merrill Company, 1965.

Vance Papers. Vol. 18. State Archives, Raleigh, n.d.

Walser, Z. V. *Flashes of Wit and Humor of the North Carolina Bench and Bar: An Address at the Annual Meeting of the North Carolina Bar Association, at Morehead City, July 2nd, 1908.* N.p., n.d.

Whitaker, Richard Harper. *Whitaker's Reminiscences, Incidents and Anecdotes.* Raleigh: Edwards and Broughton, 1905.

Whiting, Robert Rudd, comp. *Four Hundred Good Stories.* New York: Baker & Taylor, 1910.

Wolfe, Thomas. *The Hills Beyond.* New York: Harper & Brothers, 1941.

————. *Look Homeward, Angel.* New York: Charles Scribner's Sons, 1929.

Index

A Note about the Book

Designed and composed by The University of North Carolina Press, Chapel Hill, North Carolina, the text was set on a Compu-Writer II in eleven-point English, leaded two points, and the display type is eighteen-point English italic. The volume was printed by Thomson-Shore, Inc., on sixty-pound Hopper Natural Bulk Opaque and the endsheets on eighty-pound Text Graphic Weave, both manufactured by Georgia Pacific. Illustrations are from Joseph Crawhall, Impresses Quaint (Newcastle upon Tine: Mawson, Swan & Morgan, 1889) provided through the courtesy of the Rare Book Collection, Wilson Library, The University of North Carolina at Chapel Hill. The binding is Holliston Roxite by John H. Dekker & Sons.